THE
UNIVERSAL EYE

THE
UNIVERSAL EYE

THE WORLD OF TELEVISION

TIMOTHY GREEN

STEIN AND DAY/*Publishers*/New York

First published in 1972
Copyright © 1972 by Timothy S. Green
Library of Congress Catalog Card No. 76-160345
All rights reserved
Published simultaneously in Canada by Saunders of Toronto Ltd.
Designed by David Miller
Stein and Day/*Publishers*/7 East 48 Street, New York, N.Y. 10017
ISBN 0-8128-1424-X

Contents

Preface

The idea for this book came from a conversation I had in Geneva in 1968 with Neville Clarke, then director of the European Broadcasting Union's news exchange. Without his initial prompting and then continuing help it would never have been written. My special thanks, therefore, go to him.

Over the two years that I have been working on the book several hundred broadcasters in forty countries on five continents have taken time out to talk to me about their own television scene. I have appreciated their courtesy and hospitality immensely. In particular, I am most grateful for the assistance and encouragement of Sir Hugh Greene; Sir Charles Moses, Secretary General of the Asian Broadcasting Union; Michael Type, assistant to the Secretary General of the European Broadcasting Union; Hamdy Kandil, Managing Director of the Arab States Broadcasting Union; Josef C. Dine of the Corporation for Public Broadcasting; James Dodd of NBC International in New York and Alistair MacKenzie of NBC International in Mexico City; Fenton Coe of NBC, Burbank, California; and Richard Connelly of ABC. Barney Keelan at the Independent Television Authority in London kindly allowed me to use the ITA's library, where Linda Coles and her staff were constantly helpful.

The problems of understanding material in many languages were overcome by the multilingual talents of Yvonne Milliet, Jacqueline Nicolotti and Irena Podleska. My wife, quite apart from putting up with my spending almost a year away from home to undertake the overseas research, has been an invaluable editor. Pat Chan and Louise Sweeting have typed the book with speed and precision.

T. S. G.
Dulwich, 3 August 1971

7

1

Introduction:
The Universal Eye

Man's first step on the moon on July 19, 1969, was watched by an estimated 723 million people in forty-seven countries—rather more than one
fifth of the world's population. No other event in history has ever been so
immediately seen by so many of the human race and, as a television critic
put it: "In that one gesture TV's priority at the center of man's future
historic development was symbolically demonstrated." Never before has
the earth been so nearly one community, one village, all gathered together
eagerly before millions of glowing screens. Capitalists and communists,
rich and poor all sat down as one to see and hear Neil Armstrong a
quarter of a million miles away take his step for all mankind.

The ghostly pictures from the moon must have been rather like the
first flickering images that men like John Logie Baird conjured up on tiny
screens in the privacy of their workshops less than fifty years ago. Yet
today the pictures travel in a microsecond from moon to earth, there to be
distributed instantly to a hundred million homes on every continent. Just
three satellites, each little bigger than an oil drum, poised in space 22,500
miles above the equator over the Atlantic, Pacific and Indian oceans throw
an electronic girdle around the earth. Pictures of a moon launch from
Cape Kennedy can be beamed instantly from an earth station at Andover,
Maine, up to the Atlantic satellite, which bounces it down again to the
giant receiving dishes of earth stations in Europe, Africa or South America; while the same signal, shot upward from the earth station at James-
burg, California, radiates via the Pacific satellite to Japan, Hong Kong
and Australia. It is the satellite that has truly made the world an "electronic village."

Television is so much a part of most of our lives nowadays—in
America the average set is on six hours a day, in Japan for five and in

9

Britain four—that we often forget just how young it still is. Although the world's first regular television service started in Britain as far back as November 1936, television has only gotten into its stride in the last two decades. In 1950 there were no more than 5 million television sets in the world. The United States, Britain and the Soviet Union had television, but there was none in France, Germany or Japan. Just twenty years later more than 250 million sets were scattered around the world in 130 countries. The United States alone had 84 million in 1970, Western Europe had 75 million, the Soviet Union 30 million and Japan 23 million. Only in Africa and much of Asia is television still a curiosity; the whole of Africa south of the Sahara has fewer sets than San Francisco or Marseilles; China has scarcely 200,000 sets among its 750 million people and India a mere 20,000 for 600 million—one set for every 30,000 people, compared to one for every 2.5 people in the United States.

Many might say the Chinese and Indians are fortunate. Elsewhere television is the handy scapegoat for those attacking the ills of our society, the target for brickbats for promoting violence or permissiveness and wasting our time with trivia. Malcolm Muggeridge regards the television camera as "the greatest destructive force of our time; the great falsifier"—an opinion which does not for a second prevent him from being a tireless and highly entertaining performer in front of it. And an American professor of sociology argues: "Next to the H-bomb, television is the most dangerous thing in the world today."

That judgment depends on what use is made of it. I spent an evening recently in a small village in India with a crowd of farmers who were watching their "prime time" show—a lesson in sugar cane planting. The potential for television there, as in so many countries of the Third World, is enormous as a means of education in health, hygiene, farming, as well as reading and writing. Often there are no schools or qualified teachers, so that television can make the difference between some education or none at all. I remember talking to a UNESCO communications expert just back from South America, where a particular project for primary education by television was bogged down in political wrangles. "The delay," he said, "means that thousands of children just miss out on school completely—they'll be grown up and working before we get started."

Even when television, either for education or entertainment, does get off the ground in developing countries, its effect is often blunted by the fact that a set costs more than most people earn in one year or that electrification does not extend beyond the main cities. "What we need," a Peruvian television executive remarked to me, "is kerosene TV."

Despite such drawbacks, television finds its feet in all kinds of out-of-the-way places. Ethiopia has a tiny television station installed in six rooms of the city hall in Addis Ababa; the whole setup was installed in nineteen days and the one studio is not much bigger than a family living room—yet they produce nearly half their own programs. Their budget for a year is about $200,000—less than the cost of one episode of *Bonanza.* And the most unlikely television station of all, perhaps, is perched on the Rock of Gibraltar. It serves just 6,000 television sets and gets by on little over $100,000 a year. Yet the staff of twelve produce almost half the five hours of programs each evening using part-time cameramen. Obviously it is not very sophisticated, but at least the local effort is being made. Television programs may cost over $200,000 an hour in America or $50,000 an hour in Western Europe, but a great deal can be done for far less. Even the commercials, which may cost $50,000 to make in the United States, can be done cheaply. In the West Indies, for instance, the television announcer sometimes whips off his shoes and holds them to the camera, saying, "Buy fine shoes like these at Joe's store on Bay Street."

Setting out at the beginning of 1970 to review television in some forty countries on five continents, I anticipated that I would find that outside the major countries the American package show reigned supreme. That may have been true ten years ago, but no longer. In television these days everyone is quite determined to do his own thing. They may have little talent and no money, but they all find there is no substitute for local programing. "You can show them films from other countries for a while," said a consultant who helped to establish television in the Sudan, Kenya, Aden, and Sierra Leone, "but what they really want to see are their own people debating, arguing, getting in their sly jokes about one another." When I spent a morning in Nairobi talking to the controller of television for Kenya his phone was abuzz with politicians and businessmen all trying to get on the Voice of Kenya's evening talk show, *Mambo Leo.*

Not that the universal appeal of the western or *The Lucy Show* is over. Nothing can touch *Bonanza,* which is watched week in and week out by 400 million people in eighty-two countries, from Poland to the Philippines and Nigeria to Nicaragua. *The Lucy Show* goes out in Cantonese, Spanish, French and German. But only a handful of American programs are big international sellers. NBC International reckons to earn 40 percent of their income from the sale of *Bonanza, High Chaparral, Get Smart* and *I Spy.* MCA Universal's two trump cards are *Ironside* (known variously as *Der Chef* and *L'Homme de Fer* overseas) and *The Virginian.*

But this hard core of best sellers cannot fill the screen for more than a few hours a week. Although television is still primarily an evening pastime—only the United States, Canada, Japan and Australia start at crack of dawn—something like sixty to one hundred hours of new programs are required each week in countries with two or three channels. Homegrown productions, therefore, are accounting for up to 85 percent of output in many countries. Against them American shows or British exports like *The Saint* and *The Avengers* have a harder time pulling audiences. In South America, nowadays, nothing can rival the *telenovela* in popularity. These shoestring soap operas about poor country girls who find fame, fortune and lovers in the big cities often fill the screen for four or five hours an evening, playing out the dreams of the poor. "Against that competition the chances of selling some stupid American situation comedy are dying," said an American program salesman in Mexico City.

The flavor of the top programs varies, like the cuisine, from country to country. The Japanese's greatest passions are for samurai dramas about sword-wielding warlords in feudal times, and "hard training" dramas depicting team efforts to achieve some sporting or business victory. The Germans all sit down together to watch detective stories and a real life crime series in which the police enlist their aid to catch the crooks. The night that particular program goes out every wanted man in Germany sits quaking in his hide-out ready to run if he is mentioned. The Norwegians, a rather serious-minded people (they rejected *The Lucy Show* on the grounds that children ought not to speak like that to their mother), came up with a highly original *Idebanken (Bank of Ideas)* that picked the brain of the viewer to solve such problems as what is the best way to get a handicapped person in a wheelchair off and on a train. One viewer designed a small hydraulic platform with which many railway stations in Norway are now equipped. And the Irish—well, who can beat the Irish at talking? They have a Saturday night *Late Late Show* that is as rowdy as an Irish pub. They simply get a studio full of farmers, bricklayers, or even women's lib members, who are needled a little at the start by the host, and they are away. "Almost every Saturday it's a ding-dong battle," said Irish television's director of programs. "One week we had 120 priests and started asking them what they knew of sex, marriage, and how to run a house. They were almost bashing each other by the end." The week I was in Dublin there was a slight variation: the *Late Late Show* featured frog racing.

Television's parochialism is really overridden only by a handful of world events: the moonwalks, the Olympics, and the Ali-Frazier fight.

The fight, in particular, caused the most poverty-stricken of television stations everywhere to forget their budgets for a night. Countries like Jordan and Pakistan, which normally pay no more than $50 or $60 an hour for imported shows, lashed out with $2,000 for the fight, their normal outlay for about a week.

Although the satellites hovering above the equator have introduced the era of global broadcasting, language barriers thwart much international programing. What has developed, however, is "electronic imperialism" where a common language is shared. Spanish television, for instance, is carving out a market for its programs throughout South America. Egypt is trying to establish its superiority in television in the Arab world. And the French earnestly give programs away free to their former colonies in Africa and Asia. The Americans, in addition to conventional program sales, often offer, through the United States Information Agency, to pay the satellite costs involved for nations wanting to take live coverage of crucial Presidential speeches. Even the Russians are slowly easing into this electronic empire building; in Cairo, along with westerns, television shows Russian folk dancing and solemn films on industrial safety or productivity.

The headache for everyone, of course, is the cost of television. As Michael Garvey of Irish television put it, "We get through money at a paralyzing speed." Much as everyone would like to make nearly all their own programs they often have to fall back on cheap, imported shows and, increasingly, on coproductions with other broadcasting services. The coproductions, which tend to be historical spectaculars like French and Italian television's version of *The Aeneid* or the BBC and Time-Life's *History of the British Empire,* may cost up to $1 million and would be quite beyond the resources of a single organization. "We have to do these joint enterprises to stay in serious television," said Aubrey Singer, who oversees these epics at the BBC.

The majority of nations now flesh out their budgets with advertising. Ninety of the 130 nations with television accept commercials for all or part of their income. In Europe, the stronghold of public service broadcasting financed by annual license fees, everyone except the Scandinavians, Belgians, and the BBC in Britain top up their budgets with small quotas of commercials. Even the communist countries have advertising pushing new lines in consumer goods or spelling out the joys of a Black Sea holiday. The precaution, however, that most countries take when they go commercial is to seal off the advertiser from the programs; governments and broadcasters look aghast at sponsorship's cramping effect on American television and determine not to get trapped in the same mire.

The real bogey for many television services is the politician, not the advertiser. In the communist camp television is naturally a tool of the Marxist revolution, but elsewhere it is also frequently a political preserve. In developing countries television is usually under the umbrella of the Ministry of Information—and anyone trying a coup d'état must capture the TV and radio stations and transmitters as an early priority. Parts of Western Europe face the same threat. Charles de Gaulle kept French television firmly under his thumb as long as he was President, and in Spain and Portugal the screen reflects the wishes of their right-wing dictators.

This political control is likely to increase. Already in South America governments are taking over commercial stations that have previously been privately owned symbols of prestige for wealthy families. Even in Britain, politicians who would otherwise be accounted liberal stump the country saying, "Broadcasting is too important to be left to the broadcasters."

The new era of global television opened up by the satellites is making politicians much more aware of the chance of propaganda from overseas showing up on screens in their domain. Scientists are already forecasting direct-broadcast satellites in the 1980s, which will radiate pictures that can be picked up by a simple antenna attached to the television set in every home. The prospect of being able to tune in direct from London to television via satellite from New York, Moscow or Peking inevitably means that governments will become more concerned in controlling the airways than they were when the television signal only jumped a few miles. As Lew Kuan Yew, the prime minister of Singapore, puts it: "I may be its slave, but it is my lamp."

THE
AMERICAS

2

The United States:

The Commercial Colossus

Although television in the United States is unequaled anywhere in wealth and output, the Americans remain a remarkably underprivileged nation in what they are actually offered on the screen. The money, to start with, is enormous. The $3.5 billion spent buying advertising time on America's 650 commercial stations each year is more than is available to all the other commercial and public service television systems of the remainder of the noncommunist world combined. Procter and Gamble alone, the largest advertisers on American television, spend nearly $200 million a year sponsoring programs or buying "spots," which is just about the annual income of the BBC's television service. The three major networks—ABC, CBS, and NBC—each earn more from advertising every year than any national television service outside the United States, while their combined profit of $226 million for 1969 was about the same as the entire revenue of French television that year. Yet never was so much spent on so little. American television has not been daring enough to step out and explore the immense opportunities offered by such riches. Instead, it has been imprisoned in a narrow world, whose confines are defined by the advertisers rather than by the broadcaster or the viewer.

There is, of course, nothing wrong with commercial patronage. As one American advertising executive remarked to me, "After all, Renaissance art was commissioned. Even Rembrandt was commercial: the lace on the doublets in his paintings is perfect—to please the local lacemakers —and the right people have the correct prominence in his groups. He combined all these commercial requests and came up with a work of art."

But are the American advertisers, the major patrons of today, spurring television on to similar creativity? "Ah, the advertiser's job is to buy ratings, not to raise the public taste," said the agency man. "We want numbers, 'tonnage' of homes. Sponsoring the New York Philharmonic as opposed to blood and guts just doesn't work. Television is still making cave drawings instead of painting the Mona Lisa."

In a nutshell, that is the dilemma and the tragedy of American commercial television. The patrons that feed it so generously are preoccupied with tonnage, not with tone. Apart from the fledgling public television service that now blends some two hundred educational and community stations into a "fourth" network, American television is chiefly in the business of selling goods.

At least no one makes any pretense about it. "We have to think of our advertisers and shareholders all the time," said a vice-president of NBC. "Look, no American network could put on a program like *Civilisation* for thirteen weeks, they'd take a bloodbath financially. You'd have to put it on in the early evening to catch children, and that would kill the whole night." Then he added, shuddering at the thought, "And all our viewers would sample the competition on the other networks, they might like it and stay with them. We're boxed in by the fact that we are a profit-oriented industry."

Although American television, as a result, is often a "wasteland" (as Newton Minow, a former Chairman of the Federal Communications Commission, once dubbed it), there is also much to its credit. In many things, from entertainment specials by Frank Sinatra or Barbra Streisand to coverage of the Apollo moonwalks and documentaries such as CBS's *Hunger in America* or *The Selling of the Pentagon,* the networks have set professional standards that few other television services can match. The western has become American television's classic production: around the world 400 million people in eighty-two countries relax with *Bonanza* at the end of a hard day's work. And it was Edward R. Murrow who, in the 1950s, really pioneered the whole craft of television journalism in his remarkable *See It Now* series. The trouble is that these days such programs are occasional jewels in fare that is otherwise, as one critic put it, "As bland as a diet of oatmeal three times a day."

The audience eats it up obediently. The sixty million American households who own a television set (42 percent had color and 34 percent at least two sets in 1970) blithely leave it turned on for a slightly longer period each day year by year. In 1950, sets were on for 4 hours and 35 minutes a day; in 1970 for almost 6 hours. American women watch television for 4 hours every day; their husbands for just under 3. Teenagers also view for about 3 hours a day; those aged 6 to 11 for 3½ hours and tots, aged 2 to 5, face the electronic babysitter for 4 hours. This daily dose means that by the time the average American student graduates from high school he, or she, has spent 15,000 hours watching television, compared with a mere 10,800 in the classroom. "Only sleeping time surpasses television as the top time-consumer," a report on children's viewing remarked.

The addiction is encouraged by the sheer volume of programs. Turn on your set almost anywhere and you have a choice of half a dozen or more—ten in New York—channels, many of them running eighteen or nineteen hours a day, some nonstop. WCBS in New York, for instance, shows old movies right through the night. The last one comes on around 4:30 in the morning. Once, when I was in Chicago to appear on a talk show, I arrived at the television station in the evening to make an advance tape. I inquired when the show went out. "Two-thirty," said the producer. "Which afternoon? Tomorrow?" "No, no," he corrected me, "two-thirty tonight."

Talk shows and old movies are a good way of filling up time at relatively little expense. Indeed, the guiding philosophy of many smaller stations, in particular, seems to be "if in doubt pop on another movie"; forget your program worries for an hour and a half and just collect the money from the commercials. Most weeks there are about 130 old movies shown over New York's stations alone—a veritable history of the American cinema. All in the space of seven days during April 1971, for instance, one had the choice of Errol Flynn in *Dodge City* and *Istanbul,* Marlon Brando in *Viva Zapata,* Gary Cooper in *Friendly Persuasion,* Ronald Colman in *Prisoner of Zenda* and Bob Hope in *Paleface.* Any passionate admirer of Susan Hayward could have watched her five days in a row in *Tulsa* at eleven o'clock in the morning.

Since relatively few American stations are actually geared up to originate programs, with the exception of local news, they are enormously dependent on networked programs from ABC, CBS, and NBC. The choice of fresh material is especially narrow for stations not affiliated with the networks. Along with showing movies, they have to rely heavily on rerunning old network shows or cheap syndicated quizzes and panel games. Shows such as *To Tell the Truth* (an innocuous little guessing game in which a regular panel tries to sort out a real contestant from two pretenders) are available in five half-hour packages every week, costing as little as $40 a time, plus the cost of videotapes. The high cost of programing prevents most producers from turning out anything of better quality or more sophistication for syndication to independent stations. Shows have to be sold in at least eighty to a hundred good markets (everyone in commercial television speaks of "markets" rather than cities) to break even, and few people take the risk. One notable exception is Group W, the broadcasting offshoot of Westinghouse Electric Corporation, who try to originate both documentaries and talk shows, which can go on their own five television stations and then into general syndication. Group W, for instance, launched David Frost's 90-minute talk show for five days a week and it swiftly became one of the most critically acclaimed new programs on American television in recent years. Yet even that was barely breaking even in early 1971, although it was on over 70 stations, including important independent ones in New York, Los Angeles and Washington in the golden hours from 7:30 until 11:00 each evening which everyone calls "prime time."

Virtually all the major new programing therefore is seen over the ABC, CBS and NBC networks. The real duel for leadership over the years has been between the Columbia Broadcasting System (CBS) and the National Broadcasting Company (NBC). The American Broadcasting Company (ABC) has always been number three, although recently it has chipped away more and more at the leadership of the two giants. Like Avis trying to beat Hertz out of No. 1 position in the car rental business, ABC claims they try harder. But the history of American broadcasting, both in radio and television, is really the growth of CBS and NBC. CBS, under the constant guidance of William S. Paley for over forty years, has grown from a small east coast radio network in the 1920s to a communications empire with a net income of over $1 billion a year. Its television network embraces five owned stations (the most that any group is permitted to own in the United States) in New York, Los Angeles, Chicago, Philadelphia and St. Louis and over 190 affiliated stations. CBS's other activities include everything from filmmaking to book publishing and owning the New York Yankees baseball team. They have also been a pioneer of the dawning cassette age through their Electronic Video Recording division, which has devised one of the main systems (EVR) for playing cassettes.

NBC is even more closely interwoven with the American business establishment as a subsidiary of the Radio Corporation of America (RCA), which, quite apart from making television cameras and sets, radios and record players, is a major producer of highly sophisticated electronic equipment for defense and satellites. Every new employee at NBC gets a little booklet which tells him proudly, "RCA is a major figure in maintaining the United States defense posture. There is hardly an area of national defense in which one or another of RCA's operating divisions has not played a key role." RCA also owns the Hertz car rental business, a publishing house and even an organization called Banquet Foods, which supplies meals for all occasions. The television network itself covers NBC's five owned stations in New York, Washington, Chicago, Los Angeles and Cleveland and over 200 affiliates, together garnering over $600 million each year in advertising revenue.

Only ABC has not yet become a communications mammoth, because a plan to merge it into the mighty International Telephone and Telegraph stable was refused by the U.S. Government as being against the public interest. Even so, its television network of five owned stations in New York, Chicago, Detroit, Los Angeles and San Francisco, plus 170 affiliates, attracts something over $450 million a year of advertisers' money.

Since federal broadcasting regulations, administered from Washington by the Federal Communications Commission (FCC), prohibit anyone from owning more than five television stations, the affiliates of each network spin the real distribution web for programs. Their tastes and prejudices, not surprisingly, have considerable influence on the programs put out by the network.

Although an affiliate station usually agrees to take a minimum of eight hours of network programing each week, it has no obligation to accept any specific one. It can "bump" the network whenever it chooses and replace it with a program of its own. Normally, affiliates are only too happy to take the lot: the full three hours of network programs in prime time each evening, together with the soap operas and game shows that while away the daytime hours, and the late night talk shows of Johnny Carson, Merv Griffin and Dick Cavett that keep the patter and chatter going till one in the morning. However, many individual stations, particularly in the South, are more wary than the networks of controversial programs and serious documentaries. Often less than half a network's affiliates take documentaries—they just throw on an old movie instead. The rejection of more serious programs by affiliates is a constant headache for the networks. They have a difficult enough time persuading many advertisers to buy time on a program not conceived as mass entertainment without affiliates also playing truant.

In the large cities there is normally an affiliate of each network, but in smaller communities with one or two channels the stations often pick and choose their programs from all three networks. The classic example has been KTBC-TV in Austin, Texas, a highly profitable station owned for many years by Lyndon Johnson and his family (the controlling share-

holding is actually in the hands of his wife, Lady Bird). KTBC is an affiliate of both ABC and CBS and can take its pick of the most successful
programs from each.

The affiliates receive a share of the advertising revenue of each network program they carry, according to the size of their market. The real
gravy, however, is the earnings from the national or local "spot" ads
placed directly with the stations, which they can pack into station breaks
during or between network shows. Strictly speaking, advertising in networked shows in the three hours of prime time in the evening is supposed
to be limited to six minutes per hour, with another ceiling of twelve minutes an hour outside prime time. But many stations slip in up to fifteen
minutes on the hour. The Federal Communications Commission, the li-
censor of TV and radio stations and watchdog of the industry, once blew
the whistle on a station that was proposing thirty-three minutes' advertising in an hour.

The affiliates themselves are often subsidiaries of publishing or industrial groups. Cowles Communications, which ran *Look* magazine, is in TV;
so is the Post-Newsweek empire which owns the *Washington Post* and
Newsweek; Condé Nast—publishers of *Vogue* and *House and Garden*—
have interests in four television stations, and the publishers of the *Chicago
Tribune* and New York *Daily News* have stakes in three. Time-Life owned
five stations until 1971, when they sold them out to another major publisher, McGraw-Hill. In all, 106 American newspapers or magazines had
major holdings in television in 1970.

The largest nonnetwork group, however, is the Westinghouse Electric
Corporation, whose Group W subsidiary controls stations in Baltimore,
Boston, Philadelphia, Pittsburgh, and San Francisco. Although Group W's
stations are all affiliated with the major networks (two with NBC, two
with CBS and one with ABC) they have been striving in recent years,
under the energetic direction of their president, Donald H. McGannon, to
emerge as a programing group in their own right. Apart from developing
two syndicated shows—those of David Frost and Mike Douglas—Group
W has embarked on a wide range of documentaries. In 1968, for instance,
they established an Urban America Unit to make four or five special
reports a year on the problems of America's cities.

But it is one thing to produce programs, quite another to break the
hold of the three networks on prime time so that they can be shown to
best advantage. McGannon's real strategy was to persuade the Federal
Communications Commission to pronounce a new ruling in 1970 (quickly
dubbed the McGannon rule) that from September 1971 onward the net-

works would be permitted to provide only three hours of programing in evening prime time, instead of the traditional three and a half hours. (Strictly speaking, the new rule applied only to stations in the top fifty markets, but such is the value of advertising time in the top fifty that it is not worth the networks' investing in programs at all if they cannot be shown there.)

McGannon hoped that, by turning half an hour back from the networks to individual stations each evening, the scope would be greater for Group W and other producers to display their wares. He believed also that the whole spectrum of programs might be widened. The rewards of winning a slice of prime time are considerable; the earning power of a program in the evening is about six times that during the day. Most evenings, when up to forty million Americans are looking at television, advertising costs anything from $40,000 to $80,000 a minute, depending on the rating for a particular show. By day, advertising commands a more modest $10,000 a minute. Prime time, therefore, is the seductive lure which the networks have guarded jealously. The potential advertising revenue to *each* network *every* night of the week is somewhere over $1 million. Indeed, few American television executives seem to spend time thinking about anything except prime time. Walk into any of their offices in the networks' skyscraper headquarters on Sixth Avenue in New York (or any advertising agency office on Madison or Park Avenue) and there, prominently displayed either on the wall or beneath a glass desk-top, is the crucial chart mapping hour by hour the rival offerings of ABC, CBS and NBC during prime time. Everyone's thoughts and energies are on juggling the position of their network's programs in that schedule to maximize the audience. Moves are planned with concentration worthy of an international chess master. Programing for the less lucrative daytime hours is handled by a separate vice-president with his own department.

Until Don McGannon promoted the new FCC three-hour rule, prime time began at 7:30 (right after the evening news) and finished at 11:00, when most stations put out their own late night news. From 1971 onward, network prime time was normally from 8:00 until 11:00, leaving individual stations to find their own programs from 7:30 until 8:00.

The target, however, is unchanged: the maximum possible audience for every single second and, ideally, as many of the audience as possible aged between eighteen and forty-nine living in an urban area. With that magic formula in mind, the next trick is to devise a series that will so entrance the public it will be good, not just for twenty or so episodes this year, but for every year in the foreseeable future. Programs establish a "track record," which is the number of years they have survived. The record is held by Ed Sullivan, whose Sunday night variety show lasted for twenty-three years before it was finally axed in 1971. Lucille Ball is now bidding for the championship: *Here's Lucy* has been running for twenty years (under various titles) and is still going strong.

Although all the networks do one-shot entertainment and documentary "specials," which are sprinkled through the season like occasional refreshing dewdrops, the real search is for long-running series of either variety, situation comedy or drama. Except for occasional short summer seasons, the notion of doing a six- or eight-part serialization of a novel or thirteen parts on *Civilisation* just does not come within anyone's thinking. When I asked one executive whether he would have considered buying something like the BBC's *Forsyte Saga*, he explained politely that if they had and it had been a success what would they have done when the twenty-six episodes were finished? "There was no follow-up for the next season." So, lacking *Son of Forsyte*, a worthwhile production cannot stand in its own right; it does not fit the known formulas. "The secret of a good series," said David Victor, one of the most successful of American TV producers, with *Dr. Kildare, The Man from U.N.C.L.E.,* and *Marcus Welby, M.D.* to his credit, "is that you must be able to see episode thirty-five or forty-nine clearly before you begin."

The priority, therefore, is for some central character or group of characters around whom incidents can be created week after week after week. *Marcus Welby, M.D.,* the most successful show on American television in 1970–71, fitted this contingency perfectly. Dr. Welby is a general practitioner and the trials and tribulations of his patients revolve around him. "The concept is very simple," said Dick O'Connell, coproducer with David Victor. "Dr. Welby is a nice man. He is presented with a problem each week and he solves it. The general practitioner is the ideal format."

So, too, are policemen, lawyers, surgeons, and cowboys. "But what could you do with a dentist?" asked a Hollywood producer. When I told him the Japanese had a highly successful series in which a dentist was in love with a lady pediatrician he was not persuaded of the potentialities for a dental TV star.

Within the given framework the television dramas go through periodic fashions. During the mid 1960s hospital shows were in vogue. Next came 1970, the "year of relevance," with everyone struggling with the issues of drugs, permissiveness and teenage delinquency. For the 1971 season, detectives were the craze, with the networks introducing variously a fat private eye called *Cannon,* a funny police team in *The Partners,* a policeman turned priest in *Sarge* (this show was quickly nicknamed *God Squad*) and a blind insurance investigator called *Longstreet*.

Once upon a time, the networks ordered thirty-nine new shows for each series per season and completed the remaining thirteen weeks of the year with reruns of the most successful segments. But the soaring costs of television production, now over $200,000 an hour, has discouraged such massive investments. Nowadays only twenty to twenty-six episodes a year are made of even proven series like *Bonanza* (and this still involves a yearly investment approaching $5 million). For a new series only thirteen or sixteen will be ordered initially. If the newcomer wins good ratings when the new season opens in mid-September, with all the flourish of a great race meeting, then a further half dozen or ten installments may be made quickly. If it flops, it is dropped with no ceremony. A replacement will be hastily shuffled into the schedule about the first of January. Everyone keeps two or three potential replacements on the stocks ready to go on as they see how the season is shaping.

All these new programs take the television year only through to late March; thereafter the reruns begin. For the next five months there is little new material on the screen with the exception of "specials" and some try-outs of series that are considered for mid-season replacements the following January. ABC, for example, tested a Val Doonican variety series from Britain during the summer of 1971 to see if audience response merited giving the singer a full-fledged slot in a more auspicious season of the year. CBS also slipped in the BBC's prize-winning *Six Wives of Henry VIII* during the summer hiatus of 1971.

The initial guides to triumph or disaster are the ratings and share of households. A good rule of thumb is that a program with over an eighteen rating (i.e. 18 percent of all television households, which is 11 million homes) and over a 30 percent share of the audience at that time is home free. These proportions depend, of course, not just on the appeal of a program, but on the competition facing them on the rival networks. A program may do very well at one time, because of weak opposition, and poorly at another because it is matched against the nation's firm favorite. A prime example of a runaway triumph was *Marcus Welby, M.D.*, on the ABC network on Tuesday nights during the 1970–71 season. The competition was the weekly current affairs program *Sixty Minutes* on CBS, while NBC had a current affairs documentary, *First Tuesday,* once a month at the same time. Neither of them attracted a vast audience, so *Marcus Welby* coasted to success. That kind of one-sidedness did not last long; for the 1971 season CBS canceled *Sixty Minutes* as a regular Tuesday offering and pitched *Cannon,* their chubby private eye, against the good Dr. Welby; NBC shifted *First Tuesday* to Fridays and weighed in with a situation comedy, *Marriage Can Be Fun.*

That little maneuver called for no great scheduling skill; any entertainment matched against documentaries was bound to do well. The real test of the program scheduler's art comes when he has to find some answer to a show on a rival network that is knocking spots off his own entertainment. Then he has to take courage—and maybe his job—in both hands. NBC, for instance, was mightily troubled during 1970 on Tuesday nights by ABC's bouncy police series, *Mod Squad,* which was edging out their own *Julia,* the saga of a well-heeled, well-rounded black widow. *Julia* vanished the next autumn and instead NBC hauled up good, solid *Ironside* to take on *Mod Squad* for the ratings at 7:30 Tuesday nights. A daring move, because *Ironside* was doing excellently in a later period on another evening; all the rules say if a program is doing well leave it where it is. But NBC felt that *Mod Squad* could be beaten only with the really big guns. "We have to hurt that *Mod Squad* rating," said a determined NBC program vice-president outlining his battle plans behind clouds of smoke from a six-inch cigar. "*Ironside*'s rating will not be so good, but neither will *Mod Squad*'s. Sometimes you just have to slug it out; both parties will get hurt, but that's the way the game is played."

While old faithfuls fight it out, new programs are cosseted like babes in arms. One of NBC's great hopes for the 1971 season, James Garner as *Nichols,* the slightly reluctant sheriff of a small western town in 1915, was placed securely between the *Flip Wilson Show* and the *Dean Martin Show.* The strategy was that *Nichols* got the benefit both of the millions watching Flip Wilson, who are too inert to switch channels when that finishes, and of further millions who love Dean Martin and will tune in early to be sure to catch him.

Although the networks nurture a new program from birth and will invest several million dollars before anything reaches the screen at the September starting gate, they make very few of the programs themselves. In fact in 1971, the only prime time series actually produced by a network was NBC's *Bonanza.* The major television producers today are the old Hollywood movie companies, who have finally come to terms with television. Twentieth Century-Fox, Paramount, Warner Brothers, Screen Gems and M-G-M are all in the game, but the clear champion is MCA-Universal.

"Universal," said a network vice-president out in California, "is just a television factory. They roll out the program as if they were on a production line." Indeed, that is just how Universal views their sprawling complex of studios at Universal City in Hollywood. "Just as General Motors turns out cars, we turn out television shows. It's a business," a Universal executive remarked unabashed. "The movie industry is a gamble; you can invest $2 million in a picture and you may get back $10 million or nothing. But with television we know precisely what the networks are looking for. They also put up much of the money and we keep tight control of the costs by strictly limiting the number of days of shooting." Most television dramas are finished in precisely six days. "And when we say six days we mean six days," said the man at Universal, banging his desk sternly. "We have writers and directors that we know can deliver on time." Although Universal itself will invest much time and money in developing a "pilot," they will never go ahead on a complete series without a firm network order.

Their formula pays off. They contributed no less than eleven prime time programs in 1971, seven of them to NBC and four to ABC. Their nearest rival, Paramount, could muster only seven, while Twentieth Century-Fox and Screen Gems had luck with just four each. Small independent producers, who did rather well from television in the 1950s and '60s, while the movie companies were still fighting shy of television, have finally been squeezed almost out of the market. In the 1971–72 season they managed to woo the networks into buying a meager eight hours of their programing in prime time.

Actually, the most successful new rival to the major Hollywood companies is Britain's Sir Lew Grade. His Associated Television Corporation succeeded for the first time in 1971 in winning prime time positions on ABC in the competitive autumn season with Shirley MacLaine in *Shirley's World* and *The Persuaders,* a fairly lighthearted crime series with Tony Curtis and Roger (*The Saint*) Moore.

While the networks pay handsomely, the movie companies reckon to make their real profits on the syndication and rerun business that follows the first network showing. There is plenty to be recouped; very few shows now cost under $200,000 an hour. The *FBI,* for instance, is budgeted at $205,000 per episode, *Gunsmoke* and *Bonanza* cost around $220,-000, the *Dean Martin Show* eats up $230,000 every week. Even with this kind of money to play with, production schedules are extremely tight. All kinds of corners are cut to save money. On *Bonanza,* for example, the whole team will go out on location for just two or three weeks in a season to shoot miles of stock footage for twenty or more episodes. The Cartwright brothers will be filmed from all angles riding across plains, through gullies, up hills and across rivers; selected clips can then be inserted as appropriate in future episodes. To ensure continuity, the brothers always wear exactly the same clothes and ride the same horses year in, year out. If the story calls for one of them to be riding by a lake, a snippet of film shot perhaps two or three years earlier can be dug out, as their appearance is unchanged.

The hectic production period out on "the coast" is from April until mid-October, when everyone competes for studio space in getting a dozen or more shows all complete before the starting bell rings for the season in September. As everything is pieced together through the summer the ever watchful eye of the advertiser is constantly peeking over the networks' and the producers' shoulders. Since the early days of television in the United States, almost all shows have been sponsored and advertisers scan scripts with eagle eyes to delete any reference that might either be controversial or tarnish the image of their product. The tales of their red penciling are legion. Once, on a Groucho Marx show sponsored by De Soto cars, one of the assistant producers was named Ford; the advertiser insisted the name Ford be deleted from the credits. Car manufacturers are notoriously shy of their cars being involved in accidents in police dramas. "They get very touchy," conceded a network executive in Hollywood, who acts as a diplomatic go-between. "No accident may imply any fault on the part of the automobile. If there really has to be an accident then they prefer the car to be hit by a train." Before cigarette commercials were banned on American television in January 1971, the tobacco companies were equally fussy. When Dr. Marcus Welby was once required by the script to recommend to one of his patients with a serious lung complaint that he must stop smoking, an advertiser who had bought time on the show was outraged; as it happened the episode was already shot when the ad agency saw the script, and the producers refused to delete what was clearly essential medical advice. Cigarette advertisers were also always unnerved by Dean Martin, who chain-smokes on his show (seemingly good for the cigarette image), but is inclined as he tosses a cigarette away to put his fingers in his ears as if it might explode.

Although some of this is simply obsession with unimportant trivia, underlying it all is the advertiser's expectation that any program with which his name is associated will not only display his product in the most favorable light, but will fit into the neat, sanitized view of life displayed in the commercials. Procter and Gamble's editorial policy, for instance, states: "There will be no material that may give offense, either directly or by inference, to any commercial organization of any sort. . . . There will be no material on any of our programs which could in any way further the concept of business as cold, ruthless, and lacking all sentiment or spiritual motivation."

Erik Barnouw, in the third volume of his history of broadcasting in America, notes that the advertisers nipped in the bud the flowering of good drama on television in the 1950s because the plays then being written by Paddy Chayefsky and others clashed head on with the sponsors' view of the world. "Most advertisers were selling magic," says Barnouw. "Their commercials posed the same problems that Chayefsky's drama dealt with: people who feared failure in love and business. But in the commercials there was always a solution as clear-cut as the snap of a finger: the problem could be solved by a new pill, deodorant, toothpaste, shampoo, shaving lotion, hair tonic, car, girdle, coffee, muffin recipe, or floor wax. The solution always had finality. Chayefsky and other writers took these same problems and made them complicated. They were forever suggesting that a problem might stem from childhood and be involved with feelings toward a mother or father. All this was often convincing— that was the trouble. It made the commercial seem fraudulent." [1]

Down on Madison Avenue one afternoon I asked the executive vice-president of a leading advertising agency his attitude to the relationship between advertiser and program. His reply was candid: "If my client is paying $60,000 a minute for advertising associated with a program, the least he can expect is that it is friendly toward his business."

This close liaison between advertiser and program maker is, of course, the main factor that distinguishes commercial television in Western Europe from the United States; in Europe programs are insulated from the advertiser's control, because sponsorship is not permitted.

Potential advertisers may be sounded out at a very early stage in planning a new series. When NBC, for instance, was kicking around ideas for a series in the fall of 1971 involving Jim Garner, they decided that Chevrolet might like to sponsor a part of it. So, a high-powered NBC team, consisting of Don Durgin, the president of the network, Mort Werner, the vice-president for programing, and Jack Otter, vice-president in charge of advertising sales, sallied forth to Detroit. "At that stage we had two versions of what the show might be," recalled Otter later, "— either with Garner as a detective in a big city or as sheriff of a town out

---

[1] Erik Barnouw, *The Image Empire*, p. 33.

west in the early 1900s, but really we were just selling Garner." Chevrolet bought. They agreed to pay $4.3 million for three minutes of advertising a week on each of the first twenty-six episodes.

Full sponsorship of programs by a single advertiser is now rare. The other three minutes of time available on the Garner program (which was called *Nichols*) was taken up by other advertisers. Most advertisers prefer to scatter their favors around: a minute on *The World of Disney,* a couple of minutes on *Ironsides* or *Hawaii Five-O,* another minute on the CBS Friday night movies or on the *Evening News* with Walter Cronkite. This avoids the sponsor's being caught with a complete disaster on his hands. Frequently in recent years, advertisers have waited very late to book their minutes, hoping that the network at the last moment, with unsold minutes on its hands, would sell them time at a "distress" price. But cautious advertisers get in trouble too. Those who wisely bought time early on the *Flip Wilson Show,* one of the biggest hits of the 1970 season, paid only a little over $40,000 a minute. When the program fast became the most fashionable of the year, NBC soon pushed up the rates to $80,000 a minute for advertisers who came late. And they opened the bidding for the 1971 season at $86,000 a minute. It pays the advertiser to spot a winner early.

The advertiser's initial concern, of course, is the amount of "tonnage" of homes that a program can attract. But he wants to know also what kind of people are watching; are they young adults, middle-aged or old people? Are they college educated? Do they live in rural or urban areas? So the networks provide him with the "demographics" of each show; that is to say a profile of the age, sex, educational background and living habits of the audience. The demographics of the network evening news, for instance, indicates that many of the audience are people in their thirties and forties of fairly good education and income. They tune in the news as soon as they come home from the office. So, what better time to promote the aspirin and the anti-acid stomach settlers that will soothe the harassed executive after a hectic day in the office and a three-martini lunch? Consequently, the commercials, which pop up every five minutes in the news, show weary men and women clutching aching heads that need assuaging, or tossing and turning in their restless beds—until they take that instant relief. Set in juxtaposition with the news they also often seem to imply that all the troubles of the world can be cured by one little pill!

The preferred demographics for most programs are that they should be seen by people aged between eighteen and forty-nine living in urban areas—for the simple reason they usually have more money to spend.

Woe betide any program whose main audience turns out to be over fifty and living in the country. That lesson was punched home firmly in 1971 when CBS threw out a whole clutch of programs including *Beverly Hillbillies, Green Acres* and *Mayberry RFD,* whose ratings were still healthy but whose demographics were senile. The advertisers had told CBS in no uncertain terms that there were too many elderly country folk watching their shows. So out they went. Similarly, NBC chopped *The Man from Shiloh* (né *The Virginian*). "That western still had a very satisfactory rating," Dr. Thomas Coffin, NBC's Director of Research, explained, "but we took it off because it was focused too sharply on the older, nonurban audience."

Luckily for western fans, the granddaddy of all westerns, *Bonanza,* which has been running since 1959, still cuts a dashing city-oriented demographic profile and has survived for the entertainment of 50 million Americans and 350 million others in the 82 nations where it is seen each week.

The pressure of trying to tailor every program to appeal to the largest possible audience of 18-to-49-year-old city dwellers is, of course, the factor that really stultifies American commercial television. The formula allows no leeway for experiment or controversy.

Consequently, it is only by conscious decision of the networks to run certain programs at a loss that many documentaries and current affairs programs get on the air at all. Although the news divisions of the three major networks employ some of the finest television journalists to be found anywhere, they rarely have the opportunity to stretch themselves to full advantage. It is almost impossible to compare the amount of regular current affairs and documentary output of public service organizations like the BBC in Britain, ARD in Germany and NHK in Japan with the American commercial networks' serious programing in prime time; the ratio is more than 20 to 1. Briefly stated, in the autumn of 1971 both NBC and CBS had just one hour of prime time per month clearly set aside for current affairs or documentary programing; ABC had no regular slot. In addition, occasional documentary "specials" were dropped into the regular schedule, preempting series. But even these are often dressed up with movie stars doing the commentary and even the interviewing in an attempt to ingratiate them with a larger audience. While I was in New York NBC did an hour-long documentary on Scotland Yard, introduced by David Niven. At one point he actually sat down to interview the Commissioner of Police; to my mind David Niven is a movie star and not a television journalist.

This state of affairs has not come about, one must add immediately, without the stoutest possible rearguard action from the news divisions of the networks. For almost twenty years, ever since Ed Murrow pioneered television journalism at CBS with *See It Now,* the network news directors have labored to keep at least an hour a week in prime time for serious current affairs programing. One can report only that they have not succeeded. Fred Friendly, in perhaps the most publicized resignation ever in American television, walked out in disgust as President of CBS News in 1966, when the network chiefs overruled his request to preempt daytime programing for live coverage of a crucial Senate Foreign Relations Committee hearing on the Vietnam war. Instead, they insisted on keeping in that famous fifth rerun of *The Lucy Show,* explaining that they stood to lose $175,000 in advertising revenue if the Vietnam hearings replaced it. Money is the key.

In the spring of 1971, I asked a CBS vice-president why his network was moving the weekly *Sixty Minutes* current affairs program from prime time and was reported to be relegating it to Sunday afternoons. He said: "Of course it's outrageous—but it's a great money loser."

The pity of it is that on the rare occasions when the television journalists are allowed to make a worthwhile documentary—as CBS has done in recent years with two memorable reports, *Hunger in America* and *The Selling of the Pentagon*—they show just how fine American television could be. The technical and professional skill and the money are available in abundance to create masterly programs, given the freedom from the stranglehold of the advertiser.

Happily, over the years some advertisers, notably companies like Xerox, Mobil Oil, Alcoa, Borg-Warner, and du Pont, have accepted the responsibility of buying time on current affairs programs that they know may be controversial or in sponsoring documentaries that do not have mass appeal. And in these instances they have no control over editorial content; it is a cardinal rule of the network news divisions that the advertisers have no control over subject or content and see the program for the first time when it goes on the air.

But this kind of institutional advertising is not always looked on kindly by advertising agencies in advising their clients how to spend money. Once when a leading oil company suggested to their agency—one of the top half dozen in New York—that they would like to undertake a campaign on television sponsoring worthwhile programs to improve their image, the agency's chairman responded, "Institutional advertising is like a man in a blue serge suit peeing in his trousers. He gets a nice warm feeling all over, but nobody notices." The oil company, to its credit, switched its account elsewhere.

The hurdles to be surmounted by the television documentary have not been helped over the last two or three years by the outrage with which Vice-President Agnew and others have responded when the networks—and CBS in particular—have tried to tackle some of the pressing problems facing the United States. The *cause célèbre,* in the spring of 1971, was the outcry against CBS's *Selling of the Pentagon,* which took a swipe at the methods the Pentagon had been using to explain—or rather sell—its Vietnam war policy. Agnew charged CBS with "propagandist manipulation"; one Congressman snapped that it was "the most un-American thing I've ever seen on the tube."

"The tragedy of this kind of reaction," one former network news president remarked to me, "is that CBS is actually getting attacked for doing their *best.* No one says a word all the time they are doing their worst with the usual run of comedies. And the fuss created over that program means that everyone from Dick Salant (President of CBS News) on down will have to spend weeks replying to all the criticism instead of getting on with making good television. The producer will be so busy explaining himself he won't have a chance to make another documentary for months."

Yet for all the resistance to documentaries and current affairs in prime time, television news gets ample allocation every day—albeit outside prime time. The 60 percent of Americans who claim that television is their prime source of news are well served. Most of the major city stations run at least an hour of local or combined local and national news in the early evening and follow this with the half-hour network news at seven. These news shows—the *CBS Evening News* with Walter Cronkite, the *NBC Nightly News* with David Brinkley, Frank McGee, and John Chancellor, and the *ABC Evening News* with Harry Reasoner and Howard K. Smith—are flagships of network prestige. The anchormen, like Cronkite, are all distinguished journalists, not mere news readers, who are closely involved with the day-to-day writing and editing. Cronkite sees his role on the *CBS Evening News* like that of the managing editor of a newspaper. And his calm, reassuring style on the air has made the *CBS Evening News* consistently the top rated of the nightly news for many years. The box office appeal of the top announcers brings them substantial rewards; Cronkite is said to earn up to $250,000 a year, while ABC, seeking to bolster the ratings for their news, lured Harry Reasoner away from CBS for a five-year contract reportedly worth $1 million.

In addition to a total of one and a half hours of news on many stations from 6:00 until 7:30 each evening, there is normally a further half-hour news roundup at 11:00 each evening. In Los Angeles, widely regarded as being a "news-crazy" city, the network-owned stations run between three and four hours of news daily. The CBS station, KNXT, even goes so far as to preempt commercials outside regular news time to report briefly on a major breaking story.

Many stations also run daily editorials at the end of the evening news. Their news staff will include a special editorial writer—just as newspapers employ editorial writers—and his remarks will always be prefaced with a statement that they represent the views of the management of that particular station. The editorials are normally concerned with local issues; they will tax city government, for instance, about delays in mass transportation improvements, inadequate schools or pollution hazards. ABC, CBS and NBC leave editorializing to the discretion of their local owned stations, which may even express differing views. When the American supersonic transport plane was canceled early in 1971 the NBC station in Los Angeles ran an editorial deploring the SST cancellation, while the NBC stations in Chicago and Cleveland applauded it.

In fact, once the high-powered world of the networks is left behind, it is possible to find individual stations that take their broadcasting role seriously. "As I see it the networks are in show business, but we are in broadcasting," said the program director of CBS's KNXT in Los Angeles. Although the station carries the normal network output, it does report extensively on the problems facing Los Angeles. "Television in my opinion largely ignores its opportunities to inform and educate and make people smarter on how to conduct their lives," said the general manager, Ray Beindorf, "but here we are trying to provide information in a palatable, upbeat way. Nearly half our programs are local and we try to preempt the network for at least half an hour of prime time each month for important public service programs." They have a regular half-hour magazine program, *Insider Outsider,* for the black population of Los Angeles and another, *The Siesta Is Over,* for Mexican-Americans.

One of KNXT's most ambitious local programs in 1970 was an hourlong report on the danger of drugs, called *If You Turn On,* which was uninterrupted by any commercials. The public reaction was so great in praise of the program that immediately afterward, not just the station's switchboard but the entire Hollywood telephone exchange was jammed completely for several hours as viewers tried to phone in their compliments. The telephone company, when they finally untangled the lines, estimated that 170,000 people had tried to phone the station all at once. "This is the way that television should go," said Beindorf.

The difficulty is that local stations, however public spirited they may be, inevitably have to fall back on mass entertainment from the networks for much of the time in order to earn their keep. *If You Turn On* cost KNXT nearly $50,000; relatively few stations are prepared to invest that kind of money in public service documentaries. "The temptation," said one New York station executive, "is always to put on an old movie, take the money from the commercials, and run."

The greatest castigator these days of U.S. television's weakness in doing just that is a bright young man named Nicholas Johnson, one of the seven commissioners of the Federal Communications Commission. Nick Johnson has become the *enfant terrible* of the American television scene— forever damning the networks for serving up "chewing gum for the eyes." "Television tells us, hour after gruesome hour," Johnson complains, "that the primary measure of an individual's worth is his consumption of products, his measuring up to ideals that are found in packages, mass produced and distributed to corporate America." He has proposed, therefore, what he calls "the one-third time rule," which would affect every network-affiliated television station. "Each station," he explained, "would have to provide one-third of its 'prime time' for purposes other than profit-maximizing programs. That's to say public affairs, cultural, educational programs—anything other than the lowest common denominator—'commercially laden fare'—we're now offered." But Nick Johnson is a voice crying in the wilderness of the FCC; his six fellow commissioners are not likely to vote for his rule.

There are signs, however, that the FCC, which for years was regarded as a lapdog of the networks, is beginning to bark. Under a new chairman, Dean Burch (the man who ran Barry Goldwater's Presidential campaign in 1964), who was appointed by President Nixon in the autumn of 1969, the FCC is demanding that the networks improve their children's programing—which for years has consisted of little but cat-chasing-mouse cartoons. (A highly profitable exercise: CBS nets $11 million a year from Saturday morning cartoons.) Burch has told the networks categorically that things must improve radically, "regardless of whether cereal or toy sales [the main sponsors of Saturday cartoon shows] reach new heights or not." "I am appalled at a lot of what my own children watch," Dean Burch told me. "We've got to have a higher proportion of beneficial programs."

The real impetus for better children's programs came, however, not from the FCC, but from the Children's Television Workshop, established in 1968 by the public service National Educational Television (NET) in partnership with the Carnegie Corporation. Nourished by an $8 million grant, Joan Cooney, the Workshop's president, set about devising a program for preschool children that would teach them the basic skills of reading and counting. The result was *Sesame Street,* an oasis of originality, vitality and color amid the desert of American television. *Sesame Street,* situated in East Harlem, is peopled by grownups, children, a seven-foot canary known as Big Bird and assorted puppet interlopers, such as Oscar the Grouch, who lives in a garbage can, and the Cookie Monster, whose sole aim in life is finding yet another excuse to down a cookie. The program ranges over ideas with all the freewheeling imagination of a child's mind. A casual drive up the street in a make-believe car leads to a kaleidescope of brisk, visual adventures; the car's license plate has the letter V on it, which triggers a cartoon about the letter V and shows ten words beginning with the letter. Then back to the car pulling up at a red stop light, waiting for Go. What letter do Stop and Go have in common? . . . O . . . and off into a cameo on the letter O.

The bright little thirty-second cartoons juggling with letters and numbers are, in fact, *Sesame Street*'s commercials! "We use the brief episodic technique of commercials to sell not products but letters and numbers," Joan Cooney explains. And at the end of each show a voice announces that it was presented by the letters J and N, or A and E, after the custom of program sponsorship.

Sesame Street opened five days a week in the autumn of 1969 on nearly two hundred educational and community-owned stations all across America. That first season some seven million children looked at it regularly; it was the first resounding hit for the blossoming public television service. The program also became an inevitable yardstick against which to measure the performance of the commercial networks' children's shows. The networks reacted quite promptly to *Sesame Street* by appointing their own vice-presidents for children's programing and began to conjure up something more original than *Tom and Jerry.* ABC launched *Old Curiosity Shop,* designed to widen the horizons of children up to the age of eleven. But this and other new programs on the networks are still forever interrupted by those "Be the first on your block. . . . Ask Mommy to get some now" commercials for candy and toys. I watched an excellent NBC children's documentary which tackled the delicate subject of explaining the dangers of drugs to under-tens. The program was potentially absorbing but, for me at least, was completely ruined by the constant intrusion of commercials for toys; there were two commercial breaks in the first ten minutes and four in all in the first half hour.

But *Sesame Street*'s success in prodding the commercial networks to rethink their children's programing is a landmark in American television history. Moreover, it has made millions of Americans aware for the first time that a fourth noncommercial network is slowly maturing.

As far back as 1952 the FCC set aside 242 television channels for educational television stations across America. Gradually over two hundred stations have been established, either as offshoots of universities and colleges or community-run channels in cities like New York, Boston, San Francisco, Los Angeles and Chicago. Most of them have lived—indeed, still live—a very hand-to-mouth existence and until the end of the 1960s were not coordinated in program planning and had no actual network. Programs were "bicycled" by mail from one station to another.

At first central inspiration came only from National Educational Television (NET), which began in the 1950s primarily as an organization advising local community stations on how to incorporate themselves and collect funds. Gradually, NET evolved into a national program-producing group, distributing about five hours of programs a week to affiliated noncommercial stations. The Ford Foundation, the largest single benefactor of educational television in America over the years ($200 million up to 1971), was its main source of income.

Then, in 1967, the Carnegie Commission on Educational Television, a detailed inquiry into the prospects for public television in the United States, reported: "We have reached the unqualified conclusion that a well-financed, well-directed educational television system, substantially larger and far more persuasive and effective than that which now exists in the United States, must be brought into being if the full needs of the American public are to be served."

The commission recommended that Congress establish a federally chartered, nonprofit, nongovernmental corporation to oversee the whole development of educational—or public, as it is increasingly known—television. President Lyndon Johnson supported the commission's view. Accordingly, the Corporation for Public Broadcasting was set up in 1967 to knit together the assortment of educational and community stations into a strong public television system. The Corporation is financed both from government and private sources. Essentially, the Corporation itself is a dispenser of funds to program makers; the Corporation is not in the production business itself. "We are the catalyst, the stimulator in developing the whole system," said John Macy, the Corporation's president. An off-shoot of the Corporation, the Public Broadcasting Service (PBS) is charged with developing the actual network—the fourth network, as it is now being called—linking together more than two hundred noncommercial stations in the United States. PBS also coordinates a network schedule comprising programs made by its member stations or acquired from overseas (mostly from the BBC). From October 1971, PBS networked thirteen hours in prime time each week, plus three hours each morning, including *Sesame Street* and a new children's reading program.

Despite this auspicious beginning, public television in America still has to overcome the crucial hurdle of its long-term finance. In 1971, the combined income of the Corporation and the noncommercial stations (many of which receive grants from state or city authorities and universities) was just over $100 million (compared, for example, to the BBC in Britain with $200 million and NHK in Japan with $250 million). The Corporation itself had a grant from Congress of $35 million for the year 1971–72. "What we really need is $100 to $135 million a year," said John Macy, the Corporation's president. Macy's goal is to persuade Congress to grant the Corporation guaranteed long-term financing, ideally provided by a 2 percent tax on the sale of television sets. But pushing that kind of legislation through Congress may be an impossible task, for if the Corporation had permanent funding, as opposed to annual grants, Congress would no longer have any direct control over it. "Politicians here are not in the mood to give that kind of freedom to a medium as powerful as TV," said Ed James, executive editor of the Washington-based *Broadcasting Magazine*.

In wooing the politicians Macy himself stresses the educational potential of the fourth network. Politicians are more likely to respond with hard cash if they feel that television can overcome some of America's education deficiencies. But he also says proudly, "We are attracting for the first time the 35 percent of Americans who normally don't watch commercial television."

This is the real potential of the new network; it is gradually widening the whole spectrum of American television. Apart from *Sesame Street,* three of its first big triumphs have been imports from the BBC—*The Forsyte Saga, The First Churchills* and *Civilisation.* They have been greeted with delight and devoured with a dedication that makes one realize just how underprivileged Americans have been over the years in their television fare. Even vice-presidents of the commercial networks could not privately contain their enjoyment. "My wife and I now watch public television all the time and so does everyone we know socially," said one executive vice-president, "but don't write that or I'll kill you."

But public television's real task for the seventies is to create a strong track record in its own program making; so far too much of its reputation is built on its BBC purchases. The network draws primarily on four production centers: National Education Television, which has been merged with Channel 13 in New York to form the Educational Broadcasting Corporation; WGBH in Boston, an educational foundation supported by, among others, the Boston Symphony Orchestra, Harvard and Yale Universities, and the Massachusetts Institute of Technology; and two California stations, KQED San Francisco and KCET Los Angeles, both financed by their local communities.

All have already established their credentials with a checkerboard of programs of much greater originality than is customarily encountered on the commercial screen. Boston and Los Angeles have jointly produced *The Advocates,* a weekly hour-long debate that has tackled such topics as gun control, marijuana, abortion, and the Calley verdict. An "advocate" for each side, supported by the testimony of expert witnesses, argues the case. And at the end of an hour the moderator asks the viewing audience to write in with a "yes" or "no" opinion. One debate on the Middle East crisis drew 80,000 letters.

San Francisco's KQED presents a weekly review of the world's press, in which journalists compare the coverage of events in newspapers as diverse as *Pravda, The Times, Le Monde* and *Die Welt.* Two programs, *Black Journal* and *Soul,* from NET and Channel 13 in New York, are the first on American television to be produced by and for the black community. *Black Journal* is a visual magazine on issues of importance to black Americans; *Soul* is a variety show. The latter has proved so popular in New York that an estimated 60 percent of black households tune in.

Yet, even now, public television still teeters much of the time on the brink of bankruptcy. The secure and adequate financing that will enable it to really flex its programing muscles is still missing. When I called on KQED in San Francisco, the general manager, Richard Moore, and program director Jonathan Rice, both of whom have been with the station from its birth in 1954, were in the midst of a perennial debate on whether or not they would have to cut staff in a month's time. "We are still flying by the seat of our pants," said Rice. "Once I actually had to borrow $1,000 from my mother and $1,000 from a friend to keep the station open. Just this morning I got a phone call saying that someone will put up the money that will enable us to televise a concert."

KQED was the first noncommercial station in the United States to draw its main support from its viewers. Fifty thousand people subscribe either $14.50 as individual members or $25 for family membership. This brings in about $1 million a year; the rest of the station's $4.5 million annual budget comes from donations, chiefly from foundations, and an annual television "auction" to which viewers contribute everything from a used Rolls-Royce to a week's free treatment at a beauty parlor. In 1970 the auction raised $350,000.

KQED's main facilities are in a converted warehouse, where the sole studio has egg boxes stuck to the walls in an effort to soundproof it from the roar of San Francisco traffic outside. This limitation has not stopped KQED from pressing ahead with some of the most original television I have encountered anywhere.

During a newspaper strike in San Francisco in 1968 the station offered the city's journalists the chance to continue their reporting on the air. The result is an hour-long evening *Newsroom*. The report is presided over by a managing editor who sits in the center of a horseshoe desk, in the style of American newspaper offices, with the reporters seated around the outside. Each reporter in turn reads his story. The editor then asks him for clarification on certain points or leads into a general discussion of the story, bringing in the other reporters for their opinions. The result is a very informal, and sometimes slightly verbose, news report; items are not strictly timed, and may run on longer than planned if the managing editor feels discussion is going well. On fast-breaking stories, reporters come in breathless while the program is on with their reports. The format was so well received that *Newsroom* outlasted the newspaper strike. The Ford Foundation then chipped in an annual grant of $750,000 to keep it going. Although *Newsroom* lacks the wide national and international coverage of news on the commercial networks, more than a third of the families in San Francisco watch it at least once a week. The noncommercial stations in Dallas and Washington, D.C., have picked up the idea and now have their own editions.

So far local programs like *Newsroom* and networked programs on public television are not making any dent in viewing on the commercial networks—because their main attraction is to people who normally watch little television. But a Lou Harris public opinion poll in October 1971 showed that the national weekly audience for the fourth network had risen to 39 million; 38% of the homes questioned had watched public television in the preceding week. President Nixon showed his recognition of its achievement early in 1971 by including a correspondent from the fourth network in a televised *Conversation with the President,* thus giving PBS new status alongside the commercial networks.

The newcomer, however, is not likely to undercut the commercial networks or cause them to alter their policies greatly in the foreseeable future. Although some commercial broadcasters will admit privately that they too put their feet up at home in the evening and watch *The Advocates* or *Civilisation,* no radical change in the networks' programs is brewing in response to PBS. Actually, they are more concerned about the potential threat of cable television eating into the market than they are about public television.

Initially, cable, or community antennae television (CATV), developed quite haphazardly in America in small towns that were just beyond the range of conventional television signals. Some local entrepreneur, often the man selling TV sets, set up a tall mast on a nearby hill to catch the distant signals, which were then carried into the home by coaxial cable. The habit caught on fast and by 1971 at least 5.5 million homes were linked into 2,700 CATV systems. The largest system, in San Diego, California, was hooked into 50,000 homes, bringing a perfect signal from Los Angeles stations more than a hundred miles to the north. Most CATV companies charge about $20 for installation and a monthly fee of $5 to $6. To begin with everyone sat back happy and watched the profits roll up. But the coaxial cable opens all kinds of new programing horizons, for it can carry a dozen or more channels into the home. Some CATV companies soon embarked on their own programing; nothing ambitious, usually a time clock, weather chart, a news ticker and a few interviews with local celebrities. One CATV company in Grand Junction, Colorado, even started television bingo. However, CATV programing has been given new impetus by an FCC ruling that from 1971 all systems with over 3,500 subscribers must originate some programs of their own.

By then the real possibilities of CATV in bringing multichannel television into every home in the United States had been realized. Suddenly everyone wanted to get in. Time-Life sold their five television stations and invested in fifteen CATV systems, the most important being Sterling Manhattan, one of the fast-developing systems in New York City. In mid-1971 Sterling Manhattan had 33,000 subscribers and estimated there were a potential 370,000 within their cable franchise area in midtown Manhattan. The system carries all the main New York television stations and originates its own programs on two spare channels, with live coverage of all ice hockey and basketball games at Madison Square Garden and a regular evening bulletin of local news. So far, none of the CATV systems has the money to produce programs on the scale of the networks, but by concentrating on very simple coverage of local events of interest, they can start to erode the networks' markets.

The commercial broadcasters, therefore, are considerably worried by the challenge of CATV over the next decade. The advent of twenty or thirty channels for every home could fragment that precious mass audience in prime time, which they have striven so hard over the years to corral. "The networks have had a hammerlock on air time for twenty years," said the director of one New York CATV system. "Now it's being challenged."

While even cable will not force an overnight revolution on American television in the seventies, a combination of circumstances have suddenly come together to throw up all kinds of options for the future. Quite apart from the birth of public television and the swift growth of CATV, everyone is waiting breathless to see how cassettes will change the cards. At the same time the FCC, which seemed a handmaiden of the networks for so long, has been flexing its muscles with the new McGannon prime time rule and is also muttering about forcing newspapers to dispense with their television holdings. "There is a ferment today, just as there was in the late 1940s when television was getting established," said Barry Zorthian, of Time-Life's broadcasting division. "The first television era is almost over and the whole audiovisual field for the next generation is being established."

3

Canada:
The Giant's Neighbor

The village of Pembina in North Dakota seems a strange place to have a powerful television station. Only a couple of hundred people live there and the nearest American town of any size is many miles away. But the advertisers who queue up to buy time on KCND-TV Pembina have their eye not on Americans, but on the half million Canadians living just north of the border in the city of Winnipeg. Apparently the investment pays off; the people of Winnipeg spend a fifth of their viewing time watching the Pembina station. Furthermore, Pembina is just one of twenty-five television stations scattered along the American-Canadian border whose signal reaches easily into Canadian homes. Consequently, Canada's two home-grown television networks operate constantly in the shadow of the American giant. The challenge facing Canadian television in the seventies is to preserve its own identity and avoid complete engulfment from south of the border.

The majority of Canadians, who spend an average of four hours a day before their sets, have displayed little loyalty to their own part-public service, part-commercial Canadian Broadcasting Corporation (CBC) and an independent commercial network, CTV. They devote up to two thirds of their time looking at American channels, whose pictures are received just as clearly as the Canadian output because many homes in the major Canadian cities are wired by cable to powerful community antennas. Only ice hockey, that enduring Canadian passion, which is televised every Wednesday and Saturday even throughout the long, harsh winter, can lure them by the millions to their national channels. At other times even these rely heavily on imported American shows; for years the Canadians have been the best customers anywhere of the American networks.

Amidst the American onslaught the lone outpost of truly Canadian

43

television has been the French-speaking province of Quebec, where the language barrier has simply forced both the CBC's French network and private commercial stations to create, rather successfully, their own programs. The CBC's French-language network proudly claims that they make more French-language television programs than ORTF in France. But elsewhere every television executive is haunted by the American specter at his shoulder. "We have absolutely no cushioning from the Americans," said the program director of CBC's English network. "I spend sixty seconds of every minute thinking about their challenge in making up my schedule."

To compound the problem, Canada is about the most awkward country in the world to provide with a comprehensive television system. Quite apart from having two official languages, English and French, requiring dual programing, the geography is a nightmare. As James Finlay, CBC's man in London, put it, "We are twenty-one million people rattling around in half a continent; a thin line of people spread across four thousand miles through seven different time zones. Our network would reach from London to Moscow and far beyond."

Yet for that reason broadcasting in Canada also assumes great importance as a lifeline holding the nation together. Canada has no national newspapers and precious few magazines; while the theater and films have always been overshadowed by the U.S., responsibility for maintaining a distinct Canadian identity has fallen to radio, and increasingly, to television. "I don't think Canada could survive without the CBC," a television news director told me in Toronto.

Faced with this problem, the Canadians are now scrambling to preserve their television from what one TV critic called "wall-to-wall Hollywood in prime time." The impetus came from an investigation into the future of broadcasting, the Fowler Report, which declared in 1965: "The Canadian broadcasting system must never become a mere agency for transmitting foreign programs, however excellent they may be. A population of twenty million people surely has something of its own to say, and broadcasting is an instrument by which it must have an opportunity to express itself."

Following this report, a Canadian Television and Radio Commission to oversee broadcasting was established in 1968, under the energetic guidance of a French Canadian, Pierre Juneau. He has wasted no time in attempting to Canadianize Canadian broadcasting. Juneau has insisted that at least 60 percent of the programs put out both by the CBC and by the private commercial stations must be of Canadian origin; moreover, this

60 percent ratio must be maintained in prime time from 6:30 until 11:30 each evening. And to prevent the networks running all American programs for the remaining 40 percent he has also set a ceiling of 30 percent of programs from any one country—which effectively means the United States.

Yelps of protest, especially from the commercial stations, greeted this stern pronouncement. "They are telling us to produce more Canadian programs, but they are not giving us any money to do it," complained Murray Chercover, president of the CTV network, "and it's a fact of life that the further we have to make our money go, the less we're going to get for it in the way of quality."

Juneau is unmoved. He realizes that it will take time to build up Canadian talent, the best of whom have traditionally been lured away by the gilded coffers of the American networks. There has to be a beginning. "You can't have first-rate Canadian programs without some," one of his staff said. "Perhaps only 20 percent of it is first rate to start with, but that's better than none."

The real question, however, is whether these fine intentions are viable. Although the CBC, for instance, is conceived as a public service organization with a clear mandate to "contribute to the development of national unity and provide for a continuing expression of Canadian identity," it depends on advertising for a quarter of its income. Advertisers are not known to be impressed by high-sounding phrases about "national unity"; they want big audiences. Already in cities where the CBC faces competition from both the local CTV network and American stations, it has rarely gained more than 15 or 20 percent of the audience. Canadianization could mean, initially at least, an even smaller share of the audience, making the CBC even less attractive to advertisers. Not an appealing prospect, especially as the Canadian government is most reluctant to step up the official grant which provides the rest of CBC's income; it even "froze" the grant during 1970–71.

The CBC's declared intention that its "prime objective for the seventies is the repatriation of the Canadian air waves" is further complicated by another local quirk. The CBC does not own all the stations in its network.

It owns about a dozen stations in major cities, but the majority of stations on both the English and French networks are privately owned affiliates, whose income is dependent entirely on advertising—they do not share directly in CBC's government grant. The advantage they have is that they get all CBC's networked programs (about forty hours a week) free;

and if CBC has sold a networked program to a national advertiser then the affiliates receive a slice of that income.

Inevitably, there are incompatibilities in a network that comprises both public service and commercial stations. "We are uneasy bedfellows," admitted a CBC executive in Ottawa. The affiliates always want network programs that will attract maximum audiences to boost the price of their own local ads. Devising an acceptable program schedule is like trying to walk a tightrope that is being tweaked from both ends at once. "Mickey Mouse could make up an American network schedule," said Norman Garriock, program director of CBC's English network. "It's all numbers and dollars. But I defy him to come and make up mine."

But the CBC is not deterred from trying to originate as broad a spectrum of programs as its $200 million a year budget allows. In an attempt to nurture young Canadian writers, they have set up a special fund to enable them to devote time and thought to producing television plays. No one expects miracles overnight. "It's going to take a long, long time to build up Canadian drama," admitted a senior drama producer, "but at least we are giving writers the chance." Also to its credit the CBC devotes at least one hour of prime time on four nights a week to serious documentaries and current affairs—which is precisely sixteen times longer than is allocated regularly by American networks over the border. One of their best in recent years was *The Magnificent Gift,* a dramatization of the founding of the Hudson's Bay Company, which eloquently showed the downfall of the Indians as they confronted the fur traders and were swept aside in the relentless pursuit of imperialism. CBC's overseas reporting has also been aided by Canada's political determination to remain independent of the United States on such issues as the recognition of Communist China. CBC teams have been able to visit China and North Vietnam for firsthand objective reports. "We are certainly not insular," said John Kelly, the deputy director of information programs. "We try to look at every part of the world through Canadian eyes."

Inevitably, the dominance of the Americans does have some influence on the nightly news. CBC news simply cannot afford to use satellites regularly for its own news coverage, but if NBC, for example, is using the Atlantic satellite for pictures of riots in Belfast, CBC can pick up a feed of those pictures at little cost out of New York. However, if NBC decides not to use the satellite, the CBC will wait for its own filmed report to be flown across the Atlantic and will show it a day later.

The Canadians also have to bow to the Americans in making up the evening's schedule. The secret is to place all the American entertainment programs early in the evening, in the hope of winning viewers who will then remain faithful throughout prime time. With the exception of hockey, which can hold its own against all comers, most Canadian programs are held back until nine o'clock, after such American goodies as *The Partridge Family, Laugh-In,* and the *Dick Van Dyke Show.*

The commercial CTV network of twelve stations, which covers all the major cities of Canada except Quebec, but does not penetrate so much into rural areas, presents an equally Americanized front. Looking over its schedules it is hard to believe that it is not actually an American station. With the exception of ice hockey on Wednesday night, no Canadian show gets a look before 9:00, by which time everyone will have been mesmerized by *Bewitched, Andy Williams, Dean Martin, Carol Burnett* and *Here's Lucy.* Not that CTV seems to be hiding many Canadian gems away. Their most popular local program is known as *Pig and Whistle,* which is a variety show set in a pub with a singing landlord. Frankly, as I watched it, I wished he'd stick to serving beer.

The most heartening viewing in Canada is from CBC's French network of six owned stations and nine affiliates, with its headquarters in Montreal. Apart from two stations for French-speaking communities in Winnipeg and Edmonton, all are in the province of Quebec. Although Montreal and much of Quebec are within the range of American television stations, the French-speaking Canadians have shown enormous loyalty to their own network, which has responded with a remarkably wide range of programs. "What I'm aiming at is a real divorce from the normal North American way of scheduling," said Jean-Marie Dugas, the director of programs for the French network. "We may live in North America but we are an island of French speakers. I want to capitalize on that."

He has established a close working relationship with the French-language television services of France, Belgium, and Switzerland, joining with them in coproductions. The late night movies are culled from all over Europe. The week I was in Montreal one had the choice of good films from France, Italy, Hungary, and Britain. But the network has really established its reputation on its own local production. In 1970, only two of the top fifteen programs were not made in Canada. Moreover, in complete contrast to CBC's English-language network, the most popular programs were not ice hockey or variety, but local comedies or drama series —*tele-romans,* as the French call them. The *tele-romans* are normally about family life in and around Montreal. One of the most successful, *Rue des Pignons,* is a rather more cosmopolitan version of *Coronation Street.* "Our viewers feel a great affinity for these programs," explained

Jean-Marie Dugas, "because three quarters of all the people in Quebec province actually live in and around Montreal. They have a great feeling for this city—there are about twenty-five news sheets every week full of gossip of who is sleeping with whom and everyone knows about everyone else. So characters in our *tele-romans* set in Montreal are very familiar to them also. Really we have this great advantage that we are making programs for one city."

This in itself is something of a rarity in television, for elsewhere drama series, although they may be set in one city, are normally made for a nation at large.

Blended with the *tele-romans,* which are good, lightweight entertainment, is a considerable amount of more serious documentary and drama programing. Every Sunday evening, a two-hour program, *Les Beaux Dimanches,* from 8:30 until 10:30, presents concerts, ballet, operas and plays. During the 1970–71 season *Beaux Dimanches* presented twelve original plays by Canadian authors, a dramatization of Steinbeck's *Of Mice and Men* and two full-scale operas, Gounod's *Faust* and Humperdinck's *Hansel and Gretel* (the competition from the American channels over the border at that time for bilingual viewers was *Bonanza* and the *Ed Sullivan Show*). Not that CBC's French network is a heavyweight channel; it has its own share of imported American programs—*Bewitched,* charmingly retitled *"Ma Sorcière Bien Aimée,"* is the most popular—and such British fare as *The Avengers,* rechristened *Chapeau Melon et Bottes de Cuir* (Bowler Hat and Leather Boots—a much more intriguing title than the English original). "I'm trying to be purist *and* commercial," said Jean-Marie Dugas.

The French Canadians' hard work at their own programing has been duly rewarded by the building in Montreal of a $66 million television center, with twenty-six radio and seven television studios, which comes into full use in 1972. The CBC are proudly heralding it as the most modern television center anywhere—improving, they hope, even on NHK's impressive facilities in Japan. From the top of the 320-foot hexagonal tower that rises above the studios you have a fine view not only of the whole of Montreal, but out across the St. Lawrence River to the hills of Vermont and upper New York State. However, despite the view of the United States from the roof, television in Montreal is standing firmly rooted on Canadian soil.

The English-language networks are not so solidly placed. Their new determination to withstand the American avalanche and match the French in establishing their own identity now faces an even more demoralizing threat—cable television, which is spreading faster in Canada than any-where else in the world. A quarter of all Canadian homes had cable TV in 1971, bringing in not just the Canadian channels but at least three, and sometimes six or seven, American stations. In cities like Vancouver, British Columbia, and London, Ontario, two thirds of the homes have cable TV with a choice of ten channels.

The Canadian Radio and Television Commission has been racking its brains as to how to best counter the growth of CATV. It insists that all cable systems must carry Canadian stations as a priority but, as the basic systems being used can fit in twelve channels, that is no problem. Any threat to stop the development of CATV is greeted by loud complaints from communities not yet connected that the CRTC is depriving them of their civil rights in denying access to television programs which are already piped into many other Canadian homes.

Thus within a very few years it is likely that almost every Canadian will be able to tune into ten or a dozen TV channels. This will fragment the existing audiences for CBC and CTV, seriously undercutting their attraction to advertisers. "Just look at the top ten advertisers in the U.S. and Canada," said the managing director of one leading Canadian commercial station. "They are the same and all are controlled out of New York. Quite soon the Americans will be able to place their advertising for the Canadian market on *American* channels, which will be seen in every home here. What is the future for us?"

The CBC, with its large government front, clearly stands the best chance of survival on this bleak scene. The dismal commercial prospect is not interfering with its determination to improve Canadian television in the seventies. Furthermore, a new stimulant will soar into the sky in 1972 when Canada launches a domestic communications satellite—the first in North America. The satellite, operated by the Telesat Canada Corporation, will have ten operational channels, of which three will be used exclusively by the CBC. Two of the channels will distribute English-language television programs; the third will extend the coverage of the French network. The satellite will also expand the television network throughout the far north, bringing the Eskimos and miners living in those barren lands into the Canadian fold. But even this, while giving a few thousand more the opportunity to watch television, will not roll back the American giant. That will cast a shadow over every effort to Canadianize Canadian TV.

4

Latin America:
Tele-novela Land

Television in Latin America can be as uncertain as local politics. Stations mushroom overnight, flourish for a year or two and then vanish in bankruptcy or in a cloud of dust from a guerrilla's bomb. One station in Guatemala, with an American general manager, gets a brisk burst of machine gun fire every few weeks from gunmen in a passing car as an anti-American billet-doux. In Venezuela a new channel, heralded as the most modern in Latin America, opened with great promise but, unfortunately, the transmitter had been placed on the wrong mountain. A few villages in the jungles of the interior, if they had had electricity and TV sets, would have received a fine picture, but the teeming two million populace of Caracas had barely a glimmer on their screens. The station lost $13 million. In Costa Rica engineers erected a transmitter on top of a volcano, beaming excellent pictures throughout the country; then the volcano erupted and the transmitter was engulfed in lava. A station in Buenos Aires must have established a record by having forty-three general directors in less than twenty years.

Along with other mishaps, political revolutions are coped with as briskly as the weather forecast. "Our last revolution was very gentlemanly," said an executive of Teleonce—Channel 11—in Buenos Aires. "Three soldiers came along from the presidential palace and just told us to broadcast the takeover of the new president."

Despite the prompt arrival of soldiers at the hint of a coup, television is owned and operated by the state in only three Latin American countries—Cuba, Chile and Colombia. Elsewhere it is hard to find the programs among the commercials; many countries allow sixteen minutes of commercials in one hour. That is not quite as profitable as it sounds, because too many stations are chasing too little advertising. The entire television advertising kitty in Latin America is no more than $180 million a year (which is just about the same as the BBC television budget in Britain), yet many of the major cities have five or even six channels. Both Lima and São Paulo had seven until 1970, when one channel in each city quietly faded away. "There are so many stations," remarked a European program salesman after touring the continent, "that you feel there is one on every corner, just like the tobacconist's."

Although television has a mass audience in Latin America, a set is still beyond the means of millions of families. In Brazil, for example, there is one television set for every 15 people (compared with one set for every 2.5 people in the United States), while in Peru the ratio is one set for every 30 people. The problem, of course, is not just the cost of the sets; large rural areas have no electricity supply. "What we need," said a director of Channel 5 in Lima, "is a kerosene-powered TV set."

Actually, even if one existed, many would still be outside the range of television for it is concentrated almost entirely in the centers of population. Major cities within a country are often not linked by microwave; video tapes and films travel from one local station to another by bus. Only in Mexico, Cuba and Colombia has there been a concerted effort to build a nationwide microwave link. The Brazilian government is slowly linking up its main cities, but the whole country will not be hooked in for several years. In Buenos Aires, when I asked the general manager of Teleonce if Argentina might have a complete network in this decade, he replied a little sadly, "Perhaps this century."

The issue, of course, is not a simple one. The distances involved are enormous; Western Europe could be lost comfortably in the jungles of Brazil. The real answer, many experts feel, is a Latin American satellite, which would not only give complete coverage of individual countries but would link them together. The existing Atlantic satellite, which the Latin Americans already use for international football games, moonwalks and, since 1971, a daily news film exchange with Europe, does not help the distribution problems within their own continent. But for the moment a Latin American satellite is beyond both budgets and political cooperation. Although television organizations are now cooperating much more closely, political agreement between regimes as diverse as those of Brazil and Chile, or Argentina and Peru, is hardly likely.

Moreover, the concept of public service broadcasting is only now emerging; the few government educational channels that do exist are so far starved of money and expertise. "The trouble is," lamented an executive of the Argentine government's own Channel 7 in Buenos Aires, "that we never have a government in power long enough to formulate a broad-casting policy. The aims of the channel as a result are something of a mystery."

Television licenses in the past have been granted mostly to wealthy supporters of governments. A friendly politician, rather than broadcasting skill, has been the main requirement for winning the right to open a TV station. In Costa Rica a dentist ran a TV station for a while until it lost so much money he had to accept expert help from a more professional Panama channel. Latin American families that first made their wealth in rum, sugar, oil, cattle and newspapers have frequently tried to extend their empires into television. Indeed, it seems to have become quite fash-ionable in countries like Venezuela for the most powerful family businesses to operate a TV channel. Family rivalries may be perpetuated in the com-petition between their private channels. The clash between the Chiari and Elata families in Panama to win the highest ratings for their respective stations reminded an American adviser there "of the Montagues versus the Capulets in *Romeo and Juliet*."

The ease with which people previously made great profits in radio in Latin America, where stations multiply like amoebas (there are 365 in Brazil and 200 in Peru) convinced many innocents that TV offered equally easy loot. "People operate radio stations here almost from their bathtubs," remarked an American television executive in Mexico City. "Commercials are often paid for in merchandise. It's highly profitable." Television pro-grams, however, cannot be paid for solely out of free cases of whisky or soap flakes from a sponsor.

Nevertheless, the most successful television entrepreneurs in Latin America have been, without exception, men who graduated from running radio networks. There are only a handful of them. Goar Mestre, who gave Cuba the world's first complete TV network in the 1950s before departing for Argentina, after Castro's arrival, to become the czar of television in Buenos Aires. Emilio Azcarraga, a rather grand old man, controls the three channels of Telesistema in Mexico. In Peru, Genaro Delgado Parker, president of Panamericana Radiofusion, has produced the most successful soap operas in Latin America, while in Brazil the late Francisco de Assis Chateaubriand Bandeira de Mello founded Diarios Associados, which controls fourteen of the country's fifty-two stations. Two other men are bidding for leading roles—Alexandro Romay, a brash former disc jockey in Buenos Aires, whose Channel 9, which runs mainly live variety shows, is giving Goar Mestre very tough competition; and Dr. Roberto Marinho of Brazil's new TV Globo network which, after several years of considerable losses, has finally become the most popular channel in Rio de Janeiro and São Paulo.

The wealthiest empire founded on the profits of television in Latin America is undoubtedly that of Emilio Azcarraga in Mexico. "Azcarraga," says one of his friends genially, "is the Metro lion of Mexican TV." He began his career in the 1930s as a representative of RCA records in Mexico City. While plugging RCA, he also recorded local Mexican artists and migrated into radio to promote his records. Early in the 1950s he applied for a license to open a television station, although the credit for opening the first channel in Mexico (indeed, in Latin America) goes to another successful radio man, Romulo O'Farrill. O'Farrill's XH-TV opened in Mexico City on August 31, 1950. Azcarraga's station opened shortly afterward. For two or three years the two men fought a bitter rivalry to win audiences and advertising. Finally, President Miguel Aleman suggested tactfully that it was time to stop squabbling and concentrate on developing television. He urged Azcarraga and O'Farrill to merge.

They took his advice and, absorbing a third station in Mexico City, formed Telesistema Mexicana, with Emilio Azcarraga as undisputed leader. Telesistema is still the most formidable television combine in all Latin America. It operates three channels in Mexico City, owns stations in Monterrey, Guadalajara, and Tijuana and has nineteen affiliates in other cities. The main channel in Mexico City is networked throughout the country. Azcarraga has also moved into cable television by the simple expedient of picking up signals from American stations near the Mexican border, relaying them to the capital and feeding them into homes by cable. He has built a television production center in Mexico City, which he conveniently leases out to his three channels. The programs produced there are also ideal fodder for the myriad little TV stations in Guatemala, Nicaragua and Costa Rica that cannot afford to make their own programs.

The profits from all these enterprises have been substantial. Over the years Azcarraga has branched out into numerous other activities (158 different companies according to one count), including car sales, real estate and a grand hotel in Acapulco. He even owns a football team, whose matches may be televised only on his own channels. This enthusiasm for soccer led to some highly embarrassing moments for Azcarraga just before the 1970 World Cup football competition in Mexico. Azcarraga's son, without his father's realizing it, secured all the television rights to the competition and then set about making a deal individually with each country that wanted Telesistema's pictures. Much to the dismay of the BBC in Britain, he sold the British rights to Independent Television. Only after many spirited exchanges was the commercial network forced to back down and agree that on an event of such importance the BBC must also be able to carry the pictures.

Telesistema's monopoly has been challenged since 1968 by several new commercial stations, backed by a group of Monterrey businessmen. The newcomers, whose money has been made largely in breweries, do not yet appear to understand that making television is a different process from making beer. For Emilio Azcarraga, whose fortune is founded in television, they are no great threat.

While Azcarraga's energies have been concentrated in Mexico, Goar Mestre has been roaming at large through television elsewhere in Latin America. He is a big avuncular man in his late fifties who chain-smokes Romeo y Julieta cigars in his blue-carpeted office on the top floor of the television center he has built in Buenos Aires for Proartel—his TV production company. After graduating from Yale, Cuban-born Mestre went into business in Havana, in the early 1940s, as the local agent for Kolynos toothpaste and Jell-O. Quickly becoming dissatisfied with the radio commercials made for these and other products on the radio stations then existing in Cuba, he went into radio in 1942 to improve matters. He built up the CMQ radio network throughout Cuba, and also operated two local stations in Havana, one giving nonstop news and time checks interspersed with commercials, the other broadcasting classical music to satisfy his own tastes. In the early 1950s he stepped naturally into television. The relatively small size of Cuba enabled him to establish two networks, each of seven stations. They were linked together by eighteen microwave hops. Mestre thus takes credit for being the first man to create a television system covering the entire population of a country—an achievement which played conveniently into the hands of Fidel Castro when he campaigned to make himself known to the Cuban people after the fall of Batista.

"When Castro came into Havana we simply turned television over to him lock, stock, and barrel," Mestre recalls. "He was in my office all the time. While he was in the hills as a guerrilla he had never realized the power of TV but, once he became president, he quickly saw that this was the one way to reach the Cuban people in their homes. Then you couldn't keep him off. He was the prime-time show. He never spoke for less than four hours, and his record was six hours and fifteen minutes nonstop. He just chatted on and on, repeating himself, hammering home his points about social services, better education, no more corruption. He had the style of a star performer, with that big beard and his olive green uniform; all through he'd smoke away at his cigars and sip coffee and cognac."

A Swiss journalist visiting Cuba in those early days noted, "I have seen the Bouglione Circus, Cinerama atrocities by Cecil B. de Mille, Arab festivals and Broadway parades, but never have I witnessed a show to hold a candle to Fidel Castro's television marathon. . . . What is government by television? A cheap newspaper gimmick? No, for with his nonstop TV show, Fidel Castro has actually created a new form of government that is just as original and will prove no less significant in its historic effects than the Greek invention of the ballot. . . . For six million Cubans the sole expression of their government's will is the television speech." [1]

The joke in Havana then was that one could rely on the electricity supply only on the evenings when Castro was due to make another television harangue.

Castro's command of television quickly left Mestre out in the cold. "I bailed out and came to Argentina." There he started his own television production company, Proartel, and won a license for Channel 13. Since the only real rival then was the chaotic government channel, he had little difficulty in making Channel 13 the prime station in Buenos Aires: on the air fifteen hours a day, with almost 80 percent of the programs produced locally. He also established a limited network of ten stations in other cities. However, the blanket coverage he achieved in Cuba has not been repeated, because there is still no microwave network throughout Argentina. The government will not let him build one, although it keeps promising to build its own.

His success in Argentina prompted Mestre to embark on a variety of television forays in Peru, Colombia and Venezuela. They were much less rewarding; the Venezuelan expedition, in particular, was disastrous, for it was there that the transmitter was placed initially on the wrong mountain.

Beyond the Andes in Lima another would-be television empire builder, Genaro Delgado Parker, has been employing his ingenuity to prevent Peru's left-wing military regime from taking over his and the other four commercial stations. His father has long been established in radio in Lima, but Genaro and his two brothers, Hector and Manuel, have graduated into television. Manuel runs Channel 5 in Lima, Hector looks after their overseas operations, while Genaro heads a holding company, Panamericana Radiofusion, which coordinates all their activities. When the brothers first went into television they quickly found that their ambitions were thwarted by very strict budgets. The total television advertising revenue

[1] Jean Ziegler, International Press Institute, 1960.

in Peru is a mere $7 million a year, shared among five competing stations. "We decided the only way for us to develop was to make our programs for all Latin American markets," said Genaro. "We've been very lucky. We started in 1966 and so far we've sold our programs in fourteen countries, which isn't bad for a small Peruvian company."

Encouraged by this success the brothers have been moving into television outside Peru. They have a stake in one station in Argentina and another in Puerto Rico, where they have also established a production company. In Lima, Genaro Delgado Parker shows visitors to his office a large model of the new television center he hoped to build—if he could have obtained guarantees from the government not to nationalize television. That plan, however, was thwarted in November 1971 when the Peruvian government announced it was taking over 51 percent ownership of all local commercial television stations.

This take-over marks an accelerating trend of government intervention in broadcasting throughout the continent. It has helped speed the retreat of the three major American networks and Time-Life, who all embarked on a great, but unhappy, flirtation with Latin American television in the early 1960s. The Americans were tempted into Latin America, not just as a market for their programs, but to sell stations equipment and television sets in the belief that television there could be just as profitable as in the United States. The broadcasting law in most countries forbade their actually owning a television channel, but the Americans found a local partner who obtained the license, then pumped in capital, equipment, and know-how. The prospect seemed most attractive. A network like NBC, which is owned by RCA, could fit out the station with RCA equipment, have a ready outlet for its programs and reap, they thought, great advertising profits. In Venezuela the American networks bought into every single TV station; NBC joined the local Phelps family in Channel 2 in Caracas; ABC went into Channel 4 with the Cisneros family (which had made its fortune bottling Pepsi-Cola), while CBS and Time-Life linked up with Goar Mestre from the Argentine and the Vollner family, whose main interests were sugar and rum, to open Channel 9.

In Argentina CBS and Time-Life worked with Mestre on his own Channel 13, NBC invested in Channel 9, and ABC joined a group of local Jesuits who were hoping to propagate the faith through television over Channel 11. Further investments were made in stations in Brazil (where Time-Life backed the developing TV Globo network), Peru, Panama and Guatemala. And everywhere it was the same story—huge losses.

"We simply overestimated the market," said an NBC executive who spent several years helping his network bail out of Latin America as gracefully as possible. "For a while everyone thought it was the new frontier. We quickly found out it wasn't. There were just too many stations."

In Venezuela, for example, the advertising revenue available was about $22 million a year, but the combined budgets of the three stations in which the Americans had stakes came to $24 million. Once they realized their mistake the Americans tried to retreat, but often the losses of the stations were so great that no one locally would buy out their interest. They have either had to retain the investment hoping for better days or sell out to their existing partners on extraordinarily generous credit terms.

A simple miscalculation about revenue was not the sole cause of the American failures. Their Latin American invasion began just as nationalist feeling was gaining momentum; Argentinians, Peruvians and Brazilians resented the American domination. "The Americans failed to realize that television here is a different animal from television in the United States," said Goar Mestre. "People in Argentina don't mind the occasional American program, but what they really like are shows with local flavor. We make 78 percent of our own programs."

Local programs, in fact, are pushing American imports right out of Latin America. Moreover, because the whole continent, with the exception of Brazil, speaks Spanish, there is a fine pool of programs in Spanish which can be conveniently swapped between individual countries. Peruvians can watch Mexican programs, Venezuelans can understand shows from Colombia or Argentina. Prime time everywhere is now given over entirely to local programs or those produced in neighboring countries; American shows are relegated more and more to the afternoons or late at night. "Program directors know they can beat any American series hands down by putting their own *tele-novelas* against it," said an American program salesman sadly in Mexico.

The life's blood of Latin American TV is the *tele-novela*. Two or three of these soap operas frequently follow each other right through prime time. In Mexico, Telesistema's Channel 2, the main network covering the whole country, runs *novelas* back to back every day from 4:15 until 7:45. In Panama, 8 till 10 every evening is *tele-novela* time. In Argentina they prefer them in the afternoon; Goar Mestre's Channel 13 carries nonstop *novelas* from 3:00 until 6:00. Every *novela* has the same essential theme: a poor but beautiful country girl comes to the big city, works as a maid in a rich household, is seduced, has an illegitimate baby but prospers and opens a chic boutique or marries a millionaire playboy. Variations on the theme are endless. TV Globo in Brazil scored a great success with *Pigmalião 70,* which simply reversed the normal Pygmalion roles, so that poor country boy comes to the big city, is taken up and educated by a rich, beautiful, sophisticated, sports-car-driving lady.

"The story of a successful *tele-novela* must be the story of many people in Latin America," explains Genaro Delgado Parker in Lima. "It's not melodrama, it's not crime. It's like the lives of many of the viewers— or how they would like their lives to be. The dialogue is simple and unsophisticated. The characters aren't all bad or all good."

Delgado Parker's own Panamericana Radiofusion has been responsible for two of the most successful *tele-novelas—Simplemente Maria* and *Natacha.* Both of them have the same poor-country-girl-starts-as-servant-in-big-city-home theme; the only real difference is that Natacha marries her lover and Maria does not. *Simplemente Maria* has been seen in every single Latin American country and also on Spanish-language stations in New York, Los Angeles and Miami; Brazil, Argentina and Venezuela have all made their own versions. At the latest count around 400 episodes had been made. *Natacha,* which started rather later, easily notched up 260 episodes and Delgado Parker told me, "Maybe we'll make 400 in the end." *Simplemente Maria* has also been made into a film; when I was in Lima the lines stretched all around the block from the movie theater.

The production of *tele-novelas* has been honed down to the barest essentials. Most half-hour episodes cost between $1,200 and $2,000, depending on how little the producers can get away with paying the stars. Location scenes are almost unknown; the *novelas* are normally churned out in one studio with a couple of sparsely furnished sets. Three episodes are shot in an eight-hour working day. The secret of such swift productions is a midget radio receiver plugged into the ear of each actor, which dispenses almost entirely with the time-consuming business of memorizing lines thoroughly or learning detailed stage directions. As the action proceeds before three cameras, a prompter in the control room reads the script and stage directions into a small radio transmitter so that the actor hears his lines in his tiny earplug. He just follows orders or repeats what he hears.

The Mexicans are particularly brisk at this business. One morning I stopped by a Telesistema studio where they were making about the hundredth episode of a saga called *La Cruz de Mariza Cruces,* in which a poor country girl goes to work as a maid on a Mexican ranch, gets pregnant . . . etc. Work on making three episodes that day had started at 10:00 and by 11:15, when I arrived, they had already completed one in its entirety. Now the director, a splendid Mexican with a short, clipped beard and a frock coat, was busy briefing his cast for the next chapter. He ran over the main points of the script for a while but, by 11:30, they were all set to shoot the second half-hour episode of the morning. The prompter hunched over his microphone, everyone adjusted his earplugs and they were away. "Mariza, stand up, move to your right and say 'I am yours forever,' " snaps the prompter. The actress responds accordingly. In another corner of the set a man in white tie and tails holds a woman in a low-cut evening gown in his arms and, on instructions, they start jogging up and down before a camera to simulate dancing. Cut to an empty set; an old man comes wandering slowly on, looking puzzled and confused. To me it is not clear if that is how he should look or if his earplug has broken down. Never mind. Minor errors are overlooked. The important thing is to finish the episode before lunch. At least they do only three episodes a day here. At Channel 8 in Caracas, Venezuela, they reckon to do three episodes on weekdays and four on Sundays.

The mass audiences for the *tele-novelas* are, however, hardly stern critics of production techniques; for them a story with which they can identify is all-important. "The secret of the *novela* is a good, strong script," said Goar Mestre. In the slums of Rio, Buenos Aires or Lima the tale of local-girl-makes-good is far more compelling than *Ironside* or *Bewitched,* which are completely beyond the experience of very simple and frequently illiterate people. They are entranced by the *novelas. "Novelas* keep them mesmerized," said a young television producer in Buenos Aires. "For an hour or two they forget the conditions in which they are living—perhaps it even stops them from making revolutions."

Besides the *novelas* the other hallmark of Latin American television is live variety on Saturdays and Sundays lasting anywhere from six to twelve hours. These marathons are a potpourri of singing and comedy acts, quiz games and interviews, normally hosted by one breezy master of cere-monies who becomes, almost inevitably, the number-one television per-sonality. The Argentinians have the greatest passion—and stamina—for these nonstop programs. Goar Mestre's Channel 13 offers a seven-hour Saturday show, *Sabados Circulares de Mancera,* hosted by a chatty, slightly aggressive young man with unruly hair, named Nicholas Mancera. Pitted against Mancera's meanderings Alexandro Romay's Channel 9 offers eight and a half hours of *Sabados de la Bondad.* The show is introduced by Hector Coire, but Romay himself, a slim, brisk figure with a toothbrush moustache, can rarely resist the temptation of stepping down from his director general's chair on Saturday evenings to participate, often without prior warning, in the show. He has been known to stroll into the studio, hold out a commanding hand close up into the camera lens, call "Wait a moment," and launch into a series of outlandish anecdotes about totally mythical adventures that have befallen him. This unexpected arrival of the boss gives the show a spontaneity that makes up for the technical gaffes which are almost inevitable in such a feat of endurance.

One night when I was watching the show (and being vastly entertained by it) a leading Argentine pop singer, Sandro, apparently got lost behind the scenes during the commercial. The host, Hector Coire, meanwhile, was leading into an elaborate introduction heralding his entrance: trumpets blared, the cameras switched to the top of a staircase. "Sandro," yelled Coire, as teenagers in the studio audience squealed with delight. No sign of Sandro. Coire cued him again: "Sandro." Still no lithe figure bounding down the stairway. Coire, slightly taken aback, turned and walked over to the teenagers and started interviewing them to gain time. While he was in the midst of that chat Sandro finally strolled, unnoticed, down the stairway.

The eight-and-a-half-hour Saturday show is really just a warmup for Sunday, when *Feliz Domingo* (Happy Sunday) lasts a straight twelve hours, from 11:30 in the morning until 11:30 at night. The formula of quizzes and pop singers is the same. While this exhausts the host, Orlando Marconi, the camera crews and even the studio audience, the ordinary viewer simply tunes in once in a while, as if he were dipping into a visual Sunday color supplement.

The popularity of these protracted live shows has pulled Alexandro Romay's station back from the brink of financial disaster. When he took over, he inherited such a pile of debts that he had no money to buy outside programs and precious little to make his own. Undaunted, he rounded up a pool of local out-of-work actors and pop singers and started building live studio shows around them. The lack of polish was more than compensated for by everyone's enthusiasm. By 1969 Romay was seriously challenging Goar Mestre's Channel 13 for top audience ratings in Buenos Aires. Not only was Mestre forced to respond with live shows; the habit is now spreading fast throughout Latin America. In Mexico Telesistema has started *Siempre el Domingo*—Always on Sunday—which lasts seven and a half hours; in Brazil you can watch the *Silvio Santos Show* for five and a quarter hours on TV Globo each Sunday afternoon, and the moment that finishes switch to *Diarios Associados,* where Flavio Cavalcanti is just beginning his four-hour stint (every time Sunday falls on the sixth day of the month Cavalcanti's show runs, by some curious twist of logic, for six hours).

The Brazilians have also launched the one international variety program on television in Latin America—*The Rio Song Festival,* a close cousin of the Eurovision Song Contest. Staged as a grand spectacle in a stadium in Rio, it has all the excitement of a football game and is the television event of the year. In 1970 more than forty countries from Europe as well as Latin America entered songs and singers in the contest, which was broadcast live by satellite throughout the continent. Globo even imported color cameras so that the finale of the competition could be sent in color by satellite direct to Europe.

But the era of endless song and dance on Latin American television is drawing to a close. Rather belatedly, many politicians there are beginning to realize the potential of television both to educate the millions who cannot read and write and to mold them to their own designs. Castro has very efficiently demonstrated in Cuba how to bring a country to heel by television; but Colombia has set the best example in Latin America of opting out of the *tele-novela* circuit in favor of television as a cure for illiteracy and disease. The Colombian television service is one of the poorest on the continent (it has to get by on $5 million a year) and is closely government-controlled, but it has attempted to provide some form of public service. When I visited Abraham Zalzmann, the director of television at the National Institute for Radio and Television (Inravision), he was reading the Pilkington Report, seeking further guidelines from that detailed investigation into British television. Inravision controls all the studios and transmitters in Colombia, but leases out time to commercial program companies in the evening. By day, however, the Inravision network is used for programs for schools, financed by the evening commercials. Inravision has established one of the most complete networks in Latin America, covering almost 95 percent of Colombia's population of twenty million scattered through the foothills of the Andes. They have achieved this by building the highest television transmitter in the world, perched over 13,000 feet up on an Andean peak, and by establishing the longest jump between microwave links in the world—260 miles between two mountaintops.

One full network is already in operation, plus a second local channel in the capital of Bogotá which puts out adult education programs in the evenings. A second national network, devoted entirely to educational television, should be complete by 1973. This new channel will broadcast education programs nonstop from eight in the morning until midnight. "Without television," Abraham Zalzmann explained, "it is quite impossible for us to educate everyone. Education is not compulsory in Colombia because there are not enough teachers or schools. Television can fill that gap."

The major task is to ensure that every community is equipped with a television set; in 1971 there was only one set for every twenty-five people in Colombia. The four hundred dollars needed to buy one is quite beyond the means of millions. The government and overseas aid agencies are therefore proposing to establish community receivers around which all the children or even the adults in a village or a street can gather. The United States has supplied 1,500 sets for schools to receive daytime programs, while several hundred more sets have been distributed to local teleclubs for adult education programs each evening on the local Bogotá station. "These teleclubs are not only to teach people to read and write," the director of educational programs pointed out, "but to explain to people the basic facts about public health and hygiene, housing construction and agriculture."

While the Colombian experiments with educational television are still in their infancy, a UNESCO educational television expert remarked that "the Colombians are really the only people in Latin America who are seriously trying to use television to advantage."

Everywhere, however, the pressure is on to increase educational broadcasting. All commercial stations in Brazil now have to broadcast at least five hours of educational programs each week and the government is building its own network of forty educational stations. The new tone of television was evident when I called on the CBS representative in São Paulo, who for years has happily sold *Gunsmoke* and *Hawaii Five-O* to Brazilian stations. I found him busy writing a new catalogue of all educational and documentary programs available from CBS. "Until now the stations here have been concerned only with ratings," he said, "but they've had it made clear to them that if they don't change their programs the government will." He was sending out, as a gentle hint with his new catalogue, the full text of a speech by Brazil's President Medici chiding the television industry for being so slow to mend its ways. "This is not the first time I have had to speak like this," the President pointed out sternly. "I have reminded you before that it is not enough just to have five hours weekly of educational programs, but essential to raise the whole level of programing; poor-quality programs must be forbidden as a rule on television; the creative talent of Brazilians must not be destroyed by television."

The cry for educational television is, of course, often a convenient cloak to cover government maneuvers to strengthen its hold on television. Stations whose editorial policies are embarrassing to the government can quietly be nationalized as educational channels. But most of them are fully aware of the dangers and steer an obsequious course rather than risk losing their income from commercials. Open censorship is not always necessary; news editors are well drilled in what not to cover. "We practice self-censorship," a television news editor, who once worked for the BBC, admitted in Buenos Aires. The Mexican government, which was incensed by television coverage of student riots in Mexico City just before the 1968 Olympics, has since enacted a law that enables it to claim 12.5 percent of all television time to explain its own policies to the people.

Clearly the happy-go-lucky age of television in Latin America is past. The days when any rich family with good political connections bid for a television license are finished; the Americans are bowing out, trying hard to forget the losses they have had. "Television in Latin America is at the crossroads," said Alistair McKenzie, who has spent more than fifteen years representing NBC interests there. "The beginning of 1970 was really the turning point. Now the politicians are stepping in everywhere. Chances of selling some routine, stupid comedy are dying. In the future the preoccupation will be the moral and educational content of programs; frankly I don't blame them."

WESTERN
EUROPE

5

Eurovision

The nerve center of European television is concealed high up in the roof of the Palais de Justice in Brussels. Outside, the broad flight of steps up to the cavernous entrance hall of the Palais is bustling with lawyers, policemen and witnesses, but tucked away in the far corner of the entrance is a tiny elevator that soars nonstop toward the roof. The door slides back to reveal a narrow gallery running along inside the roof of the entrance hall: the lawyers suddenly look like dwarfs, scurrying back and forth far below. At the end of the gallery—quite a nerve-wracking walk, for there is only a metal handrail—a door leads into first a kitchen and then a warren of attic rooms. There half a dozen young men in their shirtsleeves sit before a panorama of television monitors that glow with the call signs of Europe's television stations. Very shortly, at 5:00, the screens will come alive with film of that day's happenings all over Europe—an avalanche in the French Alps, a riot in Belfast, a football match in Italy, a disarmament conference in Vienna. Just now, the young men, who come from the Netherlands, Britain, Belgium, West Germany and Sweden, are busy checking their circuits with television stations as far-flung as Dublin and Lisbon, Tunis and Belgrade, Rome and Copenhagen. They talk in English or French, alternating back and forth easily between the two languages. Occasionally, when some capital is slow to respond they show a moment's irritation: "Can't the twit switch that circuit?" There is no time for delays, precisely at 5:00 they must have the whole of Europe and three North African countries hooked in together for what they call EVN 1—the first session of a twice-daily exchange of news film. Another exchange, EVN 2, will follow at 7:00. Before that, however, they have to funnel all over Europe live coverage by satellite of the landing in the Pacific of an Apollo spacecraft back from the moon. They must also cope with special transmissions between individual European capitals as various foreign correspondents make their personal reports home for the evening news. Later in the evening they will relay an important football match from London to half a dozen other television services across Europe.

The hideout beneath the rafters in the Palais de Justice is the control room for Eurovision, the European Broadcasting Union's (EBU) unique multinational program exchange. Twenty-seven television stations in twenty-two European countries are linked to this network, which extends also to Morocco, Algeria, Tunisia, and to Intervision, Eurovision's counterpart in Eastern Europe and the Soviet Union. Yugoslavia, although a communist country, is an integral part of the Eurovision, not the Intervision, network. The lone European nation not on the network is Iceland, which is too remote. Iceland does have television—broadcasting for about three hours a night six days a week (never on Thursdays)—but has to rely on all its imported programs coming in by air freight.

Brussels became the technical center for Eurovision from the beginning because, when the network started to evolve in the mid 1950s Belgium was a convenient central location for European telecommunications to converge. Moreover, most of the early multinational program exchanges were between Britain, France, Belgium and the Netherlands (for Queen Elizabeth's coronation in 1953, for instance). The Palais de Justice, then the tallest building in Brussels with its dome rising to 360 feet, was ideal for a technical post, as antennae placed inside the dome could pick up television pictures over great distances.

Nowadays, the pictures from the crossroads at Brussels can be relayed instantly to all the 75 million television sets in Western Europe. By 1970 there was one set among every five people; only in Spain, Yugoslavia, Portugal, and Greece was television not a commonplace in every home. Portugal, for example, had one set among twenty people, Greece had one among fifty. Television in these countries is still a rarity outside the large cities. Little villages in the north of Portugal have only one or two sets in bars and cafés. "The people here have still not got accustomed to watching television in their homes," said Dr. Antonio Bivar, director of international relations for Portuguese television. "For centuries they've gone out to bars every evening and they still prefer to go there and watch the television among their friends. It's just the same in the south of Italy, people don't like sitting at home."

Everywhere in Europe television is primarily an evening attraction. No one yet has programs with breakfast, although many start up at lunch time with entertainment for housewives. In small nations like Norway and Denmark part of the evening's viewing is considerably repeated during the next day for night-shift workers. Italy has one major feature program each evening starting at 9:00, while in Portugal there is virtually no entertainment before 10:00 in the evening.

The Portuguese, incidentally, have the most curious legislation I encountered anywhere in the world regarding television programing. All public entertainment in Portugal has to be licensed as being suitable either for ages up to six, up to twelve or over seventeen. Since television viewers cannot be segregated by age groups *all* programs must be deemed suitable for viewing by twelve-year-olds. This totally limits their television output. As a Portuguese television executive lamented: "Can you name me a modern play that is suitable for twelve-year-olds?"

A limitation that most European countries have in common, however, is on television advertising. Television almost unanimously earns its living from annual license fees; the advertiser is kept at arm's length. While there is plenty of popular entertainment to attract large audiences, the public service concept prevails. The statutes of broadcasting organizations invariably require them to "inform, educate and entertain the public." Just two countries, Spain and Monaco, have wholly commercial television, while Britain alone has the dual system of one commercial network earning its living from advertising and the two networks of the BBC supported by license fees. The cheapest license fees in Europe are in Ireland and Portugal, which charge about $15 a year; the highest is $34.80 in Sweden. Several countries charge extra for licenses for color sets—the Swedish color license, for instance, costs $54.10. License income, however, cannot always meet the rising costs of television. Gradually many of the public service broadcasting organizations have come to accept strictly limited blocs of commercials between programs to supplement their budgets. West Germany allows twenty minutes of commercials in four blocs between 6:00 and 8:00 each evening and none thereafter. France permits a mere eight minutes per evening. The advertiser, therefore, is often privileged to get any advertising time at all; he may get only a quarter of the spots he applies for, as the networks are quickly overbooked. Direct sponsorship is usually forbidden.

The pace of development has been set primarily by the British and the West Germans. The British were the moving force behind the establishment and expansion of the European Broadcasting Union, and their professional standards have set targets for others to match. Moreover, their programs have been shown more widely throughout Europe than those of any other nation except the United States. Since many of the smaller countries, such as Holland and Sweden, do not bother to dub they are also seen in English, thus contributing gradually to breaking down the language barriers. The West Germans, on the other hand, have invented a color television system, PAL, which has been almost universally adopted by their European neighbors with the notable exception of the French, who, with typical Gallic independence, have opted for their own color system, SECAM. The British and the West Germans, together with the French and Italians, dominate the program scene. Only they have the resources to mount really large-scale productions or series. In any overseas crisis, for example, one of these "big four" will inevitably move swiftly to book satellite time for news film transmission. The Belgians, Finns or Swiss—with much less money—normally wait until one of the four has booked the satellite and then take a feed over the Eurovision network, splitting the satellite charges. They cannot afford to go it alone.

The smaller nations almost always operate in the shadow of their big neighbors. Since television is unconfined by Europe's political frontiers, all kinds of international overlapping occurs. The ordinary family in Brussels can, with a good aerial and a modified television set, view no less than ten channels in five countries. Besides Belgium's own two channels—one broadcasting in French, the other in Flemish—they have a choice of two channels from ORTF in France (three from 1972 onward), three from Germany, two from the Netherlands and one from Luxembourg. The Danes, the Dutch, the Swiss and the Irish are also swamped by foreign television, although the actual choice of channels is never so extensive. This encroachment certainly stimulates small nations to improve their own programs and technical standards, but it may also precipitate them into second channels or color before they can really afford it. The Dutch, for instance, have to try to match the West Germans, since their viewers demand the same quality. However, most of the time viewers remain fairly loyal to their own national channels, with perhaps only 10 or 15 percent of viewers regularly tuning to foreign channels. The exception is Ireland, where Radio Telefis Eireann (RTE) in Dublin has to compete with two strong British signals beaming down from Belfast and across the Irish Sea from Wales. Where reception is best two thirds of the Irish homes watch British commercial television; the remaining third are split between the BBC and their own RTE. Irish television was originally started in an attempt to distract the local people from British television. "We were set up as a shield against incoming material—to stop people watching programs from across the water," said Michael Garvey,

RTE's controller of television, "which is a rather negative way to start."

The reaction of the smaller services is often to link up with the major networks next door for the more costly entertainment programs, provided that languages are compatible. The Austrians, for instance, undertake many coproductions with the second German network, ZDF. The Irish have a deal with the BBC in Britain whereby they can show programs from the second BBC network, BBC 2, which has little coverage in Ireland, before the BBC repeats them on its powerful first channel. Complications set in when a single country has television services operating in more than one language. In Belgium, where the French- and Flemish-language services operate quite separately, each with its own staff, the French network RTB works closely with ORTF in France while the Flemish RTB coproduces with the Netherlands and repeats many of their plays. Switzerland is even more diverse; she has a French-speaking network working out of Geneva, a German network from Zurich and an Italian network from Lugano. The Geneva station regularly coproduces with ORTF—whose programs can easily be picked up in Geneva—and Zurich works with the Germans and the Austrians. This does not mean that the smaller nations do not produce their own programs: most of them are making 60 percent or more locally, but they simply lack the budgets to embark alone on expensive series. Irish television, for example, has a budget of only $10 million a year compared with $420 million available to television in Britain.

Europe's three smallest stations, Tele-Monte Carlo in Monaco, Tele-Luxembourg and Gibraltar Television exist mainly by running old films and American series, interspersed with commercials. Moreover, many of their viewers are in the surrounding countries. Tele-Monte Carlo covers the French Riviera east to the Italian frontier and west to Marseilles; Luxembourg's pictures radiate to France, Belgium, and West Germany. Although they all kick off the evening with local news and magazine programs, and Tele-Monte Carlo and Tele-Luxembourg undertake some joint quizzes with ORTF in France, their chief attraction is old movies and series. They are the only stations in Europe which still rely heavily on American material. Tele-Luxembourg and Gibraltar Television receive a small part of their income from license fees, but essentially all three rely on commercials for survival.

The freedom from advertising pressures enjoyed throughout most of Europe is frequently offset by government control instead. The restrictions and pressures vary greatly from country to country. French television was tightly regulated under President de Gaulle, but has an easier time under

President Pompidou. Up in Finland, where television reporting suddenly lurched to the left under one director general in the late 1960s, conservative politicians moved in with their own party secretary as his replacement after a general election. General Franco's government in Spain keeps a firm grip on television which, although it earns all its income from advertising, is actually a part of the Ministry of Information and Tourism. The Ministry keeps close control over television news; there is plenty of film of General Franco and his heir apparent, Prince Juan Carlos, but strikes or the demonstrations by students at the University of Madrid pass unmentioned.

With or without political control, broadcasting organizations in several countries, including West Germany and Italy, try to present an impartial front by a near series of checks and balances. If the director general is a socialist, his deputy will be a conservative—and so on down the line. Promotion, therefore, can sometimes depend on the right party affiliation rather than ability. News and current affairs reporting under such circumstances often lack objectivity, as each side busily tries to edit out points that might offend its own supporters.

The most unusual attempt to break out of the straitjacket of political checks and balances was made in Austria. For many years radio and television there were organized strictly on party lines; if one job was held by a conservative, the next went to a socialist and, as the joke used to go, a third man was also required to do the work. "Both radio and television were sterile and insignificant," said Alfons Dalmas, the chief editor at Austrian television, ORF. "We didn't risk anything at all on the news—even a foreign story about British socialists would be banned because it might help our socialists."

Then in 1963 a young Vienna newspaper editor, Hugo Portisch, published a virulent attack on this stifling balance of power and, beneath his editorial, printed a coupon asking those in favor of broadcasting reform to complete it and send it to him. The paper received an avalanche of 300,000 replies. Thus encouraged, Portisch decided to take advantage of a clause in the Austrian constitution which says that if 250,000 signatures can be obtained in a plebiscite pleading for a new law Parliament must debate the law they propose. Portisch organized a plebiscite which drew 832,353 signatures. This pressure led to a new broadcasting act decreeing that in future ORF and the persons employed by it are independent. Since then Austrian television has exploded with all kinds of news coverage. Portisch himself, having inspired the revolution, became a leading television personality overnight—a cool soothsayer for all seasons, traveling the world making documentaries and giving his own personal view of the week's events every Saturday night in peak time. His program draws some 70 percent of the Austrian audience, rivaling *What's My Line?* and *The Man from U.N.C.L.E.* in popularity.

Such a revolution, however, is hardly likely to deter politicians in Austria, or elsewhere, from meddling in television affairs wherever they get the chance. Moreover, they all love appearing on the box themselves. Many party public relations men keep score to the nearest second of the amount of time their leaders are given on television to ensure that they are on at least as much as—and ideally more than—their rivals. Political reporting is expanded in West Germany, the Netherlands, Sweden, Denmark and Norway by regular television coverage of important parliamentary debates. The West Germans, in particular, often run the debate all day and through the evening if the Bundestag is discussing major issues of economic or foreign policy. The real outsiders are the British; Parliament has consistently refused to allow either radio or television access to the House of Commons. This is a major weakness of British television, which otherwise enjoys a considerable reputation for its freedom from political control.

Every European country, however, firmly resists advertising by politicians or parties at election time. They view with dismay the millions of dollars spent on American television by politicians in search of power. The usual procedure is to allocate time for party political broadcasts, with every party being granted time according to some prearranged formula—either the number of candidates it is fielding or its registered support. The Dutch, whose television is organized entirely by farming out so many hours a week to a variety of political and religious pressure groups, have this down to a fine art. The twelve political parties represented in the Dutch Parliament are entitled to ten minutes each four times a year, with extra time at elections. The British parcel out party political broadcasts at a secret conclave of party leaders with representatives from the BBC and the commercial network; all broadcasts are shown on all channels so the viewer cannot escape.

Just how effective such broadcasts are is another matter. A careful survey of the effects of television on British general elections by the Television Research Unit at the University of Leeds has shown that election television fulfills mainly an educational role in providing voters, who have already made up their minds, with information about party policies.

"There was no evidence to show," the study concluded, "that the viewing of party broadcasts has affected voting or the attitudes of electors to the Labour and Conservative parties." [1]

Television journalists with whom I have discussed this conclusion in several European countries agree—party broadcasts preach to the converted. What every television editor prefers, but can rarely achieve, is to persuade party leaders to sit down for face-to-face confrontations during elections, or at least to interviews with leading journalists. Most European leaders, however, have learned the lessons of the Kennedy-Nixon debates in the United States; everywhere presidents and prime ministers decline to confront their opponents on TV.

The British Prime Minister during those debates, Harold Macmillan, remarked afterward to a senior BBC executive that any premier who exposed himself with the leader of the opposition was a fool; it was bound to be to the opposition's advantage.

Harold Wilson tried a different tactic during the 1966 general election in Britain; he timed many of his speeches to coincide precisely with the BBC's main news at 8:50 each evening. He knew the BBC was covering them live and he had it carefully arranged with an aide to signal to him the moment he came up live on the news; then regardless of what he was saying to the meeting he immediately plunged into what he wanted the television viewer to hear, sometimes leaving the local audience floundering at the transition. The BBC finally circumvented this by recording all his speeches and editing the section they wished to show. As one of their governors told me, "We couldn't tolerate this news editing by the Prime Minister."

Considering the political pressures brought to bear on many European television organizations, their international activities through the European Broadcasting Union are remarkably free from politics. Within the EBU, broadcasters from right-wing dictatorships like Spain and Portugal work side by side with colleagues from socialist Yugoslavia and Sweden. Right from its birth, at a conference convened by the British Broadcasting Corporation at Torquay in February 1950, the EBU has prided itself on being a noncommercial, nonpolitical, nongovernment outfit serving the needs of professional broadcasters. Its staff is multinational; the administrative director is a Swede, a naturalized Frenchman runs the legal department, a Yugoslav directs the program coordinating center and a Belgian is in charge of the technical operations. Although Brussels serves

---

[1] Jay G. Blumler and Denis McQuail, *Television in Politics: Its Uses and Influence.*

as the technical center, the EBU's headquarters are in Geneva. Along with thirty-three members from thirty countries in its own broadcasting area, the EBU has fifty-four associate members in thirty-four other nations as far away as Japan, Australia, Nigeria and Peru, which makes it the world's premier broadcasting union. Indeed, outside the communist bloc there are relatively few major broadcasting organizations which do not belong.

The prime role of the EBU has always been as a clearing house for its members' programs, particularly in sports and news. The real incentive for the original establishment of the Eurovision network was the European passion for sports; every television organization needed coverage of major football games, international skiing, boxing championships and, of course, the Olympics. The EBU, speaking for all its members, was able to coordinate these arrangements. During 1970, for instance, 518 out of 645 programs handled by Eurovision were sports and over 90 percent of all programs were news or sports. Nowadays, the EBU sends a team, composed of producers and technicians drawn from various television services, to negotiate for all Europe at Apollo moon shots or the Olympics. A handful of men—Vittorio Boni and Ernest Braun from Italy, Tomas Garcia from Spain and Richard Francis from the BBC in Britain—have established themselves as the EBU's top troubleshooters for these occasions. Consequently, instead of a host of individual broadcasting organizations all scrambling to secure their own arrangements, the EBU's team fixes coverage for all. If satellite transmissions are required the EBU books the satellite and distributes the pictures to everyone through the Eurovision network from Brussels. Thus only one satellite charge is applicable and it is shared by all. The EBU bills its members for satellite time or other special circuits on what is known as the Rossi scale. This was devised originally by Richard Rossi, a Swiss banker, and is based on the number of television sets per country; small nations appropriately pay less than large ones. The great advantage is that it enables countries like Switzerland, Belgium or Norway to receive exactly the same caliber of coverage as the wealthier Germans or British (who could, if necessary, afford to go it alone). "The strength of the EBU," said Vittorio Boni, director of international relations for Italian television, "is that it has won the very best coverage of world events for *all* European viewers."

The value of the EBU's clearing house is demonstrated daily in the news exchange, which enables television news in even the poorest European countries—and North Africa—to present a wide view of that day's events not only in Europe but around the world. The major news film agencies of Visnews, UPI-ITN and CBS are all linked into the news exchange, so that they contribute film from all five continents.

The daily exchange begins at 10:45 each morning, when the Brussels technical center links up Geneva with all Europe's television services for a story conference. The conference, in sound only, is conducted by an EBU coordinator in Geneva and a news editor of one of the participating countries. Each country shares this job in turn, with a fresh editor taking over every two weeks. When I was in Geneva the EBU coordinator was a bright-eyed Irish girl, Katie Kahn-Carl, who had previously worked for RTE in Dublin. She began by saying "Good morning—*Bonjour tout le monde*" to the newsmen listening all over Europe. She briefly mentioned there were no satellite bookings that day and turned the conference over to a Belgian in Brussels, whose turn it was to handle the conference that fortnight. He proceeded to ask each country in turn what news film they could contribute that day. Germany offered floods on the Rhine, Italy had a cycling race, Switzerland came up with world skiing championships, France had floods and President Pompidou leaving for the United States. Next the agencies made their offers: UPI-ITN had guerrilla activity in Jordan, Visnews had demonstrations in Chicago against the Vietnam war and a speech by Spiro Agnew in Minneapolis. Then came a list of stories available from Intervision in Eastern Europe, including what was described as a "report from a tank farm on the occasion of the day of the Soviet army" and a Polish congress of Christian youth from Warsaw. As each item came up the news editor would inquire, "Anyone interested?" And organizations who wanted it could stake their claim. Normally if one country alone requested the story it would be turned down for lack of interest, but if two or three responded "Yes" it was at once accepted. Finally, the conference was thrown open for anyone to request coverage from another organization of a story they had not proposed. The Italians wanted to know if the BBC had film of Mia Farrow's twins in London, several people asked the BBC if they had a report on a Scottish doctor who was experimenting with "test tube" babies. The BBC said they would find out and advise Geneva later.

With the conference over, the Geneva coordinator worked out a formal story list, which was then telexed to everyone with a request that they advise Geneva by 1:45 which items they required. The conference merely established there was sufficient interest in a story; the full list of who wanted what came later. As the day proceeded there were some changes on the list: the guerrilla film was scratched because of a delayed flight from Beirut; the Germans came on the line with a late offer of armed police surrounding a plane at Frankfurt airport that was suspected of having a bomb on board. Fast-breaking stories can always be slipped in at the last moment before the first actual exchange of film takes place at 5:00. Important stories may warrant a special linkup of their own late in the evening, but as most of Europe's television services put out their main news before 8:00 it has to be an event of exceptional significance. If a sudden news break requires a satellite booking, Geneva will at once ask the British, Germans, French and Italians if they are interested. The moment one or another agrees, Geneva books the satellite and advises everyone by telex that they too can participate if they wish. The final list of EVN 1 and EVN 2 normally totals eight or nine stories; most are transmitted at EVN 1 at 5:00, while EVN 2 is really a late edition for film that is delayed getting to the studios in the originating country or for events in the early evening. During 1970 a total of 3,798 news stories were transmitted on the news exchange, of which 275 items were contributed by Intervision from Eastern Europe and the Soviet Union. The biggest users of the exchange were the small nations with no foreign-based correspondents or cameramen; in 1970, for example, Yugoslavia took 2,810 of the 3,798 stories sent on the exchange. Austria took 2,808 and Switzerland 2,569; the rich ARD network in Germany, by contrast, accepted only 528.

Normally the exchange gives a good panorama of the day's major events but, inevitably, political pressures in some participating countries mean that film of strikes, riots or other happenings reflecting unfavorably on that country are not offered. The Italians and the Spanish do not contribute reports of strikes, and the French, during the de Gaulle period, never seem to have covered any demonstrations against the General. Even the British are reported to have withheld film of a soccer riot in Scotland after pressure from the Football Association. But these curtailments have not marred the overall success of the exchange, nor aroused animosity at the daily conference. If a country does not offer coverage of a riot, others will sometimes ask politely if it is available; when they are told "Sorry, no," the matter rests. Actually what often happens is that one of the agencies will have covered the trouble, so that from London Visnews or UPI-ITN will offer film of strikes in Madrid, when Spanish television has nothing to contribute. Alternatively, there is nothing to stop one country from sending its own team to cover trouble in another, but they will have to send the film home by plane, not via Eurovision linkups.

The news exchange was extended early in 1971 by the addition of linkup five days a week with television stations in South America. This side-bar exchange, coordinated through Spanish television in Madrid, makes the Eurovision pictures available by satellite to Brazil, Colombia, Peru and Venezuela and receives in return their top stories of the day which are injected into the Eurovision network. Although language barriers limit program exchange primarily to news and sports, the EBU also coordinates such assorted multinational activities as "The Largest Theater in the World" and the Eurovision Song Contest. For the theater series, well-known European playwrights are commissioned to write an original play for television. This is then shown, more or less simultaneously by all the guaranteeing nations, as separate productions in their own language. The first play was Terence Rattigan's *Heart to Heart;* others have included *Rainbird* by Clive Exton, *Enclave* by Ingmar Bergman and *Pitchi-Poi* by Billetdoux. "Largest Theater" also commissioned Benjamin Britten to write an opera for television and he responded with *Owen Wingrave,* based on a Henry James short story. Thirteen countries, including Britain, France, Germany and Sweden backed this commission. The advantage of this cooperation is that it enables the playwright or composer to be tempted with a very substantial guarantee if half a dozen or more countries agree at the outset to perform the work. There is also the satisfying inducement that the production will reach an immense audience all over Europe. *Owen Wingrave* was probably seen by an initial audience of three million people, more than could see it in an opera house in half a century.

What really makes the people of Europe all sit down together before a television set, however, is the annual Eurovision Song Contest to choose a popular "song for Europe." Something like 250 million viewers all over Europe, including five nations of Eastern Europe, watched Monaco win with "Un banc, un arbre, une rue" in 1971.

The only thing that rivals the song contest for popularity is another international contest (arranged directly between broadcasting organizations, not through the EBU), *Jeux Sans Frontiers,* or, as the British prefer to call it, *It's a Knockout.* This caper begins with heats between towns in each country and then, in midsummer, becomes international. The contest is essentially a series of obstacle races over the most wacky courses that the ingenuity of television producers can devise; there are tests along greasy poles over swimming pools, wall scaling, trying to pitch footballs through impossible combinations of hoops or into buckets. In Britain the program attracts nearly as many viewers in August (the traditional worst month for television) as the most popular series in the winter. And I recall walking down the Champs Elysées in Paris on a hot July evening and being attracted to an enormous crowd goggling at a shop window. Struggling through, I found they were looking at *Jeux Sans Frontiers* on a color receiver in a showroom.

The attraction of these international programs is that costs are shared. Even the wealthiest television services in Europe have fallen on difficult days as production expenses soar. Drama now costs up to $50,000 an hour; an opera nearer $150,000. The trend to coproductions, therefore, is expanding rapidly although most are being negotiated outside the framework of the EBU. The Italians, French and Spanish have established a particularly close working relationship on a host of historical series from *The Odyssey* to *Caligula*.

Even though these coproductions split expenses, budgets are sorely tested. Most countries have now reached a plateau in sales of television sets, so that license fee income does not rise much each year. The license fee can be increased, but this is often a touchy political issue. If advertising is already accepted in some limited way, then the temptation is to meet rising costs by stepping up advertising time from, say, fifteen to twenty minutes a day. Belgium, Sweden, Norway and Denmark, the only countries not yet to capitulate to the advertiser, all have strong advertising lobbies; many people believe that financial pressure in the 1970s will force them to yield. That would leave the BBC in Britain as the lone European broadcasting organization in which the advertisers have no toehold.

6

Britain:

An Enviable Reputation

British television is in the enviable position of being widely regarded as the best in the world. Although at home the two channels of the British Broadcasting Corporation (BBC) and the commercial network of Independent Television (ITV) face all kinds of broadsides for serving up trivia and pap, encouraging violence and fostering the permissive society (to cite but a few of the evils laid at their doors), overseas they are often seen as examples of what television should be. "The BBC is a magic word," remarked a television consultant who had helped set up television in half a dozen countries of Africa and Asia. A Canadian broadcaster with similar international experience echoed, "The finest TV by far is in Britain. You start there and go rapidly downhill."

There are, I believe, two reasons why people admire British television: first, its relative independence from both political and advertising pressures; and secondly, the sheer range and high standard of programs available—that along with *The Saint* come *The Forsyte Saga, Civilisation* and hard-hitting plays like *Cathy Come Home* on the plight of Britain's homeless.

American movies caricaturing the British way of life often include a scene of a television announcer saying, "And now Professor Throstlethwaite will give an illustrated lecture on the development of the bagpipe in Glencoe." Actually, what one is more likely to see from Glencoe is the former Olympic runner, Christopher Brasher, now a BBC producer, introducing live coverage by five color cameras of a hardy bunch of British mountaineers challenging some formidable mountain crag there. That may be equally boring for nonmountaineers but it shows how British television, and the BBC in particular, hauls its cameras out and about all over the country to catch something of the action and flavor of life. (They also had a go recently in sending a camera team on a Mount Everest climb.) The wide vistas thus unveiled mean that television offers something of interest to almost everyone some of the time. It is not constantly in pursuit of the mass audience.

The program spectrum, within a single typical week in June of 1971, besides that Glencoe climb, encompassed an hour-long profile of Ingrid Bergman, the final installment of a dramatization of Guy de Maupassant's novel *Bel Ami,* a report from the United States on *The Black American Dream,* about the history and perspective of the Negro civil rights movement, four new plays written for television, documentaries on a Hovercraft journey across Africa, Harrods (the Knightsbridge store), the Paris Commune of 1871, and Brazil's passion for football. Although all these were sprinkled through prime time, they still left plenty of room for the customary mélange of simple entertainment—comedy series, police dramas and a few American imports such as *Flip Wilson* and *Alias Smith and Jones* on BBC, *Hawaii Five-O* and *Peyton Place* on ITV. (Imported programs are limited to 14 percent of program time on both BBC and ITV, which is one major reason for such flourishing homegrown productions.) The British passion for sports was fully indulged; the BBC gave over most of one evening to soccer for the European Cup Final between Amsterdam and Athens, both BBC and ITV went horse-racing for *The Derby* (neither channel ever trusts the other to cover the major sports events adequately), there was plenty of daytime cricket and even a visit to the European karate championships in Paris.

This broad base of programing has been achieved because the British have brewed up, like a fine blend of tea, a formula for organizing their television that is not repeated exactly anywhere else (the nearest parallel is Japan). The subtlety of the concoction is that, while competition exists between the BBC, supported by about $240 million a year from license fees, and ITV, supported by a similar sum from advertising, there is at the same time complementary programing between the BBC's first and second channels. The complementary programing means, as the BBC's genial managing director, Huw Wheldon, is always putting it: "Boxing on one channel and nonboxing on the other. The two channels are central to our operation. With them you can please quite a lot of the people a lot of the time. The success of television in Britain is that we've got both complementary and competitive networks."

The two greatest stimulants over the years have been the introduction of commercial television in 1955 as a challenge to the BBC's monopoly and then, nine years later, the opening of the BBC's second channel. Both have forced program controllers to rethink their whole approach—something that has never happened, for instance, in American television.

In the beginning, of course, there was the BBC. Long before the days of television it was already a formidable institution, molded by its first director general, Lord Reith, to his image as an upright and moral force in the land. It gave the public what it thought was good for them, not what they wanted. Furthermore, Reith kept the corporation, established by Royal Charter, sternly out of the hands of politicians. When Winston Churchill as Home Secretary tried to take over the BBC as a means of propaganda during the General Strike of 1926, Reith rebuffed him.

Thus the BBC, although regarded as a part of the Establishment, became entrenched not only as an independent institution unmoved by the whims of successive governments, but as an impartial one also. As Lord Hill, the Chairman of the BBC, states: "The BBC espouses no causes; it tries to hold the ring in argument." Naturally its independence and impartiality have been assailed many times. Sir Anthony Eden, as Prime Minister during the Suez crisis in 1956, murmured about controlling the BBC but was ignored. The violence between Protestants and Catholics in Northern Ireland since 1969 has sorely tested the BBC's impartiality; while Harold Wilson, both during his years as Prime Minister and in the opposition later, often complained that the BBC was pursuing a personal vendetta against him. But although individual reporters and producers inevitably sometimes allow their personal opinions too much weight, the overall image is still one of reasonable impartiality. Furthermore, the British broadcasters enjoy a degree of freedom rarely shared by their colleagues in France, Italy, Spain, Portugal or Austria. The very lack of political restraint in Britain makes the BBC (and ITV) a much more lively forum and attracts to its staff many of the most intelligent and progressive people in the country. It has become highly fashionable to work in television and, roaming the corridors of the BBC and ITV, it often seems that no one is much over forty. In Britain it is clearly a medium of the young.

The BBC is presided over by a chairman and eleven governors, all officially appointed by the Queen in Council and chosen for their achievements in various walks of life—the governors in 1971 included a city merchant banker and the secretary of the Union of Post Office Workers. None of them need have any prior knowledge or experience of broadcasting. The chairman of the governors since 1968 has been Lord Hill of Luton (who was previously chairman of the Independent Television Authority, which rules the commercial network). Although many people saw his appointment as a political one to curb the BBC's forthrightness, it should be remembered that Lord Hill is a Tory and was appointed by a Labour government. The executive power at the BBC, however, lies with the director general and it is he who sets the style of the corporation. Hugh Greene (now Sir Hugh), director general from 1960 until 1969, and Charles Curran who succeeded him, are both professional broadcasters who worked their way up through the BBC. Their basic guide is the royal charter which decrees the BBC disseminate "information, education and entertainment."

Regularly scheduled television programs were first started by the BBC, then still under Lord Reith's guidance, as far back as November 1936. The first live outside broadcast was the coronation of King George VI in May 1937. All television operations were suspended during World War II, but resumed in June 1946. For nine years after that the BBC's television monopoly was preserved until, in 1955, commercial television burst rudely upon the scene. The lobby that fought and won the battle for commercial television was a small but dedicated one; essentially a triumvirate of Norman Collins, a former controller of BBC Television, Sir Robert Renwick and Charles Orr Stanley of Pye, the TV and radio manufacturers. Collins was the moving spirit; he had been passed over for promotion at the BBC and resigned. He determined "out of sheer bloody-mindedness" to attack the BBC's entrenched monopoly—and won. Lord Reith, although no longer director general of the BBC, was appalled at this assault. "Somebody introduced Christianity into England and somebody introduced smallpox, bubonic plague, and the Black Death," he fumed in the House of Lords at the time. "Somebody is trying now to introduce sponsored broadcasting. . . . Need we be ashamed of moral values, or of intellectual and ethical objectives? It is these that are here and now at stake." As it turned out commercial television was not quite the plague Reith feared. The programs for a start are not sponsored; advertisers simply buy spots and are most carefully fenced off from any association at all with programing. Moreover, ITV was like a bucket of cold water thrown at the BBC; for a while the corporation staggered back, drenched, to catch its breath, then, vastly refreshed, it came out fighting.

From a monopoly position the BBC tumbled until by the late 1950s it was barely getting 30 percent of the television audience; almost everyone was looking at ITV, whose directors, after a few shaky moments themselves to begin with, were making fortunes that even they had never seen in prospect. Television advertising jumped from $4.8 million in

1955 to $160 million by 1960. As Lord Thomson said, in a famous phrase that both he and others have since regretted, "A television license is a license to print money." While ITV counted up the money, the BBC was at first inclined to fall back upon a pompous insistence that "come what may it would not change its principles." But a corporation that takes the public money for license fees cannot do so with very good grace if most of the public is not looking at it (a situation that had never faced the BBC before, because no one had anything else to view). Then, by great good fortune in 1960, the tall, slightly ungainly figure of Hugh Greene shouldered his way into the scene as the new director general at the BBC. A professional journalist and broadcaster since the 1930s, Hugh Greene had no doubts about what must be done. "I wanted to open the windows and dissipate the ivory tower stuffiness which still clung to some parts of the BBC," he wrote later. "I wanted to encourage enterprise and the taking of risks. I wanted to make the BBC a place where talent of all sorts, however unconventional, was recognized and nurtured, where talented people could work and, if they wished, take their talents elsewhere, sometimes coming back again to enrich the organization from which they had started. I may have thought at the beginning that I should be dragging the BBC kicking and screaming into the sixties. But I soon learnt that some urge, some encouragement was what all the immense reserve of youthful talent in the BBC had been waiting for, and from that moment I was part of the rapidly flowing stream." [1]

As Hugh Greene was busy cultivating the climate that enabled the BBC to blossom in the 1960s, there came a television milestone—the Pilkington Report. A special Committee on Broadcasting was established in 1960, under Sir Harry Pilkington (of the famous glassmaking firm), to review the broadcasting scene and make recommendations for the future; it reported in June 1962. The history of British television often seems divided, like B.C. and A.D., into two clear eras, Before Pilkington and After Pilkington. Sir Harry and his colleagues came down in their judgment very firmly on the side of the BBC. "The BBC know good broadcasting," they reported. "By and large they are providing it. Our broad conclusion is this: that, within the limitations imposed by a single program, the BBC's television service is a successful realization of the purposes of broadcasting as defined in the Charter." By contrast, there was hardly a good word to be said for ITV. "We conclude," said Pilkington,

---

[1] Hugh Greene, *The Third Floor Front*, pp. 13–14.

"that the dissatisfaction with television can largely be ascribed to the independent television service. Its concept of balance does not satisfy the varied and many-sided tastes and interests of the public. In the field of entertainment—and not least in light entertainment—there is much that lacks quality . . . the service of independent television does not successfully realize the purposes of broadcasting as defined in the Television Act."

The BBC's reward for shaping up so well was the award of its second television channel, BBC 2. The chastised Independent Television was more tightly regulated under a new Television Act in 1964 (the commercial network is authorized by Act of Parliament as opposed to the BBC's Royal Charter from the Queen, which subtly implies the Corporation's superiority). In the future, ITV schedules would be subject to much closer scrutiny. Moreover, an increasingly stiff tax levy was imposed on television advertising; by the end of the 1960s as much as 25 percent of advertising revenue was being siphoned off at once by the government. The rosy days of commercial television's profits were numbered.

Pilkington, therefore, set the pattern for British television at least until 1976, when both the BBC's Royal Charter and ITV's Television Act come up for renewal. In retrospect, the report was rather too harsh on ITV for, whatever its faults, it had given the BBC a much needed jolt into the second half of the twentieth century. The tonic administered, the BBC, with Hugh Greene giving it its head, came bouncing back to win the audiences it had lost. Quite rapidly during the mid-1960s the BBC climbed in popularity until it could claim that viewing was roughly 50 percent BBC and 50 percent commercial. The precise share rather depends on whose figures are accepted; the JICTAR audience survey of sets in use, prepared for ITV, normally shows ITV a nose ahead—about 55 percent to 45 percent; the BBC's own audience research department, basing its calculations on actual viewers, as opposed to sets in use, often indicates the reverse. The balance is really very fine and shifts from day to day and week to week. The JICTAR calculations also show that the average British set is tuned to ITV for 2.7 hours a day and to the BBC for 2.3 hours during the winter; viewing drops off on both during the summer. The crucial point is that the BBC feels it is justifying the annual license fees of $17 for black and white and $29 for color, and that its programing is fulfilling its responsibilities to the public at large. "I couldn't give a damn if we are getting between 40 and 60 percent of the audience on average over a month," said David Attenborough, the director of programs for BBC television, "but if we had only 25 percent—which would mean we were on the way to even less—I'd be worried. Equally, at 70 percent I'd think we were not being daring enough, not trying out enough new ideas."

Attenborough sees the BBC as an electronic publishing house that selects from the community "the voices that are most interesting, most amusing, most prophetic, most gifted, most informed and most significant and enables the rest of the community to hear them."

Although the BBC may draw upon many talents it does prefer to keep the major part of its program making to itself. So much so that the "television factory" of seven studios at the BBC Television Centre, right by the White City Stadium at Shepherd's Bush in London, turns out, along with three other studios nearby, almost 80 percent of all BBC TV programs. The drama department alone produced 604 original productions in 1970. The BBC has never adopted the widespread European and American habit of contracting out programs to independent production companies. Only NHK, Japan's public service broadcasting corporation, really matches the BBC in generating its own material. The BBC is extraordinarily proud of its sheer efficiency in program making. A report by McKinsey, the international management consultants, revealed that "BBC television programs are produced more economically, considering cost and quality, than anywhere else in the world." Money, of course, is a constant worry. The Corporation received about $240 million from license fees in 1970, of which television was allocated $180 million. But producing 6,000 hours of television a year soon eats into that.

The two channels, BBC 1 and BBC 2, are presided over by a controller with his own budget, who has responsibility for programing and scheduling. BBC 1, being the original channel and the only one covering all of Britain, is designed as a more popular channel and naturally carries major sporting and news events. The annual Miss World Contest, which is often the single most popular program of the year—attracting half the British population—is a natural for BBC 1; so was the Ali-Frazier fight, which was watched by 27.5 million people. Indeed, the image of BBC 1 in the public eye is really that it is the channel to which one automatically turns, without even bothering to check, for great soccer matches, royal occasions or moonwalks.

BBC 2, which by 1972 had achieved about 90 percent coverage of the population, remains much more of a minority channel; it reckons to be doing well if it gets a 20 percent share of the audience for some programs, but mostly gets under 10 percent. Its audience is inclined to be educated, middle-class and some of its programs reflect their tastes. BBC 2 also carries the television programs of the Open University, which began in 1971. The Open University is a separate institution from the BBC, but both its radio and television courses are prepared in partnership with the Corporation. The second network, however, is not conceived either as an educational or minority channel (unlike the purely educational channel of NHK in Japan). BBC 2's role is to provide an attractive alternative to what is on BBC 1. Therefore if BBC 1 has a serious program that may draw a small audience, BBC 2 comes up with lively entertainment attracting many millions of viewers. Every Monday night, for instance, BBC 1 puts out *Panorama,* the flagship of its current affairs programs, at 8:00, while BBC 2 shows a western, either *High Chaparral* or *Alias Smith and Jones.* Furthermore, programs such as *The Forsyte Saga, The Six Wives of Henry VIII, Elizabeth R* and *Civilisation,* which have consolidated the international structure of the BBC in recent years, were all born on BBC 2. They were transferred later to BBC 1 for reruns (the controllers of both BBC 1 and BBC 2 hotly deny they used the second channel as a testing ground, but the track record does rather indicate it). Robin Scott, the controller of BBC 2, told me, "I see BBC 2 as a companion walking slightly behind BBC 1, rather like the Duke of Edinburgh following just behind the Queen. But both are personalities in their own right."

BBC 1's personality, especially with Paul Fox as controller since 1967, is a blend of show business and journalism. Fox, who came up the BBC ladder via sports and current affairs, admits, "I like to see big events rapidly on BBC 1." He is very sensitive to accusations that his channel is "too popular." Fox loves to point out that BBC 1 spends 47 percent of its total budget on drama, news and current affairs, and that in the peak evening period, serious programs, excluding drama, take up 22 percent of the time. News and current affairs are particularly important; they take 25 percent of the budget and provide 30 percent of the total programs.

Robin Scott at BBC 2 puts more emphasis on drama, less on current affairs. "I give a higher proportion of my budget to plays than BBC 1," he told me. "We're doing twenty-eight plays a year, and I spend readily on them because in drama the more money you spend the better the returns." He also sees the second channel as an ideal platform for occasional lengthy assessments of British or world problems. "You cannot be profound in the short form," he said. "I want us to do more programs of ninety minutes or more. We've already done this on the issues over London's third airport and the Common Market."

Scott and Fox work closely together in mapping out their schedule to achieve maximum contrast hour by hour and to ensure that most of the time program changes occur at the same moment (so that on the air each channel promotes the other: "Just starting on BBC 2 . . ." says the announcer, "while here on BBC 1 . . ."). "Robin and I have no secrets from each other," said Fox. "Our competition is ITV."

Some critics of the BBC complain that competing with the commercial network should be beneath the Corporation's dignity and that it should ignore commercial television. The BBC fields that charge easily enough by pointing out that what they are really doing is indulging in the art of competitive scheduling. Over the last few years they have become adept at understanding that television phenomenon, "the Inheritance Factor." "This," Huw Wheldon points out, "is the fact that one of the main ingredients in the size of any audience is the size of the audience which was watching the program which preceded it." The understanding of this factor was one of the vital points in the BBC's climb back to parity with commercial television. ITV has long kicked off prime time at 7:30 two nights a week with *Coronation Street* (its highly successful chronicle of life in one little cul-de-sac of a northern industrial town) and similar popular series the remaining evenings. Those audiences, being lazy, stay with ITV throughout the evening. The BBC, therefore, responded with its own popular comedy series at 7:30 to try to snatch as much of the audience right at the beginning of the evening and hold it. "By doing so," Huw Wheldon pointed out, "we were actually able, with popular competing against popular, to claim half the audience available at 7:30 and, in consequence (and it is this that matters), half the audience available for the range of programs which followed during the evening." The classic example was *Panorama* in 1965. The current affairs program was getting a six million audience until the popular *Steptoe and Son* was launched immediately preceding it—then *Panorama*'s audience soared to ten million.

Steptoe and Son and, later, *Till Death Us Do Part* were the two popular comedy shows that really helped the BBC pull back audiences. *Steptoe* began as a single drama about a crotchety old junk dealer and his son Harold, but blossomed naturally into a series. The Steptoes' junkyard, with the old cart-horse in its shed, and their living room dominated by a skeleton amid mountains of other useless bric-a-brac became the forum for glorious verbal (and sometimes physical) sparring matches between father and son, in which the writers, Alan Simpson and Ray Galton, caught the genuine tang of family bickering. From Steptoe's yard it was a short trip to Alf Garnett's rowdy little terrace house in the East

End of London for *Till Death Us Do Part.* Warren Mitchell as Alf Garnett, the loud-mouthed, balding little Cockney, saying "bloody" every other word, calling his wife a "silly old moo," castigating the permissive society, berating the "wogs," and beating his breast in patriotism at any mention of the Queen, became, for a while, almost a national hero. The series, written by Johnny Speight, who had grown up in exactly that setting in the East End, was so richly based—compared with most contrived comedy—that it became required viewing throughout the land.

The originality of Steptoe and Garnett was matched by another radical departure—Ned Sherrin's satirical review *That Was the Week That Was* (TW3), presented by David Frost. As M.P.s jumped regularly to their feet in the House of Commons every Monday to protest TW3's latest irreverences about them or the Church the previous Saturday night, the dusty image of the BBC as "Auntie" vanished forever. TW3 in fact had a relatively short life; it was killed off just before the 1964 general election, but it had set the vital precedent that enabled other novel ideas to develop.

The momentum has been maintained by the surrealist humor of *Marty Feldman* and *Monty Python's Flying Circus* and even, in a very different vein, the bawdiness of Frankie Howard in *Up Pompeii,* a weekly Roman orgy. These and many other comedy shows had sought to explore a new television humor rather than accepting the neat and cosy formulas of *The Lucy Show* or *Bewitched.* "The real achievement of the BBC," an Australian broadcaster remarked to me in Sydney, "is that it has been like an icebreaker, always pushing back the barriers."

The same down-to-earth approach is apparent in many things the BBC does. The long-running police series *Z Cars* and *Softly Softly* have, at times, taken on almost documentary form in probing the realities of crime. They do not attempt to fulfill some magic formula each week of tackling a problem and solving it tidily. Often the ending is indeterminate, as is so much police work. The caliber of writing in many episodes of both series is high, because the writers themselves have the freedom to develop their theme, to explore family tragedies without the necessity to tie up all the loose ends in fifty minutes.

This does not mean that the BBC has devised some infallible knack for drama series. They have plenty of flops, like *Ryan International,* the saga of an international lawyer based in Paris. The BBC boldly invested some $600,000 in thirteen episodes (they reckon to spend about $50,000 an hour on drama series) only to find with half a dozen shot that they had a disaster on their hands. They shot four more, hoping it might get better, and then called a halt. "We were then faced with nearly a quarter of a million pounds worth of programs on our hands which we didn't believe in and didn't want to put on," a senior BBC executive told me. What to do? "We had no spare money to mount another program, we had just about £1,000 an hour we could spend putting on a third rerun of *Ironside* instead. In the end we ran *Ryan*."

The opening is there for good writing, whether in series or single plays. Over the years the BBC has nourished such playwrights as Harold Pinter, Alun Owen and David Mercer who have really developed their craft through television. Week in, week out, the standard may not be consistently high, but this is simply one of the hazards of television; it gulps more plays in three months than the London theater gets through in a year. The important factor, compared with television in many countries, is that writers know that the BBC (and ITV) have regular weekly slots for new plays. In New York I talked with a vice-president of NBC who lamented that he had been trying to find some good young playwrights for a specially projected series, but had little luck. "They all prefer to write for the theater," he said, "and anyway it's all four-letter words and the themes are wrong." The real point is that for the last decade the American networks have given no encouragement to the learning playwright, so it never occurs to them to write for television. In Britain, television is a natural market. Writers are not the only ones to benefit; directors like Ken Russell really established themselves first on television. Russell's film biographies of Isadora Duncan, Richard Strauss and Delius for BBC paved the way for *Women in Love* and *The Music Lovers* for the cinema.

While biographies are obviously an inexhaustible vein for television, the novel is another. Galsworthy's *The Forsyte Saga,* with all its twenty-six episodes, really set the fashion. After a moderately quiet first showing on BBC 2 it became a national passion when it was repeated on Sunday evenings on BBC 1. Pubs were empty and churches advanced their evening services to enable the congregation to get home by 7:30 to join the Forsytes (only the choirboys objected—they missed *Tom and Jerry* earlier). The serial was widely regarded as "the most habit-forming discovery since tobacco." More than fifty other countries developed the habit. In the United States it was one of the vital programs in establishing the growing reputation of the fourth "public" television network; even the Russians bought it, although it was not until two years after the sale was concluded in Moscow that they actually showed it (they pleaded technical problems with dubbing).

Hard on the heels of the *Forsytes,* BBC 2 has kept up a steady raiding of the novel. They have done, among others, Henry James' *Portrait of a Lady* and *The Spoils of Poynton,* Thomas Hardy's *Woodlanders,* George Eliot's *Daniel Deronda,* and Jane Austen's *Sense and Sensibility.* They have not been dramatized at such great length (most are four, five, or six parts) as the *Forsytes* and not all have made such good television; Henry James transferred well, Jane Austen's subtleties were more difficult to capture. Novels have to be carefully selected, for there is always a danger that television, having hit one success, tries to repeat it forever and ever. The BBC tended to fall into the same trap in its historical series. The prize-winning *Six Wives of Henry VIII,* comprising a distinct ninety-minute play about each wife, was television at its very best. *Elizabeth R,* which was a natural sequence, lacked the same impact—despite Glenda Jackson as the Queen; perhaps her reign did not divide so neatly into six episodes which could revolve tightly around a single theme.

Nevertheless, the BBC is finding history an eminently visual topic. Kenneth Clark's personal view of *Civilisation* is to be followed by Alistair Cooke delivering *America—a Personal History of the United States. The History of the British Empire* will be unveiled during 1972 in thirteen installments. In both the last two undertakings the BBC is coproducing with Time-Life (which now handles the sale of BBC programs in the United States), but is retaining editorial control. "We insist on one editorial mind," said David Attenborough. "Ideally on coproductions we prefer our chaps and their money." The BBC's reputation makes that kind of deal feasible, but they are much less involved in coproductions than many European television networks.

Beyond the fairly predictable dramatization of novels and the recourse to history, the BBC have also developed a whole flurry of programs that fit into no precise slot. There is the occasional *One Pair of Eyes* series on BBC 2 in which journalists, actors, actresses, politicians and playwrights present their own highly personal report on any subject they choose. I remember a vivid one in which one of the men who helped to build the bridge over the River Kwai went back there and poked around the ruins of the camp and the railway line in the jungle a quarter of a century later. Malcolm Muggeridge is always turning up, either ambling into odd corners of India to recall his life there thirty years earlier, reminiscing about his socialist childhood, or conducting a lively Sunday evening series, *The Question Why,* on everything from Why Marriage? to Why Evil? Once or twice a year there is a testing quiz, *So You Think*

You Can Drive, which analyzes road accidents, quizzes a panel and viewers about new driving regulations, and generally shows up how sloppy most British driving is. Cliff Michelmore, the kindly uncle of TV, conducts an annual holiday series, on which he and a squad of reporters take package-deal holidays and come back with very frank reports on their value—something that no commercial network could tackle. And finally there are regular programs like *Horizon* and *Tomorrow's World* that are highly intelligent reports on science and medicine today, and the *Money Programme,* a fifty-minute weekly review of the business scene.

The broad scope of the BBC's programs is an object lesson to many television organizations around the world who counter any suggestion that they do too much popular entertainment by saying, "You can't do opera and ballet all the time." There are plenty of alternatives. Of course the BBC puts on both opera and ballet, but relatively infrequently. BBC 1 normally does just two operas a year, and the audience is modest. But productions such as Benjamin Britten's *Peter Grimes* have attracted an audience of one and a half million. As Huw Wheldon remarked afterward, "To have 3 percent of the entire population watching a Benjamin Britten opera on a Sunday evening is a startling phenomenon." And no one expects or demands that the audience be larger. But this does not prevent the BBC from spending a great deal of money on opera—most productions cost nearly $140,000 (three times the cost of drama). While they often take the shortcut of television performances of productions at the Royal Opera House or Glyndbourne, the BBC, as I mentioned previously, together with ten other European broadcasting services, commissioned Benjamin Britten in 1967 to write a full-length opera, *Owen Wingrave,* for television. When it was shown on BBC 2 in May 1971 an estimated 250,000 people watched this world premiere.

This is the true advantage of public service broadcasting; while a large audience is essential much of the time simply to justify the network in the public mind, a small audience can be tolerated quite frequently. No one expects or requires that opera or many other programs appealing to special tastes, whether snooker or archeology—both of which BBC 2 serves—draw a huge rating. Naturally there has to be some cutoff point. "You can't do programs regularly for 50,000 viewers," said BBC 2's Robin Scott, "but you can for 500,000."

That decision is inevitably much harder for ITV, for although programs are not sponsored, the advertisers are breathing down the necks of the program companies pleading for larger audiences. At least there are some built-in safeguards that prevent it from trying to maximize the audience all the time.

Commercial television in Britain is rather like a pyramid; at the top is the Independent Television Authority (ITA) and everything radiates out below with its permission. The ITA wears a variety of hats. It owns and operates the microwave links and the transmitters of the entire commercial network—which gives it the most positive of all vetoes because it can simply refuse to put on a program. Then it makes contracts with the fifteen program companies that make up the mosaic of ITV; each contract normally runs for six years, but the Authority can legally withdraw it at any time if it feels a company is not living up to its obligations under the Television Act. It has never withdrawn a license in midstream, so to speak, but it did assert itself in 1968 by refusing to renew two contracts. The ITA also draws up codes of program and advertising standards and presides over network schedules. The Authority can and does require current affairs and other serious programing to be shown in prime time. Many people argue that it is not nearly stern enough in fulfilling this obligation, but at least there are two current affairs reports, a documentary and a play networked each week in prime time, plus the half-hour *News at Ten* five nights a week, which would probably not be there without the ITA's insistence.

The ITA does have to use its judgment here. The stricter Television Act of 1964 specifies that it should "provide the television broadcasting services as a public service for disseminating information, education and entertainment." They must insure "a proper balance and wide range in their subject matter" and "secure a wide showing for programs of merit." But that still leaves much to the discretion of the ITA. The Authority is presided over by a chairman, deputy chairman and nine other members appointed by the Minister of Posts and Telecommunications and selected from many areas of public life. The first chairman of the ITA was Sir Kenneth Clark (now Lord Clark), the art historian—and, of course, much later, chronicler of *Civilisation* for the BBC—while the chairman since 1968 has been Lord Aylestone, a former Cabinet minister in the Labour Government. However, as with the BBC, the executive command at the ITA really rests with the director general. The ITA has had only two director generals in its history: Sir Robert Fraser, a quiet-spoken Australian who was the original architect of the whole system, and Brian Young, who replaced him in 1970. As a newcomer to television, Brian Young (formerly headmaster of Charterhouse and director of the

Nuffield Foundation) still has to put his stamp on commercial television; the present system is very much the brainchild of Sir Robert Fraser.

Shortly before Sir Robert retired I spent an afternoon with him at the ITA's headquarters in Knightsbridge, just across the street from Harrods, and asked him about the network he had created. "We were entering the unknown at the beginning," he said. "For thirty years there had been only the monopoly of the BBC, but we were starting a new service from scratch and we couldn't be a second BBC. There were two cardinal differences—first we had to earn our living—the BBC gets it from licenses. The importance of that distinction about earning a living is that ITV must ask itself more carefully whether it can take program risks or not. The second point is that the BBC is a program company, and we (the ITA) are not. The BBC, therefore, is in executive command of the production of programs and is responsible for their standard; we are not in that position."

The ITA, therefore, built the technical network and contracted out all the program making and advertising sales to a number of program companies. "We wanted to avoid concentrations of power," Sir Robert recalled, "and we decided not to have a centralized network." Accordingly, the ITA carved up Britain into thirteen (later fourteen) regions and made contracts with a program company for each region. Four of the original companies, Rediffusion, Associated Television, Granada and ABC, covering London, the Midlands, Lancashire and Yorkshire were approved as major network groups, providing among them the bulk of programs for the commercial channel. The remaining ten regional companies were envisaged, according to Sir Robert Fraser, "as being in a sense local newspapers." They produced a few local news and magazine programs, and contributed only occasionally to the network from whom they took the bulk of their programing. This system prevailed until 1968 when a reshuffling of contracts, when they were renewed, threw up five network companies and ten regionals. The new network groups are Thames (London weekdays), London Weekend (London Friday from seven in the evening through Sunday night), Associated Television (Midlands), Granada (Lancashire), and Yorkshire (Yorkshire). The regionals are Anglia, Border, Channel, Grampian, Harlech, Scottish, Southern, Tyne Tees, Ulster and Westward. The programing mosaic is completed by Independent Television News, which is jointly owned by all the program companies.

The fact that ITV is so diversified around the country has added much more regional television coverage than was ever attempted by the BBC. The BBC always was a national network, rather remote from people outside London. But with the coming of ITV, cities like Norwich, Aberdeen, Carlisle, Newcastle, and even the Channel Islands suddenly had their own television station putting out a nightly news magazine of local events. ITV consequently came much more directly into their lives. Sir Robert Fraser in the early days always spoke of ITV as the "people's television," partly for this reason and partly because he felt it was giving them the programs that they wanted and really enjoyed. ITV has also been the workingman's television. The BBC is much more a middle-class network. Indeed, over the years there have really been two breeds of viewer in Britain: the BBC viewer who occasionally looked at ITV and the ITV viewer who occasionally looked at BBC (probably for sports).

The commercial network tries to be more informal and relaxed than the BBC, particularly in news presentation. Independent Television News has always used its journalists as "newscasters," unlike the BBC, whose news readers do not always have a journalistic background. "Our newscasters are all reporters," said Nigel Ryan, the editor of ITN, "and I think this lends authority to our news. We like the newscasters to be lively and to address themselves to the man in the street in his language." ITN lacks the vast resources of the BBC's news division and has only one overseas staffer in Washington, D.C., but Ryan believes ITN responds faster to the news. "The BBC," he remarked cheerfully, "is rather like an octopus but we are a fast-flying wasp." At the insistence of the Independent Television Authority, ITN now rates a half-hour *News at Ten* on weekday evenings. The audience figures are highly gratifying; *News at Ten* normally notches up one or two places in the top ten programs every week. ITN has also given the BBC very tough competition on Apollo moonwalks. Both naturally have covered these exhaustively, but ITN is often just a little brighter and more inventive.

The coordination of ITV's program schedules around *News at Ten* and other serious programs required by the ITA is a matter of hard horse trading. Each of the five major companies contributing to the network is always trying to get the best times for its programs, while the ten regionals are always clamoring for an occasional opening. Officially, the juggling is handled by the Network Programme Committee, made up of representatives from all the companies, ITN, and the ITA, which meets six times a year. The real bargaining, however, takes place in a much smaller cabal, the Programme Controllers Group, composed of just the program controllers of the big five and Frank Copplestone, the controller of the network secretariat. The framework for the schedule is drawn up many months in advance and requirements for plays, drama series, and documentaries mapped out. Then each network stakes its claim. Some time slots are sacred, such as Monday and Wednesday evenings at 7:30 for Granada's *Coronation Street*. *Coronation Street* celebrated its tenth anniversary in August 1970 and its thousandth episode early in 1971; it shows no signs of flagging in popularity, regularly notching up the No. 1 position in the top ten. No one challenges its timing; the bargaining is much more on whose new series gets accepted. The toughest battles are about the weekend; no one seems to be able to agree what the network should put out. While London Weekend proposes ambitious plans for more culture, Sir Lew Grade at ATV clamors for more variety and films, especially on Saturday afternoons when the commercial network tries to outdo the BBC in sports. Since the BBC has long been the prime network for sports, Sir Lew would happily leave the games to BBC and offer a movie on ITV. "We've never really resolved it," admitted one network controller. "Our plans for Saturday have never come off, which is one reason the BBC does so well at weekends."

Once the network line-up is thrashed out by the big five, the regionals have their nibble. Of the 104 plays the network needs most years, the regionals normally produce ten (eight of them from Anglia). But it is difficult for these small companies to get programs written into the schedules in advance. "They really have to take a gamble and make the program," said Frank Copplestone, controller of the network secretariat, "then we'll look at it for the network."

The final schedule must meet with the approval of the ITA; the target is that about one third of the programs should be serious. The Authority also keep a watchful eye on specific programs to insure that they stay within required program standards. A synopsis of every play is studied by the Authority before it is made and, in conjunction with the Independent Television Companies Association, they grade every film series and movie. Each gets a certificate indicating when it may be shown; the magic hour is 9:00. "After nine o'clock," said the ITA's program censor, "the responsibility goes to the parents." The ITA's toughest rules are on violence. They decree, for instance, no hanging scenes before 9:30 in the evening. Both *The Avengers* and *The Saint* have occasionally been toned down for British audiences. A scene in *The Avengers* of a man being chased with an ax along a seafront was snipped out. The ITA decided it looked "too real." A Granada series, *Big Breadwinner Hog,* about a gang leader in the East End of London, also ran afoul of the Authority, who insisted that it be moved to later in the evening. Several ITV companies actually dropped the program. Most series, however, are made with the ITA's regulations in mind. The real trouble comes with old Hollywood movies. *Tarzan,* for example, runs afoul of ITA scissors for occasional scenes of natives being whipped. While *Blackbeard the Pirate,* with Robert Newton, had scenes of men hanging from yardarms, being flogged, heads and hands being chopped off—all of which had to come out.

The Authority is equally watchful of advertising. Commercials are limited to an average of six minutes an hour over the day, with a maximum of seven minutes in any clock hour; usually there are three breaks for advertising per hour. The ITA has established a Code of Advertising Standards and Practices designed to prevent misleading advertising—particularly of food and medicines being screened. The scripts of many ads are approved in advance, while the finished commercials for nationwide campaigns are previewed at 9:45 each morning in closed-circuit sessions linking the ITA with the program companies. Each year the ITA insists on about 800 amendments to commercials and rejects up to 150, as being misleading.

Among the five network companies the program pace is really set by Thames, the London weekday company, ATV in Birmingham and Granada in Manchester. Yorkshire and London Weekend (LWT), both newcomers in 1968, have had to fight exceptionally hard to win places for their programs on the network. Yorkshire, with great hopes for their current affairs output, found they had difficulty competing with Thames' *This Week* and Granada's *World in Action,* which enjoyed established reputations. One of their best assets has been the redoubtable Alan Whicker, an indefatigable reporter who left the BBC to help found Yorkshire. He is constantly seen leaping aboard a jet and soaring into the sunset to ask impertinent questions of Bluebell Girls in Paris one week, some South American dictator the next and then the people of a remote island in the Pacific.

London Weekend, of which David Frost is one of the mainstays (at one time he had his own program every night), has been beset by successive crises and palace revolutions. LWT was launched with great promises of adding a new dimension to weekend television with programs on the arts and hard-hitting current affairs reporting. This aim did not match the ambitions of the rest of the network which wanted good, solid entertainment on the weekend. By early 1971 barely any of the original LWT executives remained, although Frost was still a powerful shareholder behind the scenes. Then Rupert Murdoch, the Australian newspaper entrepreneur who had already breathed new life into the *News of the World* and *The Sun* since coming to London, bought a major holding in LWT.

He and Frost persuaded John Freeman, formerly editor of the *New States-man,* High Commissioner to India and Ambassador to the United States, to take over as chairman of the ailing company. Freeman himself is no newcomer to television: his BBC series of *Face to Face* interviews is re-membered as one of the best things on television in the 1950s.

While London Weekend under Freeman is still in search of a style, Granada and ATV long ago established very distinctive characteristics.

Granada, based in Manchester, has always reflected the socialist be-liefs of the Bernstein brothers, Sidney (now Lord Bernstein) and Cecil, who founded it. Lord Bernstein, as Chairman, has always presided per-sonally over every aspect of program planning, so that he and Granada are really one and the same thing. "He is the nearest that television has to a Northcliffe or a Beaverbrook," Anthony Sampson observed in *Anat-omy of Britain Today.*[2] "Originally I was opposed to commercial television on social and political grounds," Lord Bernstein told me, recounting his early days in television, "but when I saw that it was coming anyway I said, 'We can't let the big boys get away with all of it.' So we looked at the map. We decided that the *Daily Mail,* under Rothermere, would get London, so we tried for Manchester and got it. We had no big money and we turned down several newspapers—we didn't want to confer with any-one. I like to do something on my own and to my liking." While other program companies based in provincial cities have nevertheless often remained heavily London-oriented, Granada—although regarding itself as a national television company—has nourished and been nourished by Lancashire talent. Their programs, whether *Coronation Street* or *Family at War,* the account of a Liverpool family's experiences throughout World War II, reflect the harsh life of the industrial north. *World in Action,* their weekly current affairs report, is brisk and brash, compared to the BBC's prestigious and rather ponderous *Panorama* which competes with it; *World in Action*'s editing is so tight that it often packs more into half an hour than *Panorama* manages in the full hour. The sense of responsi-bility that Bernstein sought to instill in the programs also attracted the most socially aware writers, producers, and reporters, who developed a loyalty for the company not found in most other ITV groups. "You stay with Granada out of a sense of loyalty," said one of their executives, "and because it isn't run by committee. You may fight to get a program approved but, once it is approved, you can go ahead and make it free from com-mittee control."

[2] Anthony Sampson, *Anatomy of Britain Today,* p. 661.

By contrast with Granada's firm Manchester roots, the ATV Network, a subsidiary of the Associated Television Corporation, which is officially based in Birmingham and responsible for programs in the Midlands, often seems to have emigrated to New York. Certainly ATV's managing director Sir Lew Grade is forever jumping on planes to America to conclude a new deal with ABC. Sir Lew always hastens to point out to visitors, who suggest that he is concerned only with "mid-Atlantic" entertainment, that his company does its full share of documentaries and serious plays for the network. This is true, but its reputation is certainly founded on international film series like *The Saint, Department S,* and *U.F.O.* And no one outside America can compete with Sir Lew when it comes to cracking the networks there. Quite apart from having Tony Curtis and Roger Moore in *The Persuaders* and Shirley MacLaine in *Shirley's World* in prime time on the ABC network in the fall of 1971, he has also achieved network showings for variety series with Marty Feldman, Des O'Connor, Tom Jones and Val Doonican, and for Millicent Martin in *From a Bird's Eye View,* the travails of an airline stewardess. In 1970, Associated Television earned more than $36 million from worldwide program sales, including over $24 million from the United States alone. The BBC, by comparison, earned a modest $6 million from overseas sales.

Sir Lew is immensely proud of the international appeal of his programs. Before he launched into the international market, he says, no one even realized that British television existed. And the money from the overseas contracts enables the programs to be far more lavish than if they were conceived simply for the British screen. *The Persuaders* is costing $240,000 per episode. "We can't earn that from advertising here," he pointed out. Moreover, he added, "People ignore the fact that our responsibility is to the majority, not ignoring the minority." Sir Lew regards himself as "the average person in this country" and sees no reason to fill the screen with documentaries all the time. "I want to be entertained by good dramas, by variety shows, by good escapist adventure series."

Sir Lew's technique of selling a series in America before it is even made may be good for Britain's balance of payments (and has earned Associated Television three Queen's Awards for industry), but it inevitably means that programs made by a British commercial television company for a British audience are being tailored to American requirements. "The great danger of getting the American sale first is that it colors how you make the program," said the managing director of a rival ITV company. "We believe our first responsibility is to people here."

Amid the big guns of the network, the ten small regional companies wage a constant campaign to win the occasional network showing. Although they recognize that their prime job is local programing, a networked play or documentary is good for the budget and morale. Two regional companies, Anglia and Southern, have been particularly successful at cracking the network by carefully cornering special subjects and treating them well. Anglia, based in Norwich, specializes in natural history and drama. Their natural history unit under Aubrey Buxton has made a remarkable wildlife series, *Survival,* and several one-hour nature specials which have been distributed worldwide. *The World of the Beaver,* narrated by Henry Fonda, was shown on network television in the United States in prime time (in Britain it was first shown only at 10:30 at night). Anglia is also the only regional company to have a regular position in network drama—it rates eight plays a year.

Southern, based in Southampton, has concentrated on children's programs, which the ITV network long neglected. As the largest of the nonnetwork companies Southern often feels frustrated at not getting more nationwide showing. It, like many of the other companies, has unused studio capacity. "The trouble is, we come last in everyone's consideration," said David Wilson, Southern's managing director. "If Lew Grade suddenly comes up with a series, we lose our place in the network. I could double the output of our studios given more network time."

Life has not been made easier for Southern or any commercial company during 1969 and 1970 by declining advertising revenues, which fell from just over $240 million to $225 million, and the bite of the special tax levy. Although the levy was eased early in 1971 and advertising looked more promising, this did not save several companies from mergers of their sales forces. Scottish (once Lord Thomson's crock of gold) joined with Grampian in Aberdeen; Yorkshire teamed up with Tyne Tees in a new joint holding company, Trident, and Westward in Plymouth got together with little Channel out in the Channel Islands (the companies retained their individual programing identity).

Hard times, however, did not stop the commercial companies, especially the major ones, lobbying vigorously for longer program hours and a second commercial channel. In 1971 both ITV and BBC 1 were limited to 53½ hours of programs each week, plus special outside broadcasts; BBC 2 did 38 hours. Both Sir Lew Grade and Howard Thomas, the managing director of Thames, pressed the government to allow programs to start earlier in the day and finish later at night (television normally finishes by midnight). The BBC has resisted this, because they would have to match such an increase, and their budget is too tight already. They could cope with longer hours only if the license fee went up substantially. The commercial companies, of course, would simply rake in more advertising while a second, more selective commercial channel might draw in fresh advertisers, who at present use the Sunday color magazines.

Howard Thomas of Thames argued: "The only fair division is for ITV to have a second and complementary system so that we too can balance a serious program with light entertainment. Only by having two simultaneously planned channels can we maintain our present edge on the BBC." The extra channel could be started relatively cheaply—possibly operating on $36 million a year to begin with—because of all the spare studio capacity now sitting idle. The new channel would be less popular than the present ITV. "If ITV 1 is like the *Daily Express,*" said Howard Thomas, "ITV 2 would function like the *Daily Telegraph,* offering a different range of programs to a different audience and attracting new kinds of advertising. This does not mean that ITV 2 would be in any sense a minority service. There would need to be a full quota of entertainment although we should use ITV 2 as a tryout ground for program experiments."

A new channel would certainly enable ITV to cope with the rising challenge from BBC 2, which is slowly eating into its audience. "We are in a stagnant situation," David Wilson of Southern complained. "We cannot increase our audience or our advertising rates. An extra channel would give us room to maneuver." Whether one will be granted before 1976, when both the commercial Television Act and the BBC's Royal Charter come up for review, is a matter for speculation. Just as the Pilkington Report in 1962 provided one watershed in British television, the new legislation due in 1976 is likely to produce another. If a fourth channel is awarded then—or even earlier—it could provide the same tonic that came from the original advent of commercial television and BBC 2.

Such a stimulant is likely to be essential by the mid-1970s. Already there are signs that the BBC's great leap forward of the 1960s has lost momentum. The Corporation, like ITV, has its money troubles. The number of television sets has now more or less leveled off at just under sixteen million, so that the only increase in revenue is from the sale of color sets (a color license costs $12 more than a black and white set). BBC is pinning its faith for more money in the seventies on an accelerated sale of color sets (there were nearly half a million in 1971), rather than overall increases in the license. "One of the best things Hugh Greene did at the BBC was insure that color licenses cost more than black and white," said one program controller. "That is our bread and butter for the future." The limited budget, however, means that the BBC, like ITV, is reluctant to take risks. They simply cannot afford a $600,000 investment in a series that fails. The tendency, therefore, in these days of tight purse strings, is the pitch for the "safe" program. Yet it was exactly because the BBC did not have that limitation in the 1960s (when soaring television sales insured more money each year) that their programs had so much vitality. While their reputation of being the best in the world was possibly justified then, the difficulty in the future is going to be to sustain it. One way to do it might be to charge a more realistic price; the British license fee is the cheapest in Europe, except for Ireland and Portugal. (Sweden is twice as expensive.) It would be a pity to lose the reputation of being the best just for the sake of being the cheapest.

7

West Germany:
The Wealthy Patron

West German television sprawls across the heart of Europe like some great octopus with its tentacles spreading out into countries all around. Go to Brussels or Zurich, to East Berlin, Luxembourg or Amsterdam and, with a tolerable aerial, you can watch the lavish color programs of both the main German networks, ARD and ZDF. Add this strategic position to the fact that they are the richest public service network in the world and you have a formidable television system. The Germans have been major trend setters in Western Europe—they were first to accept a limited quota of commercials (twenty minutes a day) to boost the considerable existing income from license fees on their public service networks, while their color system, PAL, has been widely adopted by other European countries.

Television's disdain for the niceties of frontiers has often caused viewers in Germany's smaller neighbors to nag their television services to follow suit and, of course, to complain from time to time that programs made just for German consumption are slighting them. "Because we are smack in the center, we have to consider reactions to our programs not just among our Common Market partners but in Eastern Europe," a current affairs producer in Cologne pointed out. "People get upset by what you might feel are the most trivial things."

Even the weather, shown nightly after the news, can cause diplomatic furor. For several years the networks screened a map on which the word "Germany" stretched across both West and East Germany and even into parts of Poland that Germany occupied before World War II. The Poles protested frequently, and even many Germans admitted that the map showed Germany as it was thirty years ago. Eventually, when the networks switched to news and weather in color in 1970, the map was quietly changed. Now it shows only the major cities; names of countries and border designations have been entirely eliminated.

The responsibility of being the bosom of Europe often seems to weigh a trifle heavily on television in West Germany and make it terribly earnest. Like the Volkswagen beetle car, German television is thorough, developed with superb professional and technical skill, and immensely reliable, but can be dull to look at. One reason, perhaps, is a slight case of middle-age spread. Traveling around a number of the German stations, I was struck by how few young people there were in positions of seniority—and how few one saw on the screen. After Britain, where almost everyone in television seems to be under forty, this came as something of a surprise. "There's hardly anyone on the executive floor here in their thirties," a senior program planner at ZDF admitted. "There are just too many old people in television—and it's difficult to get them to make way for the young." Were there any bright young German David Frosts or Dick Cavetts? "No —and we haven't really encouraged the development of that kind of personality." The popular television star who immediately came into everyone's mind was a middle-aged actor-comedian, Hans-Joachim Kulen-kamff—known throughout Germany as Kuli—who ran a very successful quiz show for several years. "Kuli is just a charming comic whose jokes are straightforward and inoffensive," explained a program controller in Frankfurt.

Reluctance to pursue the cult of personality is entirely understandable in the nation where Hitler used radio with such devastating effects in the 1930s, and the legacy of Adolf Hitler has fostered the equal determination to keep central government at arm's length from broadcasting. Apart from the German post office providing transmitters and circuits, television is firmly entrenched in the hands of the regional governments. Any attempt by the federal government to establish its own television service has been sternly rebuffed. Chancellor Konrad Adenauer tried hard in the early 1960s to set up a national commercial television channel, but the Constitutional Court threw out the proposal. The judges stated categorically that, under the terms of the postwar German constitution, the federal authorities were not authorized to regulate broadcasting. "The provision of a broadcasting service is a public function," the judges declared. "If the state assumes this function in any manner, it becomes a state function." The division of West Germany after the war into three military zones encouraged this sentiment, as the British, Americans, and French each permitted the separate development of radios in their domain. From these radio stations, first approved by the occupation forces, television gradually emerged.

Today it is the *Länder,* the regional governments, who authorize radio and television stations to operate within their province. They draw up the constitutions and establish watchdog broadcasting councils. They also approve the license fee of $27.90 from which broadcasting derives its main income. The revenue from the 15.5 million sets in the Federal Republic, combined with the money from a maximum of twenty minutes of advertising a day on each of the two main channels, makes the service both the wealthiest in Europe and the richest public service system any-where. The annual income is over 2,000 million marks ($540 million). Only in the United States and Japan, with their commercial networks, is the total advertising revenue greater.

The first German network, ARD (short for Arbeitsgemeinschaft der öffentlich-rechtlichen Rundfunkanstalten der Bundesrepublik Deutschland —Standing Committee of Broadcasting Corporations in the Federal Re-public of Germany), comprises nine television stations, each being a public corporation established by the *Länder.* Norddeutscher Rundfunk (NDR), the Hamburg station, for example, was jointly created by three local *Länder* of Lower Saxony, Schleswig-Holstein and Hamburg; Westdeutscher Rundfunk (WDR), the powerful Cologne station, was authorized by the Government of North-Rhine-Westphalia.[1]

Both these stations are immensely powerful in their own right. WDR's transmitters alone reach at least 5 million sets in North-Rhine-Westphalia; only nine other *nations* in the world have as many sets as that. NDR serves 3 million sets—more than in the whole of Holland or Belgium. So although they are regional stations, they should really be judged on a par with national broadcasting organizations. After all, in the whole of Africa and Asia, only Japan has more TV sets than in the Cologne area alone.

The third station in the ARD hierarchy is Bayerischer Rundfunk (BR) in Munich. Between them, the troika of NDR, WDR, and BR provide precisely 62 percent of all the programs on the ARD network. A strict quota system, based on the number of TV licenses in each region, determines each station's contribution to the national network. WDR's slice is 25 percent, NDR contributes 20 percent, and BR 17 percent. Four

[1] Immediately after World War II, NDR and WDR ran jointly as Nordwest-deutscher Rundfunk (NWDR), covering the British zone of Germany. The original reorganization of NWDR in the postwar years was handled by Hugh Greene, later director general of the BBC.

other ARD stations in Baden-Baden, Berlin, Frankfurt and Stuttgart each contribute 8 percent to the network, while small stations at Bremen and Saarbrucken chip in with 3 percent each.

No one is permitted to specialize in fulfilling his quota. All must share the output of documentaries, light entertainment, plays, the arts, and religion. The only exceptions are the weather reports, which Frankfurt handles, a central sports desk in Cologne, and *Tagesschau,* the news unit —rather like ITN in Britain—which is attached to NDR in Hamburg. Otherwise there are nine documentary, nine drama, nine current affairs, and even nine religion departments within the ARD network.

The Germans argue that this is a fine way to maintain a well-preserved balance in programing. In drama, for instance, the viewer has the chance to see plays reflecting the tastes of nine different directors. NDR tends to put on plays of social protest, WDR has a niche in Francis Durbridge detective thrillers, Munich prefers historical dramas.

An evening's viewing, therefore, is often rather like a round-Germany tour. The announcer keeps saying: "Now we switch to Hamburg for the news, then to Berlin for a play, and later to Munich for boxing." The task of fitting together the jigsaw of programs from nine stations is handled by a coordinating office in Munich. Normally, everyone accepts the programs of others without too many qualms, but occasionally the primmer stations are reluctant to screen a controversial play or documentary. Only once, however, has a lone station refused point blank to screen a program after all the others had agreed to show it. Bayerischer Rundfunk in Munich, well known as the most conservative station in the ARD system, rejected a modern version of *Lysistrata.* "They considered it was underdressed," said ARD's program director, Lothar Hartmann. While everyone else readily showed the play, BR sulkily screened a tasteful program of their own.

Whatever advantage the ARD quota system may have in assuring that viewers see a wide variety of programs, it is very costly. "It just isn't a sensible division of labor," Dietrich Schwarzkopf, director of television programs at NDR, complained. "It doesn't make sense for every station—especially the small ones like Bremen and Saarbrucken—to maintain a complete staff for every type of program. Here, in Hamburg, we would like to concentrate on public affairs and documentaries, with the occasional comedy series, like that marvelous British show *Till Death Us Do Part.* We'd happily leave all the light entertainment and quiz shows to Frankfurt or Cologne, who are very good at them."

Costs apart, the omelette of ideas from many stations may confuse the viewer. "I deplore the dividing up of religious programs," snapped WDR's religious editor in Cologne. "How on earth can we present our viewers with a coherent discussion of the main points of modern theology and relate them to today's social conditions when there are nine religious editors on the network, often with completely different outlooks. No wonder viewers are bewildered about religion."

There is no such problem for the second network ZDF (Zweites Deutsches Fernsehen). It is a centralized network based at Mainz. ZDF was born in 1963 out of Chancellor Adenauer's abortive attempt to create a commercial federal government station. Once the courts had ruled that project illegal the regional governments got together and agreed to start a communal network charged with offering the public a clear alternative to ARD. So ZDF was founded by an interstate treaty signed by all the *Länder*.

The younger network, like ARD, derives much of its income from license fees (the actual split is 28 percent to the Federal Post Office for technical facilities, 50 percent to ARD and 22 percent to ZDF). But, because ZDF gets a smaller slice of the fee, it is much more dependent on advertising, which provides nearly half its income. The advertising revenue, however, is limited because the maximum time allowed for commercials is only twenty minutes a day, all screened between 6:00 and 8:00 in the evening; commercials are not permitted after 8:00 P.M. and never on Sundays.

The only way to increase advertising revenue is through high ratings, which enable the price for those precious twenty minutes to be pushed up and up. Chasing the ratings, therefore, ZDF set out to build its image as a breezy channel of family entertainment, as a contrast to ARD's rather stern Teutonic diet of news, current affairs, and documentaries. "We are the entertainers," said Dieter Stolte, ZDF's head of program planning, unashamedly.

Entertainment, as usual, pays off. ZDF frequently win 70 to 80 percent of the audience in prime time; occasionally they even hit 90 percent. Their greatest successes have been thriller serials.

The Germans, unlike most other nations, run their serial installments on successive nights, rather than one episode each week. So the nation is often held captive in its armchairs for three or four evenings in a row. A particularly successful international spy thriller, shown by ZDF on a Thursday, Friday, and Sunday night during the winter of 1970, almost caused the rival ARD network to abdicate from the screen. On the first night ZDF had 82 percent of the entire German TV audience; at work the next day everyone was talking about the thriller, so that night those who had missed the first episode hurried home to tune in for the second—and ZDF had 84 percent of the audience. Meanwhile, ARD, realizing that their very existence had almost been forgotten, hastily reorganized their programs facing the Sunday-evening final installment of the spy play. They delayed the showing of a documentary on Yugoslavia, because they felt that many people would normally want to see it without the temptation of ZDF's spy drama. Instead, they showed some innocuous program that no one would mind missing. It was probably a wise capitulation: 90 percent of the viewers preferred the spies that night.

ZDF has also wooed enormous audiences with a factual, crime-fighting series called *Aktenzeichen XY . . . ungelöst (File on XY . . . Unsolved)*. The show is run by an anchorman, Eduard Zimmermann, who displays all the poise and polish of Raymond Burr as Perry Mason; the difference is that he is presenting real, unsolved crimes and appealing to the public to help track down the criminals. The program goes out live ten times a year; each is built around three unsolved crimes, which are first gripplingly dramatized. After this film, Zimmermann discusses the case with the investigating detectives. He asks what vital clues are missing? Whom are they looking for? Pictures and descriptions of wanted persons or stolen jewelry are shown. Then Zimmermann tells the TV audience to phone direct to a special desk in the studio or to their local police station if they have any vital information.

The 36 million armchair detectives watching the show respond with alacrity. The first 23 editions discussed 153 unsolved crimes; of those, 82 were solved through new clues thrown up by viewers, while of 125 suspects whose photographs were shown or who were described, 82 were subsequently arrested. The net is spread even outside Germany, for both Austrian television and the German-speaking segment of Swiss television carry the show live.

The murderer of a publisher, who was slain with an ax at his weekend cottage in the country, was arrested barely ten hours after one edition featured the crime. The murderer, the film showed, had stolen the dead man's watch. The police knew the make of the watch and learned of repair marks inside the case that would enable it to be identified among hundreds of similar models. Zimmermann asked anyone who had recently bought that type of watch secondhand to come forward. Barely was the program over when several people went to their local police stations with watches they had purchased since the murder. Sure enough, the stolen watch was turned in by a viewer who recalled buying it in a Dusseldorf pawnshop. Police sped to the shop and learned the watch had been traded in by a known criminal. He was arrested and, by lunchtime next day, had signed a full confession.

The success of *File on XY . . . Unsolved* in rallying the viewers of three nations as police informants has unnerved many German criminals, far more than any conventional police dragnet. There is an air of alarm in the underworld every time it comes on. One night the picture of a man wanted for stealing cars and selling them with forged documents was shown. Immediately, a viewer phoned the studio to say the wanted man was at a certain apartment in Stuttgart. Police rushed there, found the apartment door wide open and the television set still switched on to *File on XY*. The man had seen his own picture and fled. Later the same night, however, he was caught in Frankfurt with his car brimming with forging equipment. He told the police that he was sure he would be mentioned on the program sooner or later. So, every evening it was due, he loaded up his car with a suitcase and his forging equipment, filled up with gasoline, and then sat before the television poised for flight.

Understandably, the ARD network has a hard time against such compulsive viewing, but the situation is not entirely lopsided. Their own criminal proceedings do very well. *Ironside* (known as *Der Chef*) pulls in over 60 percent of the audience. Paul Temple thrillers by Britain's Francis Durbridge do even better. Indeed, Durbridge is almost more successful in Germany than at home. WDR Cologne produce a Durbridge serial each year as part of their 25 percent share of ARD drama. Every time they notch up an 80 percent rating. Each serial is condensed into three hour-long installments and shown on successive nights. "For those three nights," a WDR executive said happily, "the streets of Germany are empty."

But ARD's reputation has really been founded on its news and current affairs programs. The main news, *Tagesschau,* at 8:00 each evening, is frequently watched by more than half the television audience, who regard ARD as the *official* channel to which one turns automatically, especially in moments of crisis, to be informed of world events. *Tagesschau* is the watershed of an evening's viewing in Germany; before come the family entertainment programs, often imported shows like *Daktari* or *Skippy,* interspersed with blocs of commercials. Afterward, with the children supposedly in bed, comes the drama, the documentaries or the current affairs, undisturbed by commercials.

Three current affairs shows, *Panorama, Report,* and *Monitor* alternate on Monday evenings immediately after *Tagesschau.* And, in the public's mind at least, each reflects the political leanings of the station which produces them. *Panorama,* from Hamburg, is regarded as a program sprinkled with left-wing commentators and producers; *Report,* from Munich, has a more conservative reputation. *Panorama,* in particular, has for years run a gauntlet of criticism for its outspoken views. Editors and commentators, judged to have overreached themselves, tumble like autumn leaves. "*Panorama,*" a current affairs producer admitted, "changes moderators like most of us change dirty shirts."

The political sympathies of many German television reporters and commentators are much more apparent than, for example, those of television journalists in Britain. Indeed, the whole staffing of many stations can turn more on political affiliations than on ability. The intendant, as the Germans call their directors general, of each station will normally belong to, or certainly be approved by, the most powerful party in his region. In the ranks below, a discreet balance is maintained between the main political parties. "The whole thing is summed up in the word *Proporz*—proportional representation," a current affairs producer explained. "*Proporz* is almost a magical word in radio and television here. It means the distribution of jobs according to the influence of parties." And *Proporz* also applies to these current affairs programs; one Monday night there is the left-leaning *Panorama,* neatly counterbalanced the next week by the conservative *Report.* WDR's *Monitor,* which alternates with them, is also regarded as left of center but is, in turn, offset by the conservative current affairs output of Sudwest Rundfunk, the ARD station in Baden-Baden. As an editor in Frankfurt put it: "You can get a nice spectrum—a palette of politics."

Besides the regular news and current affairs programs, both ARD and ZDF carry extensive live color coverage of important parliamentary debates. The federal government has permitted the broadcasters to televise debates freely since 1964. Although a request has to be made on each occasion, it is just a formality and four color cameras are permanently installed in the Bundestag. In gentlemanly fashion, ARD and ZDF alternate the coverage; if one carries the full debate live, the other will be content to run an edited summary late in the evening. "I don't believe you will find such complete TV reporting of parliamentary affairs anywhere else," said Franz Wördemann, the political editor at WDR, Cologne, who coordinates all ARD reporting from the federal capital of Bonn nearby. "We often televise debates from 10:30 in the morning right through the day and, if it is an important budget or foreign affairs debate, we'll scrap a whole evening's schedule of regular programs."

Some members did throw away their formal speeches and play to the cameras when this parliamentary coverage first began, while others (especially if their own speech was not shown) complained that equal time was not given to each party. But, nowadays, the politicians have become so accustomed to the cameras that they just get on with the proceedings. The audience, apparently, is often fascinated; ratings may be as high as 30 or 40 percent. Moreover, the televising of debates has helped to make the mass of the German public much more aware of their postwar democracy in action.

Equally thorough overseas reporting is also possible because of the wealth of German television. ZDF, for instance, maintains no less than twenty-one correspondents abroad. Both the networks can afford to send current affairs and documentary teams anywhere to cover wars or famines, earthquakes or elections. In any major crisis one would expect to find German cameramen among the first arrivals of the international press corps along with the Americans, British, and, increasingly, the Japanese.

The German viewer, therefore, never goes short on news or current affairs. Only in Japan, where the public service corporation NHK provides almost six hours of news and current events daily, is the coverage more thorough. This concern with information has made ARD a particularly serious-minded channel, so that ZDF, coming into the fray later as entertainers, naturally breathed in some fresh air.

ZDF's lighthearted success has stimulated several ARD station program controllers to demand that their network alter its image to meet the challenge. "I've been trying to sell the idea to my ARD colleagues that we must revise the style of our main network," Dietrich Schwarzkopf, of NDR Hamburg, told me. "We should offer the great information programs *Tagesschau, Panorama,* and so on, nicely surrounded by light entertainment."

While many other ARD executives and producers reject the suggestion that the network should become a "channel of joy," there is a determined attempt to develop more popular light entertainment shows. So far, the most successful have been quiz shows, especially *Kuli's Quiz* and *Einer wird gewinnen (Someone Must Win)* from Frankfurt. But the Germans never seem to have evolved comedy shows to match the BBC's *Steptoe and Son* or Rowan and Martin's *Laugh-In*. Indeed, German television is one of the very few services in Europe never to have gained even third prize in the annual Montreux Golden Rose competition for entertainment programs. Their entry in 1970, however, submitted by WDR, Cologne, showed a new and highly original attempt to create a true color entertainment show. "We tried to break out of the conventional variety show," WDR's entertainment director, Hans Huttenrauch, explained. "We hired the Dutch director Bob Rooyens to put together a program starring Dusty Springfield from England using every possible electronic trick to make it a dazzling kaleidoscope of color." *The Dusty Springfield Show* won a "highly recommended" at Montreux, and several European program controllers who saw it felt it deserved a full prize. "It was a genuinely remarkable use of color—it showed me what color television really is about," one controller told me later. "It should have won a prize for technical brilliance." But perhaps this remark is symptomatic of German television; he felt the prize should have been awarded for technical achievement, not because the show was the finest in entertainment value.

Despite the ARD-ZDF rivalry, the two networks were not intended to be in competition. ZDF, as the newcomer, is required by law to provide alternative programs to ARD. Thus, when ARD is screening *What's My Line?* on Tuesdays, ZDF matches it with a documentary or short review; when ZDF has variety on Thursdays, ARD shows a play or film, while Friday night at 9:15 is staked out for an hour's crime on ARD versus a half-hour documentary and half an hour's variety on ZDF. Major events such as international soccer matches, the Olympics, moonwalks, and parliamentary debates are divided politely between them. At the Olympics, ARD covers one day's events live, while ZDF has summaries later; next day it is ZDF's turn for the live broadcasts. Apollo moonshots have been covered alternately; ARD did all the live televising on Apollo 12, ZDF took Apollo 13, ARD Apollo 14. When Apollo 13 ran into difficulties on the way to the moon and made its dramatic return to earth, ZDF had the splashdown exclusively, although ARD was permitted to show the event later on the regular news. That crisis caused some hair-tearing across Germany as ARD program directors argued unsuccessfully with their coordinating office in Munich that they, too, should carry the splashdown live and to hell with contrast of programs for viewers. Normally, however, it is accepted that in the best interests of the viewer he should have an alternative.

The only exception is for current affairs. Each Monday evening, while ARD is putting out *Panorama, Report,* or *Monitor,* ZDF matches it with a political discussion or "cultural" documentary. Then, on Wednesdays, when ZDF screens its weekly news magazine, ARD responds with an equally serious program. Thus the viewer cannot dodge the information programs by simply switching to entertainment on the rival channel. Two evenings a week he must watch politics or culture for the good of his soul or turn off.

Actually, he has one other choice—the regional third channels of each of the nine ARD stations. No national network exists for the third channels, which began in the mid-sixties and are only on the air for three or four hours each evening. The individual stations do pool some third channel programs and even operate mini-networks (Hamburg, Berlin, and Bremen, for instance, have a common third channel), but basically this channel offers each ARD station a chance to develop its own preferences. Bayerischer Rundfunk in Munich has chosen to emphasize education, with much of the evening taken up with educational programs for adults. The opposite approach is taken by WDR in Cologne. "We try to make our third channel a complete service with news, plays, music, and documentaries," said Werner Hofer, the program director.

Hofer, who is certainly one of the best of West Germany's program directors, explained: "We are ambitious; we have an attitude of slight exclusivity and snobbishness. We try to fill the vacuum that is left by the established programs. Take Saturday night—after *Tagesschau* at 8:00, most Germans are satisfied with entertainment on ARD or ZDF, but what about the remaining 5 percent? That's my market. So we started a magazine called *Spectrum* to make detailed reports on fascinating artistic and scientific developments. We also aim to show the most exclusive highbrow movies you'll find anywhere between Hollywood and Vladivostok. We were the first station anywhere in the world to show American underground cinema. Where else can you see Andy Warhol's movies on television?"

Enjoying himself, Hofer, a slightly Pickwickian figure in purple and white striped shirt and black tie with white spots, lounged back even farther in a black leather chair until he was almost lying staring at the ceiling. He went on: "Our problem in Germany is Mother's terror; it's Mother who decides what the family watches. But, gradually, as more families buy color television, young people will be able to see programs of their own choice on the old black and white set. We want to stimulate those young viewers, to tell them about the world. We should be a radar station, picking up ideas in the theater, music, ballet, art, and education and feeding them back. More than half our viewers understand English almost perfectly, so we can present plays for them in the original language; we've done plays by Pinter and Wesker. We can do all this even on a small budget. What too few people in television realize is that the very best programs are done with the least money."

Hofer campaigns for his channel with the passion of a crusader. "Do you know?" he asked. "There was a suggestion by ARD that, during the summer of 1972 when the Olympics are in Munich, the third program should *close down*. This is the one time above all others when we should not. We've decided to invite all the countries participating in the Olympics to show on our channel one program of their choice; giving the Poles, the Japanese, the Mexicans, the Czechs a chance to show their flag on our TV screen."

Hofer's vision of this third channel at WDR is one of the most encouraging signs in German television. The pity of it is that all Hofer's enterprise and energy is going into a regional and not a national network. He was widely expected in 1969 to become director of television programs at WDR—thus overseeing their contribution to the main ARD network— but apparently he fell afoul of the local political pressures that bedevil West German television. Not only does political balance—*Proporz*—have to be preserved within the stations, but administrative councils, appointed by the regional *Länder,* have to approve senior staff. The intendant does not have the right to select his own men. Consequently, anyone who seems too outspoken or whose politics may not quite please the administrative council has a tough time making headway. Moreover, intendants may be cautious in pressing someone's case too hard, for they themselves are chosen by the regional politicians. "The election of the intendant by local political bosses has had the bitter result that television stations are too conservative—they take no risks," complained a senior production executive at WDR. "We are strangled by the mentality of politicians who may know how to run a city museum, but not a television station."

Many WDR executives and producers tried to push Hofer's case— the administrative council, however, declined to listen. But their failure stirred up a determination among many young television executives, not only at WDR but at other ARD stations and in ZDF, that they must curb the top-heavy political control of the administrative councils in favor of much broader-based groups. The old watchword of *Proporz* is being challenged by the new cry of *Mitwirkung*—participation.

"Every group has a right to be represented on television councils," said Otto Wilfert, one of the most ardent reformers at ZDF, "but we believe there should be one representative for each group. Up to now, politicians have been the majority on our council. We say give each political party one representative, and then bring in writers, university lecturers, and television producers."

The campaign has wide support. "The administrative councils have held television back," admitted a top program planner at ZDF, "and many young people with fresh ideas have not been able to break through to positions of responsibility."

The *Länder,* however, are hardly likely to surrender their control of television without a tough fight. Just as they resisted Adenauer's attempts a decade ago to create a federal commercial channel, so they will seek to check the fashionable cry of *Mitwirkung* in the seventies.

8

France:

Après de Gaulle

"La télévision c'est le gouvernement dans la salle à manger," a French cabinet minister once remarked during the de Gaulle years. De Gaulle himself certainly tried to carry the spirit of his government into every dining room in France; as long as he was president the television news at eight o'clock each evening almost invariably began with a report on his activities that day. The cameras followed him everywhere—on his peregrinations through the French countryside and on his tours overseas. His tall, erect figure always dominated the scene as he strode through the crowds. From time to time in moments of crisis there he was in closeup, raising his arms in supplication to the nation gathered before their sets, *"France, France, aidez-moi, aidez-moi."* Few politicians have been so compelling on television, and few in Europe have sought to marshal it so completely to their cause. De Gaulle made no secret of its importance in putting over his policies to the French people; he knew the press was largely hostile to him—television, therefore, must be on his side.

The story of French television, consequently, is bound up with de Gaulle. Throughout his years in power, which coincided with the years when television really spread its wings in Europe, he kept l'Office de Radiodiffusion Télévision Français (ORTF) under tight rein. And he even interfered on occasion with other television organizations' plans. Once he refused to allow the French earth station at Pleumeur Boudeau to relay to New York by satellite a CBS News program in which Jean Monnet, the architect of the Common Market, was participating. Monnet had to go to Brussels to make the program and the signal was then rerouted through the British earth station at Goonhilly Downs.

Only since de Gaulle's fall from power in 1968 has ORTF been able to establish its own identity. The organization has been completely overhauled by a new director general, Jean-Jacques de Bresson, and in 1972 will launch a new color network, giving it three in all—one black and white and two color. ORTF then will boast more television channels than any other public service broadcasting organization in the world (it also operates three radio networks). Moreover, ORTF is now the second richest broadcasting organization in Europe, with an income of over $300 million a year from license fees of $21.60 on nearly 11 million TV sets, plus a bonus of almost $100 million a year from advertising. The commercials are held to a mere eight minutes per day—but this very scarcity makes them highly prized.

France's influence in the world of television is magnified by her championship of her own color television system, SECAM, and her natural leadership in the growth of television throughout the French-speaking world. De Gaulle's grand design of developing France into a powerful independent nation with her own nuclear capability resulted also in her going it alone in color television. While everyone else in Western Europe agreed to adopt the German color system PAL, the French preferred their own invention of SECAM. The two systems are not instantly compatible, although special converters have been devised to transfer pictures from SECAM to PAL and vice versa. Furthermore, de Gaulle succeeded in persuading the Soviet Union, and consequently all of Eastern Europe, to adopt SECAM. Thus Europe is divided sharply into two color camps: SECAM to the east and west, PAL in the center. The French have also exerted great pressure on the Italians and the Spanish, who as yet do not have color, to persuade them to adopt SECAM. However, these countries appear to have resisted the French overtures and are preparing to join their other European colleagues with PAL. Undaunted, the French are still hoping that Morocco, Algeria, and Tunisia, where their influence is strong, will select SECAM when they eventually go over to color. This in turn might persuade the whole Arab world to take up the French system. Lebanon has already installed SECAM and, if the North African countries followed suit, the remainder would almost inevitably follow (although Kuwait has awkwardly gone for PAL).

The French have found natural program partners among the *pays Francophone*—the French-speaking countries of Belgium, Switzerland, Luxembourg, Monaco, and French Canadian television in Montreal. All six participate regularly, for instance, in a lively quiz, *Le Francophonissime,* which seeks to find the contestant with the best knowledge of the French language. And if ORTF buys an American movie or a series like *The Virginian,* and dubs it into French, then this almost assures its sale in the same dubbed version to the smaller Francophone countries who have less money for their own dubbing. The French-language division of Belgian television, RTB, also takes most of its drama from ORTF as it cannot afford to mount its own large-scale productions.

The French are equally active in promoting television in their old colonies in Africa and Asia. Just as broadcasting in former British colonies is frequently modeled on the BBC, so ORTF is often the example for French territories. For several years a special government department, l'Office de Co-operation Radiophonique (OCRA) actively helped in the expansion of television in North Africa, the Ivory Coast, Upper Volta, and Cambodia. OCRA was merged into ORTF in 1969, but the determination to maintain a sphere of influence remains as strong. The French-language station in Beirut, for instance, gets seven hours of programs free from ORTF each week, while in such remote outposts as Afars and Issas (formerly French Somaliland) and the island of Réunion in the Indian Ocean ORTF's overseas division handles the programing. "These small countries with very little money naturally turn to us," said Lucien Renault, associate director of ORTF's foreign department, "because we share languages and culture." The real difference in the French response is that they give programs away: the British and the Americans charge for them.

The basic concept of ORTF's role at home and overseas, as laid down in a new broadcasting statute approved by de Gaulle in 1964, is "to satisfy the needs of the public for information, culture, education and entertainment." This same document also sets out that ORTF is a "national institution of the state with an industrial and commercial character"; more simply, it is a nationalized industry.

The governing body which determines broad issues of policy is the Administrative Council, at one time composed of sixteen members, but now twenty-four. All are nominated by the Council of Ministers. They include twelve representatives of the government, five from ORTF, two from the press (one publisher, one journalist), one representative of the television audience (the president of a group known as Téléspectateurs et Auditeurs de France) and four other people from public life. The director general, who is in executive command, is also appointed by the government. During the de Gaulle years, however, ORTF enjoyed little autonomy. Finances were subject to scrutiny and approval by the Ministry of Finance and daily programing was watched closely by the Ministry of Finance and an Inter-Ministerial Committee for Information Liaison. This committee, in particular, sought to direct television news coverage;

it met most mornings to decide how to play the day's events. And, according to some ORTF journalists I have talked to, its officers might even be on the phone to the control room during news broadcasts to indicate last-minute changes.

This manipulation of the news reached its height during the May 1968 disorders. For the first few days of the strikes and student disturbances, television news underplayed the troubles and no student leaders had a chance to put their case on the screen. But television journalists, becoming increasingly restive at such blatantly one-sided reporting of the crisis, finally took the matter in their own hands, defied the management, and for several days put out remarkably impartial news and comment. Then ORTF's Friday night current affairs program *Panorama* was suppressed because it proposed to discuss the students' complaints. The journalists and some of the technicians concerned promptly called a strike and demanded greater freedom to report what was really happening. A committee of ten was formed to press their case. When de Gaulle went on television to call for calm, the committee tried to insist on equal time for opposition leaders. Interviews with these politicians were recorded but the government would not allow them to be shown. All ORTF's journalists except about twenty immediately responded by voting to go on strike. They stayed out for five weeks, while television put out an emasculated single news bulletin a day. In the end the strike collapsed and some sixty-five journalists were sacked at de Gaulle's insistence; other commentators were moved to obscure jobs on the sports desk. The General, apparently, was outraged that, in his moment of crisis, television "stabbed me in the back when I was on my knees." [1] But the journalists, for all their initial failure to gain reforms, had brought the whole matter of television censorship into the open. During the election a few months later to choose de Gaulle's successor as president, Georges Pompidou made reform of ORTF one of the planks of his campaign. He promised that in the future all sides could have their say on television.

ORTF today, therefore, is a very different creature. The Inter-Ministerial Committee for Information Liaison is no more, and all national political parties are guaranteed access to the screen. ORTF has taken over most of the responsibilities for its own finances and its previous bureaucracy has been streamlined in an attempt to give freer rein to creative talent. A new director of programs has been installed for each channel, with much greater responsibility in dispensing his own budgets

---

[1] Anthony Sampson, *The New Europeans,* p. 297.

and making up schedules. In effect ORTF is striving to make its 13,000 staff think like broadcasters instead of civil servants. "What we are really doing," said Director General Jean-Jacques de Bresson, "is to transform ORTF from a large administrative department into a proper commercial enterprise with a public service role."

A cornerstone of the reforms has been the creation of two quite separate and competitive news divisions: one for the popular black and white first channel, which covers all of France, and one for the second color channel, which covers about 90 percent of the country. The first channel's news director is a small, plump journalist, Pierre Desgraupes, who has a reputation for being moderately left wing; he has been in broadcasting for many years and made his name on a news magazine program, *Cinq Colonnes à la Une (Five Columns on the Front Page)*. He was one of the strikers in 1968 and his appointment to take over the news service caused considerable alarm among many Gaullists. But Desgraupes is balanced by the news director of Channel 2, Jacqueline Baudrier, a vivacious woman who was a strong supporter of de Gaulle, and one of the few journalists who did not strike in 1968.

Since January 1, 1970, it has been Desgraupes against Baudrier in an all-out battle to win audiences to the news on their respective channels. But more than that they had to reestablish the reputation of television news in France. "Television news," said Desgraupes, "was suspect for fawning to the government. Suspect for being accommodating by omission, by distortion, by interpretation. I want to make the news credible."

Competition is regarded as being crucial in reestablishing the credibility of television news. Both channels cover stories quite separately, each with its own reporters and cameramen. Even in overseas bureaus one correspondent works for Desgraupes, the other for Jacqueline Baudrier— a situation which, according to one ORTF foreign correspondent, "is driving us out of our minds. We have to send two reporters on every story and shoot film from different angles, so that it doesn't all look the same." Madame Baudrier's channel, of course, has the advantage of color. She has also shown a special preference for medical stories and once opened her news with a long color report of a liver transplant.

The news competition has certainly been a spur to viewing. During the worst days of the credibility gap in 1968 the audience for Channel 1's main evening news was down to 35 percent; while I was in Paris in 1970, when the news experiment was seven months old, the audience was up to 57 percent. And on the second channel, which always has a smaller audience because of its limited coverage and the fact that many Frenchmen have not bought a set that receives both channels, it was up from 2 to 7 percent. "Competition is proving a good idea," said one of Desgraupes' editors. And he added: "Many politicians now realize that the troubles in 1968 were partly as a result of television's being silent; people had no forum for their views."

Nevertheless, there is still considerable skepticism as to how free television really is. Olivier Todd, editor of the Friday night *Panorama,* resigned in June 1970 over cuts in film of French paratroops in Algiers. And President Pompidou did not help restore confidence by stating in the same month: "Being a journalist on ORTF is not like being a journalist elsewhere. Whether you like it or not, ORTF is the voice of France. You who write the news must always keep in mind that you are not talking for yourself, you are the voice of your country and your government."

But overall, ORTF's news divisions have been rejuvenated and the whole television service is finding a new sense of purpose. Moreover, most of the journalists sacked in 1968 have been rehired. ORTF received further encouragement during 1970 with the report of a special commission on the future of broadcasting. The commission, under a former Minister of Education, Lucien Paye, rejected proposals for a separate commercial television network in France. They recommended instead that ORTF be awarded a third channel. The hopes of a strong commercial television lobby, led by Jean Frydman of Tele-Monte Carlo, were dashed. The commercial lobby had based much of their argument on the British system of ITV in competition with the BBC; ORTF, they argued, needed just such a stimulant. ORTF itself, of course, has had very limited advertising since 1968, but the Paye Commission suggested that advertising time should not be extended significantly and the costs of the new channel should be largely paid for by higher license fees.

Yet even without the direct challenge of a rival commercial network, the prospect of a third public service channel in France from 1972 is intriguing. No other nation, except the Soviet Union, has three channels all belonging to one organization. Furthermore, the opportunity to start a new channel from scratch with a clean slate for scheduling occurs only rarely. The new channel will be directed by Jean-Louis Guillaud, a former head of television news, who is still in his thirties. "We are not in favor of creating either a new specialized educational or high-brow channel," he told me, reviewing his plans. "Nor are we aiming to please some single amorphous public taste. We believe there are several potential large audiences, not necessarily defined by age or where they live, but by their interests. Most men, for instance, prefer sports and information. We want to identify those groups and cater to them. We must put an end to the dogma of unity."

Finding the right style for a new channel is not easy. "Why do fewer people read *Paris-Match* these days and more *L'Express?*" Guillaud asked. "It's all a matter of style. We have to create our style too. We've already done a survey on our second channel and found there is no clear image of that in the public mind." In searching for his third channel image Guillaud is relying particularly on bringing in many young people, both from Paris and the provinces. "Television here is still done by men of the 1950s," he said. "This is a chance to create a channel run by and for young people." And he hopes that it will pay special attention to social issues. "So far French television has not paid much attention to the problems of housing or architecture or pollution. We shall try to do information programs on all these aspects of our society today."

ORTF will produce only two thirds of the programs for the new channel; the remainder will come from private producers in France together with purchases from overseas. "Ultimately I think that half of all ORTF's programs should be made outside," Guillaud said. "We need to get a much better dialogue going with our film industry and convert them into working more for television."

Initially, the third channel will put on only three hours of programs a night, from 7:00 until 10:00, which is French prime time. The French go to bed very early (68 percent of them are in bed by 10:30), so that the television evening is much shorter than in most European countries. The main entertainment for the evening—*la soirée distraitive,* as the French call it—is just from 8:30 until 10:00. By 1975 the new network will cover most of France and its output will be up to four hours each evening. Once national coverage has been achieved it will gradually take over more of the role of the present first channel, which, for technical reasons, cannot be converted to color. This black and white network, therefore, will gradually become devoted to educational programs or old black and white movies.

Until the new channel is born, however, the first channel will certainly hold its strong majority position; most evenings it has between 50 and 60 percent of the total possible audience, while the second channel, in color, usually musters between 20 and 30 percent for its more popular programs. The schedules are designed to complement each other. Thus on a typical Saturday evening, while Channel 1 offers the latest in a series of Inspector Maigret thrillers (what more natural for French TV?), Channel 2 comes up with a documentary on bird migration, followed by ballet from the Paris Opéra. On Sunday afternoon the choice is between football and an interview with the philosopher Claude Levi-Strauss. The following evening the fare is quite serious on both channels: Channel 1 has a two-hour documentary on the role of mayors in French towns, while the rival channel has ballet from the Opéra-Comique and a documentary on the future of sports in our urban society. Later in the week *L'Homme de Fer (Ironside)* fetches up against a dramatization of a modern French novel: *Le Thé sous les Cyprès (Tea under the Cypresses)* by Jean-Louis Curtis. *Ironside* is one of the few major American series on French television; the only others in prime time in June 1971, for instance, were *The Virginian* and *The Fugitive.* The French normally hold their foreign buying down to 13 percent of their output (about the same proportion as the British), of which three quarters comes from the United States and most of the remainder from Britain—both *The Saint* and *The Avengers (Chapeau Melon et Bottes de Cuir)* have been very successful.

But France is becoming much more involved in the growing habit of elaborate coproductions with other European broadcasting organizations. Their most frequent partners are RAI in Italy, TVE in Spain and Bayerischer Rundfunk in Munich. ORTF have backed all RAI's major productions of *The Odyssey, The Aeneid* and *Leonardo da Vinci* (to which they contributed a French actor, Philip Leroy, as Leonardo), while they undertook themselves the making of an epic based on Dumas's *The Three Musketeers.* They succeeded for a while in wooing director Roberto Rossellini away from RAI to make a film for them on Louis XIV.

The second channel has also evolved a highly successful new format, *Les Dossiers de l'Ecran,* every Wednesday evening, in which a film is immediately followed by a long discussion of issues raised by it. After a biography of Louis Pasteur, for instance, they got together a studio panel of people to talk about the scientist's life and work. A movie about the mysterious disappearance of Britain's Commander Crabbe, while on underwater exercises near Russian warships on an official visit to Britain, was likewise used as a trigger for debate on what really happened to the frogman. A documentary film on the hazards of driving the Route Nationale 7 to the south of France led into a two-hour debate among doctors, police, and motorists on why so many people disregard the dangers of death on the road. And while I was visiting Paris a grand debate was staged following a movie about the Tour de France cycle race. Past victors in the race, journalists, and doctors all assembled in the studio to discuss the trials of this annual cycling marathon and to answer questions phoned in by viewers from all over France. In all the channel devoted two hours and forty minutes that evening to the combined film and debate, from 8:30 until 11:10.

This is, of course, one of the advantages of having complementary instead of competitive channels; one channel can be opened up for coverage of a single topic in some depth for most of an evening, while the other presents more varied entertainment. The rapport between the channels is so close that if a new program is about to start on Channel 2 before the end of a program on Channel 1, a small 2 appears at the bottom right-hand corner of the screen on Channel 1 to prompt anyone who wishes to catch the opening of the show on Channel 2.

A serious program on one channel, however, does not necessarily guarantee a popular one on the other. ORTF never forgets the requirement in their statutes about disseminating "culture." Documentaries abound on the lives of great French writers, artists, and composers. To take just one week during 1971, for example, there were two ballet performances, a concert by l'Orchestre National de l'ORTF, a biography in color of the poet Eugenio Montale, an hour-long program on the arts (covering a surrealist exhibition in Bordeaux, a sculpture exhibition in Paris, and the Dürer Festival at Nuremberg), a biography of the eighteenth-century intellectual and composer Jean-Philippe Rameau, and a documentary on the archeologist Heinrich Schliemann's discovery of the ruins of Troy. In the same week ORTF announced a new season of eight plays to be produced for television by the Comédie Française, including works by Molière, Giraudoux and Feydeau. All good stuff but, as a foreign correspondent living in Paris put it, "rather stiff and teachy, if not preachy." [2]

The French also take seriously the question of television and violence, but their policy is to advise the viewer very thoroughly what he is in for and then leave it up to his own discretion whether he watches. Not only does the weekly program guide *Télé 7 Jours* indicate the age groups to which any film is most suited—for adults only, for adults and adolescents, or for everyone—but throughout a program considered unsuitable for children a small white rectangle is shown in one corner of the screen. Thus parents tuning in late or without checking the details are alerted at once by the "rectangle blanc" that the program may not be appropriate for all the family. ORTF's violence code also insists that if one channel is showing a "rectangle blanc" program, the other must offer something suitable for everyone.

[2] Richard Mayne, *Listener,* Vol. 83, No. 2127, p. 3.

The turmoil through which ORTF has passed during the last few years has made its overall performance somewhat erratic. As a program executive remarked, "We've never had a very methodical approach. In almost every field I think you might say we've done the best and the worst in television." However, the new autonomy that ORTF has now enjoyed for a year or two and its thorough internal spring cleaning certainly place it poised to take a great leap forward in the seventies.

9

Italy:

A Passion for History

Newspaper headlines sometimes make Italy seem a country under siege; postmen, garbagemen, and bus drivers are on strike, car workers are rioting in Milan and Turin, and the people of Reggio Calabria are fighting for their town to be named the provincial capital. A rather different Italy, however, is seen on the two channels of the public service Radio Televisione Italiana (RAI). All is peaceful in the land and the main program attraction for the evening is an excellent dramatization of Virgil's *Aeneid,* depicting the founding of Rome, or a television biography of Michelangelo. Italian television delves very thoroughly into the glorious past, but rather prefers to steer clear of the present.

The trouble is that RAI is often beset by its own political upheavals. Its presidents resign in exasperation at trying to control such a volatile organization, while other executives write furious letters to the newspapers charging that many of their colleagues are communists or fascists. The convenient thing about a historical series is that it judiciously avoids stirring up political passions. When it comes to current events everyone is desperate to make sure his opinion is aired. The main evening news, *Telegiornale,* on RAI's first channel, for instance, strains to satisfy every shade of the political spectrum. There are no less than six anchormen, each of whom helps to keep a political party satisfied that its views will be adequately represented.

This precarious political balance is preserved throughout RAI's regular staff of almost ten thousand. The director general is a Christian Democrat and he is neatly counterbalanced by a socialist as a managing director; RAI's two vice-presidents are also allied to these two leading parties. Right at the top the president of RAI is supposed to preserve some kind of neutrality between all the factions and direct the objectivity of the organization, but it has often proved difficult to find a suitable coordinator. After Professor Aldo Sandulli resigned as President, early in 1970 (the second president to depart in eighteen months), over the furor aroused by a television program examining the conflict between the Italian constitution and certain parts of the penal code drawn up during the Fascist regime, no successor was forthcoming for over a year.

Many of RAI's difficulties stem from its rather ambiguous institutional position. Unlike many other broadcasting organizations in Europe, it is not an autonomous state corporation. Instead it is owned by a state-owned industrial holding company, IRI, whose portfolio embraces a variety of commercial operations from banks to airlines. IRI, however, has relatively little say in the running of the broadcasting organization. The real power lies in the hands of a nine-man management committee, composed largely of political appointees. This management committee keeps a close watch over all programs likely to cause political controversy—and many news items which might embarrass the government of the day never appear at all. Strikes and riots often go unreported and are rarely covered in any detail. Other broadcasting organizations that request coverage of troubles in Italy during the daily story conference for the Eurovision news exchange are politely told that no film is available. If they want to report the event they must send their own team.

Such political maneuvers, however, have not prevented RAI from making some splendid expeditions occasionally, such as to cover the Pope on his travels to Africa, Asia, and South America. For these tours RAI spares no expense and mounts a veritable task force, usually led by Vittorio Boni, their director of international relations. Boni and an RAI engineer, Ernst Braun, are recognized throughout Europe as among the finest exponents of the art of arranging television coverage in out-of-the-way places —whether for a papal visit, a football match, or the Olympics. When Pope Paul went to Uganda, Boni and his team built their own portable earth station, flew it out to Africa, and assembled it there in five days so that they could bounce live coverage of the visit via satellite direct to Rome.

The Italians have shown equal showmanship in developing perhaps the most productive liaison to be found anywhere between television and the cinema. RAI makes relatively few of its own feature programs; instead it contracts them out to the Italian film industry. The film makers, after some initial reservations about possible censorship, have adapted readily. Directors of distinction like Federico Fellini, Vittorio da Sica and Roberto Rossellini are all making programs for television, and RAI has given them a remarkably free hand. "In agreeing with Fellini that he should make five special programs for us, we wanted to stretch the confines of television, rather than limit Fellini," said one of RAI's program directors.

Consequently, RAI's two black and white channels (it is the last major European nation not to have color) have programs of great originality from time to time that compensate for the more conventional diet of detective and variety shows that inevitably comprise many evening hours. These programs have even greater impact because of the Italians' rather restrained viewing habits. Television hours are still strictly limited —RAI's main channel is on the air only nine hours a day and the second channel for a mere two hours each evening from 9:00 until 11:00. The average Italian looks at television for just under two hours a day, normally from about 8:30 in the evening until he goes to bed. Before 8:30 the television audience is very small—a mere 4 million viewers out of a potential 37 million adults.

The high mark in the evening is *Telegiornale,* the news at 8:30 for which the audience suddenly jumps from 4 to 14 million. Television news is of vital importance to Italians, for relatively few of them buy newspapers (newspapers' daily circulation is only 5 million). According to Pompeo Abruzzini, RAI's director of audience research, at least 10 million people watching the TV news do not see newspapers. Immediately after the news and a short and very lively block of commercials known as *Carosello* comes the one major feature program of the evening. This normally lasts at least an hour. "Italians will not stay in at 9:00 for a short program," said RAI's director of programs, "unless we have a good feature on both channels—they will simply go out for a drink or to the cinema."

This is where the liaison with the film industry has proved so fruitful. It has coproduced with RAI everything from Maigret and Nero Wolfe detective series to a dramatized biography of Socrates, directed by Roberto Rossellini.

The rapport between television and cinema has arisen partly as a result of legislation which requires the two media to cooperate, but more because television has been able to offer both established directors and newcomers the opportunity to make films that do not have to be a guaranteed commercial success. As a public service organization, financed primarily by license fees of $20 a year on the 10 million TV sets in Italy, plus very limited advertising between programs for 5 percent of air time, RAI has the opportunity to sponsor these directors. "We enable them to make noncommercial films," explained Vittorio Bonicelli, RAI's linkman with the film business.

The scope of many of these projects has been widened by undertaking them as coproductions with other European television organizations, notably France's ORTF, Germany's Bayerischer Rundfunk in Munich (one of the ARD regional stations), and Spain's TVE. "We have tried to make European rather than exclusively Italian films," Bonicelli said. Each country chips in about $100,000 for a ninety-minute film; this covers many of the initial expenses, but the film makers themselves underwrite part of the cost because they retain the world distribution rights. This formula enables Italian (and French) television to put up enough money to attract important film makers; $300,000 or more guaranteed is an attractive proposition.

The most enthusiastic convert to television film making is Roberto Rossellini. He declares roundly that he has forsaken the cinema in favor of television as the medium of the future. His first major series was a twelve-part epic, *Stories of the Struggle for Survival,* focusing on a dozen crucial events in world history. He followed this with a dramatization of *The Acts of the Apostles.* Despite his enthusiasm for television, Rossellini's relations with RAI's bureaucracy have been extremely strained from time to time. Once he departed for Paris, vowing he would work no longer in Italy but, after he had made a film for French television on Louis XIV, he was persuaded back to RAI to undertake two ninety-minute color dramatizations of the lives of Socrates and Caligula.

The original prototype for these historical re-creations was *The Odyssey,* filmed in 1968 by Franco Rossi in a joint RAI-Dino di Laurentiis production. This seven-hour serial cost $3.6 million and took eight months to shoot. A whole village was built on a beach in Yugoslavia and three large boats launched to carry Ulysses and his men on their wanderings. Seventeen million Italians eagerly followed these television exploits of Ulysses, thus encouraging RAI to delve further into history. They promptly embarked on a dramatization of Virgil's *Aeneid* (also directed by Franco Rossi) in six one-hour installments, together with major series on Michelangelo, Leonardo da Vinci, and Benvenuto Cellini.

The historical pageant is, of course, almost limitless. RAI's coproduction plans for the 1970s include series on the building of the Suez Canal, the discovery and exploration of the Congo, and a restaging of Magellan's voyage around the world. They are equally busy dramatizing great novels: Anna Moffo is in *Anna Karenina* and Gina Lollobrigida in *The Charterhouse of Parma,* while the French director Robert Bresson has made a ninety-minute film based on Dostoyevsky's novel *The Devils.*

Although all these programs are designed initially for television serials, several of them are being refashioned afterward into films for the cinema. A four-part television serial of *Pinocchio,* for instance, later became a two-

hour feature film; *The Aeneid* and *Leonardo da Vinci* programs have also
been edited down into films.

The close working relationship between television and the cinema has
also bred much discussion on how frequently programs should be shown
on both media. "It's not enough for a film to have one night's life on television," said Vittorio Bonicelli at RAI. "Federico Fellini made a beautiful
film for us, *The Clowns,* which we showed at Christmas. This was his own
highly personal view of clowns at the circus. You really need to see a film
like that two or three times. And now I have a wonderful film by Robert
Bresson of Dostoyevsky's novel *White Nights.* I'm afraid you can't really
appreciate it in one night on television. Perhaps it should be shown in an
art theater for six months, so that all those interested could see it there first
before it is shown on television. People must be prepared for this film."

A film of such complexity is, of course, a rarity on Italian television.
The association with the cinema does not mean that Fellini, da Sica, or
Antonioni films are on every night. "What we aim for is ten or a dozen
films by such directors each year," said Bonicelli. "Fellini will make five
films for us over three years." But at least Italian television has wrung some
genuine creativity out of their film industry. "Our aim is in complete contrast to the Americans," an Italian director pointed out. "We give our film
directors a free hand to make an original program they could not do for
the commercial cinema. The American networks also have their programs
made by movie companies, but they must be made to fit an exact commercial formula. They are not giving them the chance to be creative."

Italian television is inhibited by the politicians and the Catholic
Church rather than the advertisers. Dramatizations of *The Odyssey* or the
Life of Leonardo da Vinci are nice, safe ground unlikely to cause a political furor. RAI's problems begin the moment it starts to tackle the con-
temporary scene. The great debate on divorce reform in Italy in 1970, for
instance, caused RAI to twist into all kinds of contortions. The broadcasting organization has always had close ties with the Vatican and has pru-
dently steered clear of such delicate topics—it was once reported to have
insisted on the word "divorce" being deleted from a popular song at a
television song contest. For a while RAI tried to dodge the divorce debate
in 1970 until one of the promoters of the bill charged them with "censorship" and "total lack of objectivity." RAI then held hasty consultations
and, abruptly reversing its policy, came up with ten hours of television
debate on the divorce proposals.

The divorce Italian broadcasters really pray for is from the politicians.
RAI's ten-year license comes up for renewal at the end of 1972 and many

are hoping for some new arrangement that will give broadcasting greater detachment from the whims of the government of the day. Right-wing business interests would dearly love to capture television for the private sector. Accordingly, they have been in the forefront of a sustained campaign to magnify RAI's weaknesses and to discredit its objectivity. Their campaign was helped early in 1970 when one of RAI's own vice-presidents, Italo de Feo, wrote in the right-wing newspaper, *Il Tempo,* that the majority of RAI's staff was "communist, communist-inclined, or dissident Catholic." This accusation is hardly borne out in reality, since RAI has been essentially Christian Democrat territory for many years, but it is good fuel for those anxious to undermine its reputation. However, no Italian television executives that I met seriously felt there was any likelihood at all of television being handed over to the commercial television lobby. But they do hope for some strengthening of RAI's status. "We simply must have a complete reorganization," said one senior director. "We must be less political—we are just not serving the best interests of the public at the moment. We are too closely linked with the government in power. We need instead a corporation responsible to Parliament."

Whether RAI will achieve this objective under its new licensing arrangements is by no means certain. "The politicians here see television as the new power base," an Italian journalist remarked, "especially as our newspapers have a very limited circulation. Television reaches all the people every day and the politicians are only too aware of that. It will be hard to stop RAI from being a political preserve."

10

Spain: Legacy
of the *Conquistadores*

Spanish television is a curious hybrid: a cross between European and American, with an extra touch of political control thrown in through the strong arm of General Franco. While Spain is the only European nation where the television service, Televisión Española (TVE), is an integral part of the Ministry of Information and Tourism, it is also the sole major country with purely commercial television. A Ministry of Information running commercial television hardly sounds possible at first; actually, TVE is something of a bonanza for the ministry. All the advertising revenue of upward of $55 million a year goes directly into the ministry's coffers; they do give most of it back to TVE, but use the rest to finance radio, a symphony orchestra, and various other activities. Indeed, it is an old joke in Madrid that the television commercials pay for everything the ministry does.

TVE, anyway, has no independent status of its own and its progress depends rather on the whim of the minister of the day. Fortuitously for TVE, the minister for most of the 1960s, Manuel Fraga Iribarne, was a great television enthusiast who set his heart on expansion. Consequently, TVE was rapidly equipped during his regime with some of the most extensive and modern studios in Europe, set amid pine trees in a park at Prado del Rey, just outside Madrid. Thus fitted out, TVE is emerging rather swiftly as one of the more important program-producing organizations in Europe. They turn out 80 percent of their own programs, several of which have begun to win them a fistful of international prizes. A delightful *History of Frivolity* won the Golden Rose at Montreux in 1968 for the best light entertainment program in Europe that year.

The Spanish like to point out with considerable pride that they now rank fifth in Europe, behind West Germany, Britain, France, and Italy, in set ownership; in 1971 there were just over 5 million sets. "In 1956 we had only three thousand," said Luis Ezcurra Carrillo, the director of television, who has been the prime architect of TVE's growing international reputation, "and as late as 1962 there were only 300,000 sets in Spain. Since then our rapid expansion has been closely tied to the growth of the Spanish economy—and as a commercial network we have really created for the first time here a national market for advertising." This sudden upsurge in the late 1960s has also established Spain as an increasingly important link between television in Europe and South America. "We are the bridge," said Luis Ezcurra Carrillo, "with 200 million Spanish-speaking people there."

The bridge is created, of course, by the Atlantic satellite which TVE use extensively. In fact they carry out more satellite relays than any other television organization in the world. Quite apart from relaying such European events as the Eurovision Song Contest and football matches to South America, they employ the satellite three times every day to transmit their own news programs live to their regional station in the Canary Islands. Since early 1971 they have become even more involved with satellite exchanges as the command post for the news exchange every weekday between Europe and South America. Every afternoon after lunch, TVE hooks into a sound circuit with television stations in Brazil, Colombia, Peru, and Venezuela for a story conference on news stories available on both sides of the Atlantic that day. TVE offers a roundup of the Eurovision news exchange to the South Americans, who respond with details of the film they have available. Promptly at 6:35 every weekday evening the pictures requested at the conference from South America come beaming in via the satellite to TVE in Madrid, which then injects them into the entire Eurovision network. Then, just after 7:00, Madrid relays back to South America an edited roundup of the day's Eurovision stories. Argentina, Mexico, and Chile also participate occasionally in this exchange, if they have important stories to contribute. The evening a new president of Argentina was sworn in in Buenos Aires at 6:30, TVE had full coverage through Madrid and relayed to all Europe by 7:00.

The Spanish are eager to make the most of this legacy of the *conquistadores*. Since 1967 a series of annual conventions has been held by leading Spanish and South American television executives to discuss program exchange and the common use of satellites. This cooperation was extended in 1971 by the creation of an Ibero-American Television Organization (IATO), with Spain and Mexico as two of the leading participants, to promote program exchange in the Spanish-speaking world. Now that South America is shrugging off United States domination of its television (see Chapter 4), Spain is one natural alternative source of material.

There is plenty to choose from. Spanish television's two black and white channels are on the air for longer each day than any other service in Europe. The first channel begins at lunchtime and continues until midnight (even later at weekends), while the second channel operates from 8:30 in the evening until well after midnight. The Spanish custom of rising and retiring late means that prime time begins at 10:00 and continues until 11:30. One audience survey conducted by TVE revealed that only half the children under fourteen are in bed and asleep by 11:00 and the remainder are still potential television viewers at that hour. The main features on both channels, therefore, start at 10:00. The first channel is aimed primarily at a mass audience, and the second at minority interests. "Our first channel," Luis Ezcurra Carrillo explained, "is not quite so heavy or boring as some of those in Central Europe. We try to have a dynamic, escapist channel. The second channel, however, is not under the same obligation to please the public."

The commercial pressures for the second channel to seek a large audience are reduced by the simple means of not charging a separate price for its advertising. The advertiser buys fifteen-, thirty-, or sixty-second spots which are automatically shown on both channels for an overall price; he does not have the option of buying one channel or the other. TVE's hand is strengthened in dealing with advertisers because of its monopoly. In 1969, for instance, they cut back advertising time by one third, from an average of nine minutes to six minutes per hour because of complaints from viewers about the frequency of commercials. They avoided any reduction in revenue, however, by simultaneously increasing the price of advertising by a third. The spots (there is no sponsorship) are now among the most expensive anywhere outside the United States; in prime time a fifteen-second commercial costs $2,620. The major advertisers, for once, are not the soap-flakes and food manufacturers. The top four advertisers on Spanish television during 1970 were all selling drinks—Coca-Cola was first and Cola-Cao second, followed by Veterano and Fundador brandies; Omega watches were the fifth largest spenders. The commercials are normally shown only on the hour or on the half hour, so that in a half-hour program there is no advertising break.

Although the main channel is aimed at a mass audience, it is not nonstop trivia. The Ministry of Information directs quite clearly that television must provide a public service, so two thirds of the programs are billed as information or documentaries. Imported American programs, once very popular in Spain, are now rare. During 1971 only *Ironside,* dubbed in

Castilian Spanish, was on in the peak evening period on the first channel, with *High Chaparral* on the second. Otherwise most of the entertainment is unmistakably Spanish; even the interlude music is guitar. And when I tuned in to the most popular late night talk show, *Estudio Abierto (Open Discussion)*, the chat was naturally mostly about bullfights. But there is usually a marked preference for re-creating past history, rather than looking too closely at the scene today. My own impression after looking at Spanish television is that its most prestigious shows are historical costume dramas. I did watch one installment of a long-running documentary series of forty-seven installments on Spain in the twentieth century, but the episode I saw was about great bullfighters before 1920.

The taste for the past is best reflected in the *novelas,* dramatizations of classical novels which go out every weekday evening at 8:00. When I first saw *"novelas"* on the program schedule I suspected this was the local version of the popular *tele-novelas* I had encountered in South America. But this dream of the South American mass audience is not reflected on Spanish television. Almost all their dramatizations are of nineteenth-century novels, by great writers such as Tolstoy, Balzac, Dickens, Jane Austen, Henry James, Oscar Wilde, and Mark Twain. These productions are usually in five installments run on consecutive evenings from Monday to Friday. A few have been dramatized at much greater length: Dickens' *David Copperfield* went to twenty-five installments, and his *Little Dorrit* to twenty; Dumas's *The Three Musketeers* also ran to twenty episodes and Jane Austen's *Northanger Abbey* to ten. The novels are often quite lavishly produced: *The Three Musketeers* called for fifty-six actors and four hundred extras.

This preoccupation with the past has continued in thirteen ninety-minute productions resurrecting nineteenth-century Spanish musical comedies known as *zarzuelas.* Each *zarzuela* cost $200,000 to mount (almost American-scale budgeting) and was filmed in color, although Spanish television is still all black and white. But TVE recouped much of the cost by selling the program all over Europe and South America. Their sales of such spectaculars are now earning them nearly $1 million a year. They are also offsetting costs by joining in European coproduction, particularly with ORTF in France and RAI in Italy.

Such epics, often costing more than a quarter of a million dollars, have included a two-and-a-half-hour color film of Lope de Vega's *Fuenteovejuna,* filmed on location all over Spain, with enormous battle scenes staged in ancient castles. A TVE executive confessed, "We are going through our Cecil B. de Mille-*Ben Hur* period at the moment." Not surprisingly, they too are coming up with their own versions of history. When they tackled a dramatization of the life of Christopher Columbus in cooperation with RAI in Italy, they skirted gently around the delicate topic of whether Columbus was Italian or Spanish by birth. "We didn't mention it at all," admitted one of the producers. "Columbus just turned up at the court of Spain without any explanation." When I was in Madrid they were working on a coproduction with the BBC from London on the Peninsular Wars. Both sides have a rather different outlook on that era too, but no one seemed to know whose interpretation was going to prevail. However, no doubt the battle scenes will be dramatic television.

So is bullfighting. Live coverage of a *corrida* provides TVE with one of its most exportable items. During 1971 they set up one spectacular which was beamed by satellite to bullfighting enthusiasts all over South America, the United States (on closed circuit TV, not network), and even to Japan and Australia.

The fighting that Spanish television carefully skirts, of course, is any trouble in the streets at home. While the news programs regularly show demonstrations or riots everywhere else in Europe and America, they bypass such events in Spain itself. Nor is any coverage offered on the Eurovision news exchange. Foreign cameramen who arrive to report embarrassing events either do not get the permit required to film in Spain or find themselves leaving the scene rapidly in a police car on the way to a short stay in jail until the trouble dies down. The obsession with keeping awkward scenes off the screen has even gone to such lengths as inserting fake crowd noises at a football match, where it was feared that Basque separatist slogans might be chanted. They just had a "rhubarb rhubarb" tape running all the time and turned up the volume when it looked likely that a goal would be scored.

Hand in hand with the government the Catholic Church also insures that TVE does not reflect the permissive society too closely. When I was in Madrid the program planners had been watching some screenings of ballet from Denmark. They thought the ballet very fine, but had to reject it because several of the dancers were naked. Even a very popular wildlife program, *Blue Planet,* caused considerable unease among the Catholic Church because its host, Dr. Felix Rodriguez de la Fuente, ventured to discuss Darwinism and selective evolution. Such a topic is rarely broached in Spain and, just to reassure everyone, the program also included an interview with an eminent priest who maintained that evolution in no way denied the existence of God.

Given such restrictions it is understandable that the energies and abilities of many people in Spanish television have to be directed to the rather safer ground of producing historical spectaculars set firmly in pre-Franco days. What they all privately hope for is some firm separation in the future from the mantle of the Ministry of Information. As one executive said, "Political control would still be there, but it would be good to gain our own separate personality."

11

Scandinavia:

Resisting the Commercials

I arrived in Helsinki on a dismal, foggy day in late winter; during my stay it never brightened to much more than permanent twilight. So old television standbys like *Peyton Place* and *High Chaparral* in color on the commercial programs of Finnish television were enormously cheering amid all that Scandinavian gloom. A few days later in Stockholm, Johan von Utfall, the director of engineering for Swedish television, agreed with this observation. "Color television has an extra importance in Scandinavia: our life is so gray most of the year that color TV is a revelation. It makes life seem gay."

Yet if television relieves the dreariness of winter, it is almost forgotten the moment the short summer arrives; audiences melt with the snow. Advertising rates on Finnish television—the only network in Scandinavia that allows commercials—are halved during the summer season from mid-June through August. The second channel stops broadcasting completely during those months. Swedish television, which operates the largest and perhaps most thoughtful audience-research department in Europe, actually stops its audience surveys during the summer. In Norway, all the television staff, except those actually putting out the programs, knock off at 3 P.M. in the afternoon in summer to make the most of the sunshine.

If climate is one formative influence on Scandinavian television, geography is another. The widely scattered populations of Finland, Norway, and Sweden, some of them living well inside the Arctic Circle, make the provision of complete coverage—which is demanded by the public service concept of all the broadcasting organizations—inordinately expensive. Only the flat farmland of Denmark is easily served by a mere four transmitters. In Norway, which has less than 4 million inhabitants, no fewer than forty main transmitters and 1,500 low-power repeater stations are required to take television striding a thousand miles north over mountains and fjords from Oslo to Kirkenes on the Barents Sea (where viewers can also pick up Russian television). "Many of our transmitters are 5,000 feet up in the mountains," Jan Freydenlund of Norwegian television pointed out. "In winter they are shrouded in ice six feet thick, which makes maintenance a hideous job. Our high technical costs unfortunately mean we have less money for programs."

Happily, these adversities, coupled with the inevitably tiny budgets in four nations with only 22 million people among them, have been a spur to some of the most original thinking in television anywhere in the world. One great advantage for these small Scandinavian broadcasting organizations is that if someone does have a bright idea, it stands a good chance of being implemented; it will not be lost amid clouds of corporate thinking.

Apart from Finland, where advertising revenue accounts for 40 percent of television's income, the Swedish, Norwegian, and Danish broadcasting organizations are dependent on license fees, which are among the highest in Europe. Sweden, with nearly 2.5 million TV sets, has enough revenue from a license charge of $34.75 a year to sustain two channels, which will be putting on a total of 100 hours of programs a week by the mid-1970s. The Norwegians and Danes, however, with only 800,000 and 1.2 million sets respectively, are hard pressed. They operate only one channel each for less than forty hours a week. The Danes are proposing a second channel, but this will mean pushing up their license from $30.40 a year to over $50, the highest in the world. The Norwegians, who charge a license fee of $29.40, supplement their revenue by a 10 percent tax on the sale of TV sets; even so their annual income is less than $25 million (compared with BBC television's $200 million).

During the 1960s the sharp rise in the sales of television sets at least insured each organization an increased budget every year. Now that almost every home has a set (the Swedes, for example, have thirty sets per hundred of their population, the highest proportion in Europe and exceeded only in the United States), the only way of increasing income is to raise the license fee—or permit advertising. The Swedes, Danes, and Norwegians are all resisting advertising stoutly—the final anticommercial stronghold in Europe. "We can give people three radio programs and two television channels for the same price as one daily newspaper costs them per year," argued Laurits Bindslov, director of Danish television. "We don't need commercials."

There is an understanding that any one of the three countries will consult the others before introducing advertising; for, once one gives way, the others must follow because of overlaps in viewing areas. Sweden is the pace setter since her programs can be seen in nearly half of all Norwegian and Danish homes. Indeed, the Norwegians and Danes study the Swedes' advance program schedules and tailor their own output accordingly. If Sweden accepted advertising, Norwegian and Danish firms could dodge the ban in their own countries by booking spots in Sweden.

Even with limited advertising, however, the television organizations would still rely on buying many of their programs cheaply overseas. The Norwegians are charged as little as $150 for a half-hour American program; even the richer Swedes pay only $400. All the Scandinavians depend on importing up to 50 percent of their programs, although they have largely avoided simply snapping up the cheap American screen fodder. The exception is Mainos-TV, the commercial company owned by Finnish industry, banks, advertising agencies and insurance companies, which provides the programs for part of each evening on both the Finnish Broadcasting Company's channels. Mainos-TV originates 49 percent of its own programs but otherwise buys American serials almost exclusively; in 1969 94 percent of their serial time was filled with American programs—the remaining 6 percent were French. The Finnish Broadcasting Company itself purchases about half its foreign programs from the United States and one third from Britain.

The other Scandinavian countries rely heavily on British material. The Swedes buy 60 percent of all their foreign programs from the BBC and Independent Television, and for the rest have an open-minded policy in ferreting out interesting programs from many countries.

"There is a reaction here against American series," Olof Rydbeck, director general of the Swedish Broadcasting Corporation until the end of 1970, told me. "We've made it our policy to go out and seek truly international fare." Consequently, Swedish television offers a broad mosaic of world television programs. They have ballet from Russia, a thirteen-part crime series, *The Sinful People of Prague,* from Czechoslovakia (this before the Russian invasion in 1968), children's films and documentaries from Japan, and a Polish series, *Captain Kloss,* about a World War II resistance fighter, which gained 35 percent of the viewing audience in the late evening on Channel 1.

The international outlook is substantiated in news coverage. Swedish television maintains twelve full-time correspondents overseas. "Sweden's welfare depends on trade and foreign contacts," Rydbeck said. "I have made it a deliberate policy for us to break away from the habit of considering any story here more important than events overseas. Parochialism is lingering on in television in many countries—but not, I hope, in Sweden.

One of our most important tasks is to increase our contact with, and knowledge of, the world around us."

This Swedish open-mindedness has led also to an attempt to create within the Swedish Broadcasting Company two competing television channels, each with a clear identity of its own. The concept of competition began with the start of the second channel, TV2, at the end of 1969 Although both TV1 and TV2 share the same technical facilities and a joint news department, they are otherwise given far-reaching independence. Each channel is presided over by its own director, who can make his own decisions on how to spend his annual budget, and shape his programs according to his own design. "We believe this will give greater stimulus to program producers and a wider freedom of choice to the public," Rydbeck said. "Writers and artists will not be dependent on the judgment of one monolithic organization; if the director of TV1 does not like their ideas, perhaps the director of TV2 will."

Two men of very different background were selected as the first directors of TV1 and TV2 to encourage diversity. "For TV1, which was the existing channel, we chose Hakan Unsgaard, from within our own organization," Olof Rydbeck explained, "but for TV2 we wanted someone from outside who would not be stamped with our traditions. We selected Orjan Wallquist, the editor of a socialist weekly magazine." Producers and other staff were also divided between the two channels; TV1 tended to get the older, more conservative ones; TV2 gained the young, radical producers.

Not surprisingly, TV2 quickly established itself as a channel concerned with serious social problems, which pleased some Swedish socialists, but not the Swedish viewing audience at large. Many criticized it for being too radical and diverting from the balanced presentation of ideas, which is one cornerstone of public service broadcasting in Europe. In the first few months the new channel barely won 10 percent of the audience, although three British programs bought from the BBC—*The Six Wives of Henry VIII, Softly, Softly,* and *Lulu and the Young Generation*—gained much higher ratings.

As a further stimulant to competition, the rigid format of departments for education, current affairs, drama and light entertainment within each channel has also been cast aside. Hakan Unsgaard, director of TV1, explained, "I felt my producers would prefer flexibility to work on many types of program. So, instead of departments with their own fixed budget, we have established project groups, each with producer, director and script writer. We've broken the year down into five periods of ten weeks each;

in each period a project group may work on a different subject. So a producer who has specialized in current affairs in the past may now find himself a project leader in children's television for ten weeks, before spending another period making a documentary on wildlife."

The current affairs group does not have quite such frequent fluctuations of staff because there must be more continuity in building up contacts with politicians at home and abroad, but Unsgaard reckons to change even his current affairs chief every six months.

Once a project group has been assigned a program and the budget agreed, it is then quite autonomous to proceed as the project leader chooses. A senior executive may have a special showing of the finished program if it is on a particularly controversial topic, but the basic concept is to leave producers the maximum freedom in making programs as they see them. "We've got to go to the frontiers of taste and opinion," said Hakan Unsgaard, "and every year we push that frontier a little further forward—we never go back. The real differences we have with our producers are on the length we push the frontier at a given moment."

The hazards of pushing the frontiers too far too fast have been demonstrated all too clearly in Finland. Until 1965, Finnish television developed slowly and cautiously. "Television here was passive—all memories of the past," Dr. Kaarle Nordenstreng, the Finnish Broadcasting Company's young director of research, explained. "There were codes of what not to do—don't report strikes, no slang, nothing on sex, no experimental programs." All this was changed by the appointment in 1965 of a new director general, Eino S. Repo. "Repo," said Nordenstreng, "was the liberator. He gave everyone his head. It was like working on another planet."

Many Finns obviously felt they had indeed tuned in to television from another planet. Programs on sex education were shown, while documentaries began to challenge many traditional aspects of Finnish society; the insurance companies were attacked in one devastating report; pollution by the state chemical industry was criticized in another. Television drama dropped cozy comedies in favor of dramatized documentaries attacking private ownership and the uneven distribution of property in Finland.

Many young producers felt that they had moved into the "Golden Age of Television." The average viewer, politician, and newspaper editor did not share this enthusiasm. They considered their television service had become a platform for radical left-wing ideas. The press was almost completely united in its condemnation of Repo's "liberating" policy, and the future of broadcasting became a major election issue by 1969. When the conservatives gained strength at the election, the reaction came quickly.

Repo was replaced as director general by Erkki Raatikainen, the secretary of the Social Democratic Party. Another politician, Pekka Silvola, secretary of the Agrarian Party, was made program director for television. Repo himself was shuffled to the sidelines as director of radio. "We have been politicized," complained one bitter supporter of the Repo regime.

The status of the Finnish Broadcasting Company made it an easy maneuver. The state owns 92 percent of the stock in the company and normally only gives it a broadcasting license for one or two years at a stretch. Parliament appoints all the members of the Board of Governors, and invariably nominates politicians.

Erkki Raatikainen, the new director general, was quite frank about his role in bringing a new—or, as some would say, old—look to Finnish television. "I'm the Husak," he told me—comparing Finnish television's about-face with Premier Husak replacing Alexander Dubcek in Czechoslovakia. "I have to normalize television. We've been too international, some of our programs have been too advanced. The ordinary viewer has been puzzled. Now we are going to do more down-to-earth programs on home affairs."

The young radicals in Finnish television responded dispiritedly, "The ice age has descended."

In fact, the Finnish experience is a clear warning of the reaction that can be caused if a television service changes too quickly, particularly if in doing so it appears to drop any pretense at a balanced presentation of the views of the nation.

"Repo thought you can, must, and should *use* your media," remarked Laurits Bindslov, director of Danish television, "but TV is not your own personal medium, it is not your personal machine gun."

Danish television has also been under some pressure, particularly among the producers of its cultural and youth programs, to push left-wing ideas, but has so far succeeded in holding to a more moderate balance— although one producer who repeatedly refused to stop promoting left-wing ideas was fired. "We can ask questions about the framework of society," said Laurits Bindslov, "but we must give the broad spectrum of people's feelings."

Actually, Danish television still conducts, on its one channel, the limited television service that vanished in many countries in the 1950s. On weekdays the programs are from 7:30 in the evening until 10:30; Saturdays and Sundays there are also afternoon programs. But the total is only thirty-eight hours a week, including three hours of repeats on weekday afternoons for those who may have missed programs the previous evening through working on a late shift (a very considerate policy adopted in several Scandinavian countries). The Danish approach to television is that it is something to be viewed after dinner in the evening, just as one might go to a theater or concert; it is not conceived as visual Muzak. "My family and I would never watch television while we eat," a Danish television producer told me. "Danish families like to have their evening meal in peace and then, perhaps, see what is on."

Norwegians receive even shorter television rations—just thirty-three hours a week, of which three and a half hours are repeats. Cultural and information programs far outweigh entertainment; which rates as little as 25 percent of transmission time. "We do tend to be heavy on the information side," said Jan Fraydenlund, deputy director of television programs, "and many of our programs are like visual radio shows."

Despite this conservative image, the Norwegians have come up with one of the most original television shows anywhere—*Idebanken (The Bank of Ideas)*. Idebanken was conceived by a strapping Norwegian journalist and television commentator, Erik Bye. "I got so tired of using television as a means of killing people's time," Bye told me. "I wanted to put it to a practical use. Some countries have found television very effective as a way of collecting money for charity; so I decided we wouldn't ask people for money—we'd ask people for brain power, we'd set up a Bank of Ideas. We are a small country, we can reach all our people through television, so why not pick their brains to solve our problems?"

The first problem *Idebanken* tackled, when it began in 1967, was how to improve the conditions for the fishermen working on Norway's fleet of 36,000 fishing boats; no two boats were alike, most lacked any proper toilet facilities or comfortable quarters for the crew. Bye discussed the topic with a panel of fishing experts, then asked viewers for ideas on how to mass-produce, cheaply, a more comfortable fishing boat. One Norwegian shipbuilder responded with plans for a modern boat; other ideas from viewers were incorporated. The new boats, whose progress was carefully filmed for the program, cost 25 percent less to build than custom-built boats, and combined excellent galleys, sleeping quarters, and toilets for the crews. Six of the new boats were in service by 1970. "They are the most advanced and thoroughly tested in Norway," Bye reported proudly.

From this encouraging start with fishing boats, *Idebanken* went on to tackle everything from helping rural craftsmen to sell their products in the cities to advising on how to keep schools going in the depopulated areas of Norway. "Many farmers make excellent wood carvings," said Bye, "but they have no idea how to market them. We helped them meet the right marketing people. One old chap who was making marvelous grandfather clocks got in touch with a professional buyer through our program, and he's now selling them all over the world."

Idebanken's very success, however, became a problem. The resources and staff to back up the ideas it unleashed simply were not available. When Bye did a program on how to make simple eel traps, they were swamped with 8,000 requests for more details. *Idebanken*'s suggestion on how to keep schools going in remote areas also drew the charge that the program was trying to undermine the government's policies on education for rural areas. The government had decided schools there could not be kept open. *Idebanken* demonstrated that they could. Reluctantly, therefore, the program was called off after two years. "We came under very heavy fire," Bye admitted, "although we were not trying to play politics. I'm now trying to revive the program with a separate organization to follow up the ideas that we stimulate. We must still make every possible use of television as a proper tool to get things done."

The difficulties of achieving technical excellence and sustained high-quality programs in the small Scandinavian countries may well lead to the creation, within a decade, of the world's first supranational television network. Norway, Sweden, Finland, and Denmark, together with Iceland, already work closely together in a joint organization called Nordvision, through which they exchange programs free of charge. The main exchange is in news and sports programs, but the nucleus of cooperation is there for an eventual Nordvision channel serving 22 million people (just as Denmark, Norway, and Sweden share an airline: SAS). Laurits Bindslov, director of television in Denmark, believes that such a third channel, probably using a satellite to beam its programs easily throughout Scandinavia and to Iceland, could play an important role in breaking down parochialism. "I believe a third channel could lead the debate on the future of Europe into Scandinavia," he said. "We should invite a great European personality to be its director, so that it is not just a third local channel, but gives us truly European television."

12

The Netherlands:
Fair Shares for All

No one can compete with the Dutch when it comes to giving all comers a chance to have their say on television. Where else do the League of Humanists, the Ancient Order of Free Masons, Moral Rearmament, and the Society for Sexual Reform have program time set aside for them to propound their views? The Dutch Society for Sexual Reform, for instance, is entitled to twenty minutes of television time every eight weeks. "We believe," a spokesman for the society told me, "that we should employ our program time to spread information regarding sex and human relations." Accordingly, their programs discuss everything from homosexuality, abortion, and pornography to contraception, sex education, and marriage today. Dutch broadcasting is theoretically open to every pressure group, whether social, political, or religious, within the country. They proudly point out to visitors that their television system is the most democratic anywhere.

You begin to suspect something unusual the moment you arrive in the little town of Hilversum, twenty miles east of Amsterdam, where Dutch television makes its home. Instead of operating out of some impersonal steel and concrete monolith with endless miles of corridors, the Dutch broadcasters work from a score of elegant white-painted villas scattered among the elm-lined avenues of Hilversum. Well-trimmed lawns and carefully tended flower beds surround each villa, creating an agreeable environment quite different from the frenetic atmosphere of other headquarters. So you stroll around Hilversum to call on the Catholic broadcasters, or the socialist broadcasters, each in their respective villa.

The crux of all broadcasting in the Netherlands is that any organization which has more than 15,000 members (who must all have purchased a television license) is entitled to apply to the Minister of Culture, Recreation, and Social Work for time on the country's three radio and two tele-vision networks. Initially, a budding organization will be allowed one hour of program time a week for a two-year trial period. During this probation, the organization, through its programs and other activities, seeks to raise membership to 100,000. If successful, it then qualifies as a fully fledged C-category program, making the company entitled to two and a half hours on TV each week (plus a radio allocation); but if it fails to win the magic 100,000 followers, its right to make programs lapses. Later on, if member-ship keeps rising, the C company graduates to B status, with five hours on TV a week at 250,000 members, and finally to A category, rating eight hours a week, at 400,000 members.

During 1971 four associations were rated A. The largest was AVRO (General Society for Radio Broadcasting), which is actually the least politically or religiously oriented of all the groups. "AVRO," a Dutch broadcaster explained, "is the silent majority's program company. It is conservative, pro-Establishment, for the status quo." Much more com-mitted, however, are NCRV (Netherlands Christian Radio Society) repre-senting the Reformed Protestants, KRO (Catholic Radio Society) as a platform for the Roman Catholics and the socialists' VARA (Workers' Radio Amateur Society). There were no "B" companies, but two of "C" class—the Liberal Protestants' VPRO and a newcomer, TROS. TROS began life as a pirate television station operating from an old wartime fort off the Dutch coast in 1964, but two years later achieved landbased re-spectability, with the required number of members. It is conservative, but has no special political affiliation and is generally regarded as a second platform for the silent majority. Another newcomer, the Evangelical Broad-casting System (EO), notched up 15,000 members in 1970 and is strug-gling to achieve its 100,000 members by 1972. EO is a society of orthodox Protestants concerned to raise the moral tone of programs in this permis-sive age.

Besides these seven associations, a host of twenty-seven other political, religious, and social minority interests, which claim their views are not adequately represented, are allowed occasional programs of their own. The Society for Sexual Reform, the Humanists, and Moral Rearmament (a meager half an hour a year on TV) all qualify. The twelve political parties represented in the Dutch Parliament are entitled to ten minutes each four times a year.

Every group granted TV time receives a proportional slice of the income from the television license fee of 75 guilders ($21) a year and from advertising, which is permitted in four short blocks immediately before and after television news broadcasts at 7:00 and 8:00 each evening. The spirit of fair shares for all communicators is carried even further by diverting 40 percent of the revenue from TV commercials to newspapers and magazines, who share it among themselves according to circulation. This extraordinary generosity was decided upon when television commercials first began in 1967. The press complained loudly that they would suffer from the loss of revenue and that some publications might go broke. The government mediated by awarding them a slice of TV ad revenue to soften the blow.

The assortment of program makers all cooperate with the Netherlands Broadcasting Foundation (NOS), which provides studios and joint technical facilities and coordinates the program schedules. NOS also takes care of news and sports coverage, together with special events like Apollo moonshots. Although NOS cannot dictate policy to any of the varied program associations, it is authorized to show children's and education programs if it feels these subjects are not adequately covered. For instance, they showed the BBC's *Civilisation* series under the guise of an educational program. Overall NOS produces a third of the seventy hours a week on the two color channels; the seven program associations and the potpourri of minorities fill two thirds.

"I know it all sounds most complicated," admitted Gerhardus van Beek of NOS, "but you must realize that in the Netherlands we have always had a pillarized view of society—the whole held up by an assortment of pillars. Everyone belongs to some political party or church which represents one of those pillars. So people find it natural to follow this through in broadcasting; 2 million of the 3 million people who have television licenses in the Netherlands belong to one of the seven program societies. It's all very democratic. And if your views aren't represented, you just start your own society. As for NOS—think of us as a printing plant which prints a variety of newspapers and magazines each week reflecting many shades of opinion."

Despite their special affiliations the program companies tread delicately in propounding their own creed. And all have to rely on buying many overseas programs, for the total television kitty of only $33 million a year provides slim program-making budgets.

Bonanza, The Andy Williams Show, and *The Debbie Reynolds Show* all appear on KRO's broadly based schedule. NCRV prefers a diet of brisk British thrillers such as *The Scarlet Pimpernel* and *Softly, Softly.* Both broadcast church services and religious discussions on Sundays, but they are cautious not to appear overburdened with religious programs. Indeed, they are much less privileged platforms for their faith than they were in the days of radio before World War II. Then KRO was strongly pro-Catholic, NCRV fiercely Protestant; nowadays on TV a Protestant priest will even be invited to join a discussion on KRO, although the moderator will always be a Catholic.

Beliefs are more strongly displayed in the programs of the two main political groups, the socialists' VARA and the Liberal Protestants' VPRO. During its eight hours of program time each week VARA is constantly concerned with social and political issues. They have established a reputation for hard-hitting documentaries on problem groups like unmarried mothers, divorced women, and homosexuals. "We always make programs on downbeat topics, while AVRO or TROS will do upbeat," one of their producers explained. "We'll do unemployment, while they make a program on the biggest and best new factory in Holland."

Not surprisingly, VARA has close relations with Granada in Britain. Lord Bernstein's philosophy dovetails neatly with VARA's. "Many Granada programs are naturals for us," VARA's overseas program buyer told me. "We've been running *Coronation Street* for years. Now we are taking their *Family at War,* about the Liverpool family during World War II."

VARA's program schedule occasionally seems like a British one translated into Dutch. They have run the *Forsyte Saga, Cathy Come Home,* and early *Z Cars,* together with their own productions of Harold Pinter and Alun Owen plays. Whether it is despite or because of its socialist conscience, VARA is remarkably successful at notching up good ratings. Normally only AVRO, with a diet including *Peyton Place* and *Tom Jones,* gets more programs in the Dutch top ten.

The Liberal Protestants' VPRO, which has two and a half hours of TV each week, concentrates more on message than audience. "VPRO is the least concerned of all the companies with audience ratings," a Dutch TV critic explained. "In fact, any VPRO producer whose show gets high audience ratings is likely to be fired." Nevertheless, they display some cunning in getting the word across. I watched their programs one evening. To begin with, the announcer mentioned that during the evening one of the leading local comediennes would be on, but he neglected to mention the precise time. So, instead of switching to the other channel for a while till she came on, you had to watch all VPRO offerings to be sure to catch her. They began with an earnest discussion about the problems of unemployment, prompted by the announcement that day of the closing of a large Dutch factory. Eventually, those who stayed with it were rewarded with a highly professional half-hour color show with the comedienne, before the evening closed with a program on old age. VPRO constantly teeters on the brink of losing its qualification to broadcast, for it barely has the 100,000 members required to maintain its C category. Indeed, in 1970, it was found to have only 93,000 but was generously given a year's grace to win back the extra 7,000. Apparently, its future is secure. All kinds of people rally round and join if they think VPRO might really disappear.

The scheduling of this scramble of program associations is handled by NOS. Some evenings they divide the time among two or three groups, but Monday, Tuesday, and Thursday evenings are fixed; Monday night teams the political VARA on one network with the religious NCRV on the other; Tuesdays are set aside for KRO and AVRO—again basically a religious and political balance (if one regards AVRO as being conservative); Thursdays are shared by TROS and VPRO. This Thursday combination often works in TROS's favor, because VPRO, as we have remarked, are not preoccupied with ratings. With a minority watching VPRO on one channel, TROS piles up viewers on the other. This enables TROS to achieve the highest ratings of all the main program groups— 37 percent of viewers tune to its Thursday night shows; VPRO gains a mere 9 percent. AVRO is the second most popular association, averaging a 34 percent audience; VARA chases hard with 32 percent.

Audience research has revealed special viewer loyalty to VPRO and NCRV, but the majority of viewers are not preoccupied with which association happens to be screening programs that evening. They just enjoy watching *Ironside* or *David Frost* or *Hawaii Five-O*, without realizing who is actually presenting it. And these days many of the highest-rated shows are not presented by the program companies at all, but by NOS, because they handle all the great international sports events. NOS had 33 of the top 100 programs in 1969, almost all of them sports.

Half the secret of a successful program company seems to be in producing a colorful TV guide. By law, only the seven recognized broadcasting groups can publish full details of the TV and radio schedules, so to find out what's on you must subscribe to one of the seven program guides published weekly. Most Dutch families qualify as members of an association simply by purchasing its guide. The association with the gayest magazine clearly has the advantage, because it will attract anyone who does not feel desperately committed. The most lavish weekly is AVRO's *Televizier,* which is crammed with color pictures of TV stars. It sells over 800,000 copies, giving AVRO almost twice as many members as any other program association. This lesson has not been lost on the newcomer, and former pirate TV group, TROS. TROS puts out a handy *Reader's Digest-* style guide called *Kompas.* Frankly, if I lived in the Netherlands, I would probably buy *Kompas* because of its convenient size and professional flair and thus, without particular commitment, swell TROS membership.

Each association claims that in good democratic fashion it respects the wishes of its members and puts out the programs they want; theoretically the ideal relationship between broadcaster and his audience. How well it all works in practice is debatable. Members certainly gush with ideas, but the professionals often politely dismiss them as impractical, too costly or not good television. AVRO holds an annual conference which all its 800,000 members can apply to attend. "There's lots to eat and drink and the chairman and program executives make nice speeches," said a rather cynical rival executive. "All the members clap, say 'We are the best association,' and go back home."

VARA invites its members to Hilversum twice a year and listens with a sympathetic ear. They started a consumer program discussing "best buys," following suggestions at one meeting. On another occasion their members overruled VARA's plans to drop an attractive lady announcer. No society can afford to be too cavalier with its members; after all they have the ultimate weapon. Vanishing membership spells vanishing program time.

The only weakness in all this display of democracy is that television in the Netherlands often seems slightly incoherent, because no one group of planners is sitting down to work out a comprehensive evening or week's viewing. Since each association is left to its own devices and is at liberty to screen what it chooses (guided only by a generalization in the broadcasting act that its programs must "inform, educate, and entertain"), certain topics may be ignored. Children's programs, for instance, have been sadly neglected—the children, as yet, have no pressure group of their own. Because of this lapse, NOS is now stepping in to provide better children's coverage.

Indeed, the role of NOS, not only as a central coordinating and technical organization, is likely to increase. As television costs rise each year and coproductions with other countries become more common, NOS is the natural organization to expand. And their success in gaining so many places in the Dutch top ten, with moonwalks and sports coverage, is putting them in a privileged position. But it would be a pity if NOS became all powerful, for the Dutch broadcasting system at the moment stands out as a refreshing oasis of originality. Luckily, NOS are quite aware of this. "I am sure we must take on a more definite role," a member of their board of directors said, "but we cherish our democratic television here and we don't mean to give it up."

THE

COMMUNIST

WORLD

13

The Soviet Union:
The Blue Screen

The first clue to the nature of Soviet television is the cover of the weekly TV and radio guide. No sign there of the blondes or western heroes who so frequently smile from the covers of television weeklies elsewhere. Instead, there is usually some somber portrait of a scientist, engineer or academician whose achievements will be profiled on what the Russians have christened "the blue screen." When that much-traveled serial *The Forsyte Saga* opened on Moscow television in 1971, it was discussed only in a discreet article inside. The cover and top billing that week went to "one of the best workers in the famous plant of plants, Ural Mash, who will appear in the first three broadcasts on our country's leading heavy machinery building enterprises." The cover just prior to that featured the director of the Metallurgical Institute of the U.S.S.R. Academy of Sciences, who was appearing in a series, *The Lenin University of Millions,* about the history of the Communist Party in the Soviet Union.

While American television is primarily in the business of selling goods, Russian television's concern is promoting socialist achievement. Its priority is educating people in the ways of Marxism-Leninism and stimulating their pride in the new state they have created. Films, music, plays, and sports abound on television, but the theme of Soviet achievement comes through all the time. Even the sports commentators are highly nationalistic. No one was ever more partisan in commentating on football or ice hockey international competitions—the Soviet players are all doing a grand job, their opponents are clearly having a bad day. The integrity of the referee, if he is not from the Soviet Union, may frequently be questioned. Sentiments are entirely in keeping with the basic program policy, which is shaped in the best Leninist tradition "to maintain a basic patriotic spirit . . . so that every inhabitant feels himself to be a citizen of the great Soviet Union. . . . If an individual feels himself to be a citizen of the country, he feels solidarity with the country's politics."

Lenin himself was always enthusiastic about the possibilities of mass communication as a tool of the Revolution. Indeed, the Soviet Union regards the first radio broadcast ever made there as having been Lenin's announcement from the cruiser *Aurora* in October 1917 that the communists had won the Revolution. Although Lenin never lived to know television, no doubt he would have embraced it as the perfect propaganda machine. For the Soviet Union, after all, is an immense country of many peoples, speaking some sixty different languages. Television would have given him the chance, as it does the Soviet leaders now, to be seen by all from Leningrad to Vladivostok and beyond all in the same moment—assuming, that is, that some of them stayed up fairly late at night. One of the biggest problems of organizing television in the Soviet Union is its ten time zones; early evening in Moscow is early morning in Vladivostok.

But the size of their country has not daunted the Russians from attempting to bring the blue screen into the homes of all their 240 million people. Today there are over thirty million television sets in the Soviet Union—more than in any other single nation except the United States. Well over three quarters of all the homes can watch at least one channel, while in nearly fifty cities there is both a national channel from Moscow and a regional channel. Leningrad has three channels, Moscow itself boasts four. The Russians are not content to rest at that. The main national program from Moscow will blanket the entire Soviet Union early in the 1970s, including the remotest and most sparsely populated regions. In addition, regional television centers with five channels are being built at Tashkent and Frunze in the south and at Vilnius near the Polish border. The ultimate aim is to have five channels available to every Soviet citizen.

Already their television dwarfs the development in most other countries. Thirty-five thousand people are employed in broadcasting, while the new television center completed in the Moscow suburb of Ostankino in 1970 is as abundantly equipped as any in Europe, the United States or Japan. Each of the twenty-one studios has between six and eight color cameras (the norm in the West is three or four), plus two videotape recorders. There is an additional videotape center with no less than sixty-four recorders; compare this with NHK in Tokyo, whose facilities are universally admired, which has only thirty-six. One Western technical expert, who has studied television centers throughout the world, told me he found the Moscow establishment the most elaborate of them all. And dominating the Ostankino skyline is a lanky 1,700-foot-high television tower.

The tower, which has a restaurant appropriately named the Seventh Heaven near the summit, is reputed to be the tallest building in the world. From a distance it looks like an outsize multistage rocket all set for launching.

Regular color television began in 1967, the same year that most countries of Western Europe launched their color programs. For the Russians to be able to see the Red flag in "living color" was, of course, a suitable way to mark the fiftieth anniversary of the October Revolution. Their color system is the French SECAM, which de Gaulle successfully persuaded both the Soviet Union and the communist countries of Eastern Europe to adopt (although so far only East Germans among the satellites actually have color). In the Soviet Union the changeover to color has been relatively slow. In 1971 about twenty hours out of 160 hours a week on Moscow television were in color. One drawback, as in most countries, has been the cost of color sets. They sell for about $1,000 in Moscow, and so can be afforded only by tourist hotels or workers' clubs. The difficulty and cost of constructing a complete television system for so immense a land—it is 4,500 miles from Moscow to Vladivostok—meant that the Russians could never really contemplate establishing a conventional land-based microwave network for the entire Soviet Union. The many time zones also made true network television impractical.

Regular television programing began in Moscow as far back as December 1939. It broke off during the war, but resumed again shortly afterward in December 1945. During the Stalin era expansion was slow. Because of the distances television developed on a regional basis, with the first stations in the capital cities of each of the fourteen republics of the Soviet Union. Mini-networks spread out within each republic. In all about 130 local stations were built, many of them making a good proportion of their own programs, often in the regional language. Cities like Leningrad, Kiev, Minsk, Tallinn and Riga, in the west of the Soviet Union, were also slowly linked by land line to Moscow.

However, the first Sputnik, in 1957, not only marked the opening of the space age, but pointed the way to a great leap forward for Soviet television. The Russians soon became the first nation anywhere (Canada will be the second) to use communications satellites as an integral part of their domestic television network. The first Molniya communications satellite was launched in 1965. Within two years an initial network of twenty-four Orbita earth stations was built up, mostly to the east of the Urals. The Orbita stations, close to such cities as Novosibirsk, Alma-Ata, Vladivostok and Magadan, pick up the pictures beamed to the satellite from Moscow and feed them into local networks. The initial batch of Orbita stations, which brought twenty million people within the range of television for the first time, was inaugurated as part of the celebrations for the fiftieth anniversary of the Revolution in 1967. The network has been extended with another three stations, bringing into the fold remote cities like Anadyr on the Bering Straits, opposite Alaska.

Unlike the Intelsat satellites, poised at fixed positions over the equator, the Molniya satellite goes looping around the earth in an oval orbit (it cannot be "fixed" over the equator, as the television pictures bounced back would then miss most of northern Siberia). Thus Molniya does not provide cover throughout the twenty-four hours; instead it comes swinging in over Siberia twice a day. It is in range for about six hours at a time to relay the pictures from central television in Moscow. Each Orbita earth station tracks the satellite automatically as it passes by, catching the television pictures in huge dish aerials thirty-six feet across. To cope with the harshness of Siberian winters, the Orbita stations are all designed to withstand temperatures of minus 50 degrees centigrade and wind speeds of up to 12 miles per second. The Moscow and Vladivostok Orbita stations can send and receive pictures; the others can only receive.

The satellite network has also been expanded to embrace Mongolian television in Ulan Bator, where an earth station opened in 1970. Mongolian television, incidentally, has a single channel on the air for about three hours a day, serving a few thousand sets. The Russians have talked of extending the Molniya club to the communist countries of Eastern Europe and even to Cuba. And when President Pompidou of France visited Moscow in 1970 the French earth station at Pleumeur Bodou on the coast of Brittany temporarily bowed out of its regular place in the Intelsat system and trained its antennae instead on the Molniya satellite to relay live pictures of the visit.

Obviously the Russians would like their Molniya system to be accepted eventually as a worldwide alternative to the Intelsat network for intercontinental television relays. Eino Repo, the Finnish president in 1970 of OIRT (the communist bloc's equivalent of the European Broadcasting Union), told me: "Within the next five years the Russians will be offering a fully alternative system. It will be just as practical—and a shorter distance—for pictures from Japan to France to be relayed via Molniya over Russia as via Intelsat's Indian Ocean satellite." Whether noncommunist nations will actually leap at the chance of sending their pictures via a communist satellite, when they already have their own, is another matter.

Within the Soviet Union the state has organized television on two levels; at the top is "central" television operating out of Moscow; then there are regional administrations for each of the fourteen republics. Central television is administered by the state Radio and Television Committee, whose seventeen members are appointed directly by the Council of Ministers. The chairman, who is the equivalent of the director general or president of a broadcasting organization in the West, is usually an important political figure. The post frequently seems to go to a former ambassador. Beneath him are four vice-chairmen—one each for radio, television, external broadcasting and engineering. Regional television follows much the same pattern, with the local Radio and Television Committee being nominated by the administration of each republic. All television is financed out of the state and regional budgets; there is no annual license fee for owning a set.

But Moscow is the pacemaker. The four channels there all have their own distinct role. The first channel is the flagship. It is on the air for eleven hours every day, from 9:00 A.M. until midnight, with a four-hour break in the afternoon. Most of the programs it originates are seen throughout the Soviet Union—although not simultaneously because of the vast shift in time zones. This is the general-interest channel that carries all the big news and sports events, plays and films. During the day, however, much of the time is given over to programs on industry or farming. At Tuesday lunchtime, for instance, there is a farming program that may show livestock breeding in Moldavia or the achievements of a new tea-harvesting machine in the fields of Georgia. Another daytime program, *Science in the Sunny Republic,* reports from the Institute of Deserts in the republic of Turkmeni, near the Caspian Sea, about improvements in cotton-growing in difficult climates. Then an early evening show goes to a factory in the Urals to interview the local party committee secretary and the construction bureau leader about how they are achieving their planned targets and on the need for scientific and industrial progress in their factory. All kinds of workers come in for a special pat on the back. On Food Industry Workers' Day or Fishermen's Day, special documentaries review the progress of the industry and explain five-year-plan targets. The chairman of a regional fishery cooperative explains how his collective is exceeding its planned cod and herring target for the season. And on Sunday evenings in prime time there is a concert for "the workers of the sea," in which choirs from fishermen's collectives join national artists in a musical soirée.

The emphasis on self-improvement is constant. Saturday lunchtime there is a series called *Looking After Your Eyesight.* This is followed by a program on Mongolian art. In the evening a documentary commemorates the fiftieth anniversary of the Mongolian People's Revolution, pointing out that "with the 1960s the Mongolian People's Republic entered the final stage of building socialism. In the last five years alone GNP has increased by 160 percent." The North Vietnamese get their recognition too in a diploma ceremony by North Vietnamese students who are studying at the Moscow Circus and Stage College.

The main channel, many of whose programs are distributed over the satellite network, is backed up in Moscow by the second channel concentrating primarily on the capital scene. This is really Moscow's own "regional" channel, covering events of the day, local sports, and including plenty of live coverage of concerts and ballet. The third channel, which is only on the air for three or four hours in the evening, is purely educational. On a typical Thursday evening in July 1971, for instance, its schedule began with an engineering lecture and then a German lesson. The rest of the evening included what were billed as popular scientific films; the first was about various elixirs of plant growth, the next explained the technique of superimposing pictures in films and television, and the evening rounded off with a study of the intricacies of ice skating.

Moscow's fourth channel is highbrow. It carries a heavy concentration of concerts, opera, folk singing and talks by writers and scientists plus lessons in that favorite Russian pastime, chess. The programs do not begin until 7:30 in the evening and normally last until 10:30. One evening may embrace a performance of Dvorak's Ninth Symphony, a documentary on gardening and a concert from the All Union Festival of Youth Songs, and the opera *Anna Snegina,* based on a lyrical poem about country life in Russia between the February and October Revolutions of 1917.

All this serious fare does not mean entertainment is neglected. *Pravda* and other publications often rebuke housewives for spending too much time watching variety shows. There is extended color coverage of circuses and spectacular ice shows, sometimes going on for two or three hours at a time. A highly successful quiz, *KVN,* has two teams challenging each other to do impromptu skits based on the news. Old war movies (Russian made) abound, but the latest films are also shown immediately on television. One advantage of the communist system is that films do not have to make the cinema circuit for years until they are finally released to television. The newest productions can turn up on the blue screen and then go into movie houses later. Sports, of course, are covered very thoroughly. Indeed, the only regular programs that the Russian viewer sees from outside the communist world are international soccer matches and ice hockey. In turn the ice hockey on Russian television is the one event which draws plenty of viewers from outside the Soviet Union, in Finland, where the regional station of Tallinn can be picked up.

However, a discreet survey of audience reaction to television in a Moscow suburb, which was published in the Soviet press in 1967, revealed considerable dissatisfaction with the amount of entertainment. Furthermore, it showed that many Russians wanted more travel films, as they felt cut off from the outside world. "Above all people want less persuasion and more entertainment, and there is a shrewd suspicion that it is being kept from them." One person quizzed on the survey said, "They are sly, those people in television. If there is a lecture on one channel, you can be pretty sure there's a round table discussion on the other." [1]

Actually, the choice is not quite as severe as that. Most evenings between 8:00 and 10:00 entertainment can be found on at least one channel. The choice in Moscow, for instance, at 8:00 one Tuesday in July 1971 was U.S.S.R. soccer championships on Channel 1, a profile of a worker in a vacuum cleaner factory on Channel 2, a German lesson on Channel 3 and a new film, *Bracelet 2,* on Channel 4.

The programs chosen for relay over the Orbita satellite network are a rather mixed bunch. In a single day they may include a program for amateur photographers, a children's story, a recital by David Oistrakh, football, a talk by an award winner of the Lenin Youth Organization and a play about life on a collective farm. The satellite channel normally transmits up to twelve hours a day, with the majority of the programs now being in color. News goes over the satellite network at least twice every day.

News is frequent on all channels except the educational one. The first Moscow channel has five broadcasts a day. Several of the news readers are women but, whether male or female, their style tends to be stiff and formal. The stories are often just bulletins from the Soviet news agency, Tass. If the Central Committee of the Communist Party makes any important pronouncement it will be read out in full, with long lists of the names of everyone attending the meeting.

The Soviet interpretation of what is and is not news differs markedly from that of the West. A factory that exceeds its tractor output target is news; a plane crash is not. Human interest has low priority. Sometimes the news readers will say, "And now we go direct to Tashkent," as if some major story is breaking there. However, up come pictures of a tractor sowing the first of the spring wheat that day. As one Western correspondent

---

[1] *The Times,* London, May 10, 1967.

remarked, after viewing the news on television daily for four years in Moscow, "There is no sense of occasion."

When the three Soviet cosmonauts were killed by a cabin leak on reentry in June 1971, it was six hours before Moscow television broke the story. Such dilatoriness in giving the latest space news has sometimes caused quite unnecessary speculation within the Soviet Union that something has gone wrong when, in fact, all is well. Although the Russians are now slightly more forthcoming with their television pictures of space flights, the Russian viewer has yet to be told in advance of a launching and see a live liftoff. But he has become thoroughly familiar with the regular chief reporter on space, Yuri Fokin, the amiable Moscow counterpart of Walter Cronkite. Undoubtedly, the Americans' openness with their space program has forced some relaxation on the Russians. However, it is important to remember that the average Russian viewer has no idea of the lavish coverage afforded American space flights. He sees only short, thirty-second clips of film of American flights tucked away in the news. His own country's reticence, therefore, is not as obvious as it is to regular television viewers in the West. On the other hand, the heroes' welcome accorded the Soviet cosmonauts on their return is always given massive coverage. The first Russian television I watched was in 1961 when all Moscow turned out to greet Yuri Gagarin on his return from man's first space flight; the Russians relayed the pictures through to Helsinki and then into the Eurovision network for all of Western Europe to see.

While home news on Russian television plays up Soviet triumphs, the troubles of capitalist countries are gloated over in some detail. Strikes, Vietnam war protests, riots in Northern Ireland are all shown to underline bourgeois decadence or repression of the workers. Soviet television not only has its own foreign correspondents, but subscribes (and contributes) to Visnews, the international news film agency. A full daily roundup of world news film is thus available. News and comment are closely intermingled. It is always the "aggressive Americans" in Vietnam. Russian television executives visiting Western Europe are sometimes staggered to find that news and comment there are usually kept apart. One leading television news editor, after visiting the BBC in London, finally conceded to his British host after watching the news for several nights, "You really do keep comment out!"

Both news and current affairs programs steer well clear, however, of any kind of controversy about the Soviet Union. The watchword is always *bezkonflictnost*—avoiding conflicting viewpoints. Laudatory detail prevails over dissenting comment. Even in "discussions" everyone reads carefully from prepared scripts.

This inflexibility naturally cramps television's style. Everyone is so wary not to step out of line that the results can hardly be sparkling. One Western observer of Russian television over several years summed it up: "Slowness and lack of spontaneity are among the most marked weaknesses and spring from the fact that producers cannot make independent decisions about program content." [2]

Once any decision is taken at the top it is followed obediently. When radio and television were duly ordered by the Central Committee of the Communist Party to celebrate both the fiftieth anniversary of the Revolution in 1967 and the centenary of Lenin's birth in 1970, they went at it obsessively. For the Revolution's anniversary they prepared a documentary on each of the fifty years. Despite the detail possible in fifty programs, embarrassing events and people like Trotsky were passed over without mention. A Russian television executive visiting London during the anniversary year remarked how difficult they had found it dredging up enough material for fifty programs. He also said how interesting he found a British program on the Revolution compared to the turgid ones at home.

For Lenin's centenary they went at it even harder. The tone was set by the Deputy Chief Editor of Central Television, N. Ivankovitch: "Television journalists are well aware of the honorable and responsible task entrusted to them by the Central Committee of the Communist Party of the Soviet Union, to provide complete and all-round possibilities of satisfying the vivid interests of millions of television viewers in the Lenin theme. The most experienced and talented script writers and editors, producers and teleoperators, political reviewers and artists are enthusiastically preparing television programs devoted to the Lenin Jubilee." [3]

This devotion resulted in thirty documentaries on places Lenin visited, including most of his childhood haunts, the headquarters of the October Revolution, Red Square and his study in the Kremlin. Channel 1 backed this up with a series, *Your Leninist Library,* designed "to help the broad masses of working people to acquire a better and more comprehensive knowledge of Lenin's most important works." Another series, naturally, was *They Met Lenin,* with memories trotted out by old acquaintances everywhere from Moscow to Helsinki and London. The children had

[2] Kyril Tidmarsh, *The Times,* London, May 10, 1967.
[3] *OIRT Journal,* No. 4, 1969.

Stories about Lenin and *Children of the October Revolution*—*The Grand-children of Ilich.* That was merely the warmup. There were series on *Leninism*—*The Flag of our Epoch,* surveying the worldwide impact of socialism, *Lenin and the Party*—about the development of the Communist Party, *Leninist Trials* and *We Are Reporting to Ilich*—on his lieutenants during the revolutionary flight. As one account of the festivities truly stated: "Leniniana is endless."

Amid this deluge, Russian television has found little time for programs from outside the communist bloc. Unlike the countries of Eastern Europe, where American, British and French films and television series are common, the Soviet Union has rarely taken anything from the West except news and sports. During the 1960s intermittent exchanges took place. The precedent was set in 1961 when Yuri Gagarin's return to Moscow after his space flight and the May Day parade were relayed live to Western Europe; in return the Russians showed the Queen at the Trooping of the Color in London that summer. Similar exchanges have taken place since—the Russians prefer swaps to outright buying. They also initially agreed to participate in June 1967 in the multinational *Our World* program, which linked together by satellite the television services of five continents for a two-hour live look at the world. At the last moment, however, they quietly withdrew because of the tensions created during the Six Day War just prior to the program. But since then there have been signs of a more general thaw. The real breakthrough came in the summer of 1969 when Dennis Scuse, the general manager of BBC Television Enterprises, succeeded in selling the Russians the twenty-six-part *Forsyte Saga,* for a reported price of $25,000. This is the first—and only—drama serial sold to the Soviet Union from outside the communist bloc. (In the celebration *that* called for, Scuse and four Russians downed between them one bottle of Armenian brandy, a bottle of vodka, a bottle of champagne, and a bottle of Vat 69.)

The Forsytes are an understandable choice for the Russians. Galsworthy has always been one of those authors, along with Charles Dickens, who are highly regarded in the Soviet Union. Many of his books have been approved by the censors for translation. Quite what the Russians made of the serial is another matter. The Saga started in July 1971 simply with a narrator speaking in Russian over the English voices. According to Western correspondents reviewing it in Moscow, the mixture was almost unintelligible. Naturally the Forsytes' picture of the class structure in Britain provided the Russians with a little useful ammunition. An article introducing the series in the weekly television magazine explained that "the

Forsyte family were the nucleus of bourgeois society, represented in England at the end of the last century and the first quarter of the present. Well-known features remain today."

The Forsyte sale showed that the Soviet Union is very slowly becoming a more open market. A newly created Foreign Exchange Studio, an offshoot of Central Television in Moscow, spent a reported $330,000 on foreign programs in 1969. Thames Television in London sold the Russians *Now That the Buffalo's Gone,* a documentary narrated by Marlon Brando on the vanishing North American Indian. France's ORTF joined with Moscow television to re-create *The Battle of Moscow* from World War II. From the United States CBS Enterprises exchanged *The Secret of Michelangelo* and *Casals at 88* for a prize-winning television film of the Bolshoi Ballet in *Romeo and Juliet* and a play, *Blind Rain,* from the regional television center at Kiev. NBC sold *Profile of America, Homeland U.S.A.,* and *The Vanishing 400,* a documentary on the changing character of high society in the New York and Washington Establishment. The emphasis, clearly, is on culture or programs—like the Thames documentary on the Indians—that do not show the noncommunist world at its best. As yet, however, there is no sale for *Bonanza,* the biggest television hit in most other communist countries.

Perhaps *Bonanza* hardly fits the style of Soviet television. Gun-toting westerns were certainly not in the mind of the 23rd Congress of the Communist Party which directed television, along with the other media, "to mold a Marxist-Leninist outlook and promote the political and cultural development of all the Soviet people."

14

Eastern Europe:
Cowboys and Commissars

An old Humphrey Bogart movie on Saturday night, Peter Sellers capering about in *Only Two Can Play* on a midweek evening, Rupert Davies puffing hard on his pipe as Maigret. Television in London perhaps? Sydney? Rio de Janeiro? No, East Germany. And the biggest fan club anywhere for *Bonanza*? In Poland. In the first two months of 1971, NBC supplied over five thousand photographs of the Cartwright brothers to *Bonanza* addicts there, compared with a modest two thousand in the United States. And the third largest batch of seven hundred and fifty went to Rumania, where the local cattle ranchers frequently write to the Cartwrights, care of NBC Burbank, for their advice on stock breeding.

Television in Eastern Europe does get bogged down sometimes in sermons on increasing tractor output but, compared with the Soviet Union, most of the satellite countries fit in a surprisingly high proportion of light entertainment, much of it from the noncommunist world. Take just one week in Poland in May 1971: the films shown on the two channels of Polish television were from France, Italy, Britain, the United States, and even Brazil. Saturday night there was a Joel McCrea western.

The art of the scheduling game appears to be to preserve a modest balance of programs between East and West; naturally there must be slightly more programs from communist countries than from noncommunist. East German television, for example, selects two thirds of its imported programs from socialist states, one third from capitalist. At any sign of pressure from the Soviet Union that a country is not toeing the communist line sternly enough, the foreign (and particularly American) programs are withdrawn overnight. Folklore or workers' discussions suddenly become the fashion. Rumania dropped *The Untouchables* rather sharply in the early summer of 1971 at the first rumblings of a political shakeup. "Everyone has decided to play it safe and keep his head down, so no American programs," an Eastern European broadcaster explained. Czechoslovakia also became abruptly closed to most Western programs after the Russian clamp down in 1968. Quite apart from selecting their programs from all over the world, the Czechs had previously built up a fine reputation for the annual Prague Television Festival, which attracted a high class of entry from television services everywhere. The festival has continued since 1968 but, according to regular visitors, is a shadow of its former self.

Nowadays television throughout most of Eastern Europe is as commonplace as in the West. There are 16 million sets, or one among every six people. Only Rumania trails significantly behind with one for thirteen. The undisputed leader is East Germany which, with 4.5 million sets, or one for every four people, is on a par with penetration in West Germany, Britain, and Japan. Television in East Germany, in fact, has achieved the highest standard of technical and programing skills found anywhere in the communist world. Television producers in West Germany have to concede that productions of plays by Brecht or dramatizations of Thomas Mann's novels by East Germany's Deutscher Fernsehfunk are better than their own. As a drama producer in West Berlin explained: "Although some of their plays stick too much to socialist realism, their attention to style results in first rate productions."

The East Germans, of course, are in direct competition with West German television just over the border. Every home in East Berlin and most throughout East Germany can watch television from the West. The rivalry has secured full government support, therefore, for Deutscher Fernsehfunk. They must keep pace. The East Germans, for instance, began color television in 1969, some three years before any of their communist neighbors, but only a year or so after the West Germans started their switch into color. And Deutscher Fernsehfunk's second channel is on every night of the week, while elsewhere in Eastern Europe there is still either only one channel or a second channel that functions just three or four evenings a week.

State control of television is absolute in all the communist satellites. Usually their organization is similar to that in the Soviet Union, with a State Radio and Television Committee appointed by the Council of Ministers. In East Germany there have been separate committees for radio and television since 1969. Normally, there is also a Broadcasting Council made up of representatives of the Council of Ministers, trade unions, and workers in drama, journalism, and other activities associated with broadcasting. Unlike the Soviet Union, however, television in Eastern Europe relies chiefly on annual license fees for its income, rather than a direct state grant. The fee is modest: in Poland and Czechoslovakia it is about $12 a year, in Hungary $20. Everyone supplements his income with a very limited amount of advertising, normally two or three blocs of five minutes between programs in the early evening. The commercials, however, are too infrequent to make much real difference to budgets. In Czechoslovakia, for instance, they account for well under 20 percent of television's income. Little hard selling goes on. The advertisements are really informing the public about a new style of radio, refrigerator, or tractor, rather than pressuring them into buying. The advertiser, after all, must not appear to be trying to make a profit but simply to be serving the public need.

The overall character of a country's programs reflects its degree of adherence—or lack of it—to the Moscow line. In Poland it seems to be a question of how much Western material they can get away with. Deutscher Fernsehfunk, on the other hand, despite those old Bogart movies, followed Walter Ulbricht's loyalty to Moscow. So there are documentaries like *Unknown Citizens* delving into the lives of the working people to reveal "the poetry of a normal socialist day." And the East Germans describe the two-thousand-mile-long coaxial cable that links their television with that of the Soviet Union as "a line of friendship." Like the Soviet Union, they have not yet succumbed to buying American entertainment series (as opposed to old movies). They are always playing up socialist achievement and are wary of buying programs from any of their less hard-line communist neighbors if they are at all controversial. They were most reluctant to take programs from the Czechs, for instance, during the two or three years prior to 1968, when Czech television was the most independent-minded of any communist nation. Since the Russians cracked down in Prague in August 1968, however, the East Germans have been busy making coproductions with them.

The expertise and wealth of television in East Germany also makes Deutscher Fernsehfunk much less dependent on importing programs than most communist television services. Their main channel is on the air for ten hours every day, the second channel for four hours each evening, with most of the programs in color on the weekends. The first channel begins at 9:30 on weekday mornings and 8:00 on Saturday, but the mornings are taken up mainly with repeats of important programs from the previous evening for the benefit of those working then—a practice common in television in all communist countries. (Whether many from the night shift actually watch is doubtful; audience research indicates that most are asleep, and only old-age pensioners tune in.) In the evenings both channels carry an even blend of entertainment, sports, news, and current affairs. Since the introduction of their second channel in the autumn of 1969, Deutscher Fernsehfunk have tried to give their viewers a reasonable choice. A dramatization of Balzac's *Père Goriot* on Channel 1 is matched with sports on Channel 2, or a film contrasts with the Philippine National Ballet. The exception is for news and current affairs. The main evening news is at 7:30 on both channels. Current affairs programs (as in West Germany) are usually matched against a serious documentary or cultural program. Both sides of the border refuse to put light entertainment against current affairs; the viewers must watch the serious stuff or tune out.

The East Germans also share the West German passion for thrillers. Quite apart from importing the BBC's highly successful *Maigret, Airline Detective,* and *Sherlock Holmes* series, they have produced plenty of what they call "politically engaged criminal films." One such three-part drama, *The Lady of Genoa,* unveiled a plot to steal an old master painting in West Germany. Along with the criminal fun and games, the play also knocked the unscrupulousness of the art market there. The crooks in the thrillers often turn out to be Western diplomats or millionaires from such right-wing dictatorships as Portugal.

The more serious drama is frequently drawn from the classics. A serialization of Charles Dickens' *Nicholas Nickleby,* color productions of *King Lear* and Shaw's *Androcles and the Lion,* and a mammoth three-and-a-half-hour dramatization of Dostoyevsky's *The Brothers Karamazov* spread over two evenings were the highlights, for instance, in the spring of 1971. Plays actually written for television, however, tend to take a more stereotyped, socialist line. One much-publicized production, *Irena,* was about an "encounter" between an East German mechanic and a Russian girl, Irena, who met while working on a building site. "This encounter," the producer explained, "serves as an example of the unceasing promotion of friendship existing between the citizens of the German Democratic Republic and Soviet citizens."

The theme of Soviet achievement pops up again and again. Deutscher Fernsehfunk made a documentary series, *I Serve the Soviet Union,* and a four-parter called *Shield and Sword* on the Soviet army during and after World War II. Regular documentaries during 1970 were devoted to travels through Siberia to see construction work there. A Saturday morning series of lectures on "socialist economy" contrasted its benefits with the ruthlessness of capitalism in the United States.

When the East Germans started their second channel in 1969 they emphasized that its aim was "to educate highly cultured personalities with all-around interests and a firm class standpoint. It will help to satisfy better the growing intellectual-cultural demands of the working people." They hoped that "in the sphere of dramatic art efforts will be concentrated on productions promoting the role of German television in the formation of socialist state consciousness and in the creation of our socialist national culture."

Polish television, in contrast, underplays socialism. The prospectus for their second channel, which opened in October 1970, stressed that the new channel would include encyclopedic data as well as themes fostering the cultural and intellectual standards of the society. Scientific and technical broadcasts would play an important part." No mention, however, was made of socialism.

Although Polish television lacks the resources of its East German neighbors—it had to get by with very run-down old studios and poor equipment until a new TV center opened in 1970—its schedules are a rather remarkable mélange of television from East and West. Along with *Bonanza* from the United States, the Poles have become devoted to *The Saint, The Baron,* and *Randall and Hopkirk Deceased,* all purchased from British commercial television. The chief editor of television news in Warsaw suddenly dropped everything in the midst of a conversation with one British visitor in the summer of 1971 to say, "Time for *Randall and Hopkirk Deceased,* we mustn't miss that." As for *The Forsyte Saga,* "That," a Polish broadcaster told me, "was rather like an earthquake." The Poles ran each episode twice a week; the first time through with Polish narration over the English soundtrack, the second night simply the full English-language version. "No one in Poland would answer his telephone while that was on," said the broadcaster.

The difficulty, apparently, is maintaining an equal balance with programs from the Soviet Union and other communist countries. There are no gripping drama series to be had from Moscow. The makeweights, therefore, tend to be Russian documentaries and educational programs. Set against them, the choice from the capitalist world often seems remarkably refreshing. During May 1971, for example, the fledgling second channel put on both a Japanese and a French evening, with all the programs drawn from television services in Tokyo and Paris. Another night they had Ken Russell's television film of the life of Delius. The main drawback is the lack of foreign exchange, which inhibits the Poles from buying more programs from the West. They are allowed a very limited quota, so their purchases have to be very selective. In the summer of 1971 they were carefully saving up their allocation to buy from Britain the rights to a new BBC drama series of six plays on Casanova, written by Dennis Potter.

The Poles' own popular series focus almost exclusively on World War II. The most widely shown wartime saga has been the adventures of a Resistance hero, *Captain Kloss.* The good captain, posing as an officer in the German army, fights his way out of all sorts of traps every week. The series has been a hit throughout Eastern Europe; even in Sweden it won high ratings late on a Saturday night. *Four Tankists and a Dog* scores with a humorous account of the exploits of a tank crew and their Alsatian, while *The Girls of Nowolipki Street* recounts what befell four girls, Frania, Kwiryna, Bronka, and Amelka on that Warsaw street during the hostilities. "We have a great nostalgia for that period," a Polish actor told me, "sleeping somewhere different every night, never knowing what would happen the next day. Nothing exciting has happened since then."

But it isn't all war games. Polish television has been able to draw on a lively theatrical and film tradition. Although they lack the resources to mount many large-scale productions themselves, their output during May 1971, for example, included Eugene O'Neill's *Long Day's Journey into Night,* a dramatization of Hemingway's *Old Man and the Sea,* and Mozart's opera *Don Giovanni.*

The most ambitious project, however, is a Television Technical College developed jointly by the Ministry of Education, Polish television, and UNESCO's Department of Mass Communications. Faced with a serious shortage of well-qualified technicians and engineers, the Poles have started to use television systematically to improve their technical education for adults. This technical university of the air puts on physics, math, and chemistry lessons in the late afternoon just after everyone gets home from the factory. This enables workers, who never had the benefit of a formal university education, to expand their understanding of technology. During the first year of the experiment, some 60,000 sent in for booklets to go with the television courses.

The Poles' toughest fight has been to keep their television service going with very antiquated equipment. Whatever the sparkle of some programs, they have acquired a reputation for an erratic technical performance and constant unpunctuality. Matters even went so far as the director of programs taking the leading page in the weekly TV guide in May 1971 to apologize to viewers for the "lack of punctuality" and the frequent lack of coordination between programs advertised and what actually went on. The trouble was, he explained, that people often started work on a program *after* the time for its screening had been published, so if they hit any snags it simply was not ready when promised. "And," he sighed, "our equipment is far from satisfactory. Current investments can at best only smooth over the consequences of neglect for many years." The problem, apparently, is that no one dreamed television would expand so fast and a fateful decision was made ten years ago that existing cutting rooms and laboratories could cope with all television's requirements for the foreseeable future.

These hazards, however, have not prevented Polish television from taking a much more enterprising line in the last year or two, particularly since Gireck replaced Gomulka as party leader. The most noticeable innovation has been a program called *Citizens Forum*. This is a live hour and a half in which viewers can pitch questions at ministers and leading members of the Communist Party. The first two forums in 1971 tackled housing and agriculture. Although questions may be sent in in advance, there are sixteen telephone lines (one for each province of Poland) open to the studio for supplementary questions as the program proceeds. Three outside broadcast units are also stationed in towns and villages to televise questions live. The program, which has been created at the suggestion of the communist leadership, not the television service, is an attempt to improve communication with the people. Many of the questions, apparently, are not known in advance. According to Polish-speaking Western broadcasters who have seen it, the questions are often very tough. Ministers have sometimes been quite taken aback and, lacking good briefing, have stumbled in dodging the issue. Politicians in communist countries are much more accustomed to speaking from prepared scripts. Up till now they have not had to get used to the rough and tumble of the live television interview that is part of every politician's life in the West. Consequently they often fumble.

No doubt they will shortly have to learn. The *Forum* idea is spreading rapidly in Eastern Europe. Hungary had it a couple of years before Poland. The pioneer, however, was Czechoslovakia. There the program was a vital part of the new air of independence that flowered on television briefly during the Czech "spring" of 1968. Indeed, television really showed the way to the new style of socialism that evolved in Prague that year. The renaissance was due largely to a lively and intelligent man, Jiri Pelikan, who was director of television in Czechoslovakia from 1963 to that fateful August of 1968, when the Russians invaded. Pelikan now lives in exile in Rome, while Czech television has shrunk back into a new dark age. Several writers and commentators of that period are in prison.

While the flexibility lasted, however, Czech television was an example of what can be achieved in a communist society. Not only did the international reputation of the service increase as some lively programs began to win prizes at television festivals everywhere, but the Prague Television Festival itself, with Pelikan as a genial host, became a notable event.

I asked the exiled Jiri Pelikan what he had set out to do. "My conception of television," he said, "is that it is a powerful means of democratization. In a Greek democracy the leaders could address everyone assembled in the main square. We cannot get that intimacy now, but television does enable the leaders to speak to everyone in his home. So to start with television can make everyone much better informed. But it can also democratize the culture of a country. Previously only an elite went to the National Theater, opera, or the ballet in Prague; now television can make their productions accessible to the people."

The cornerstone of his policy was to try to persuade politicians to open up on television, to make them the subject of questions and interviews, instead of reading prepared statements. A regular hour-and-a-half *Forum* was started in which ministers and leading experts on travel, housing, defense, or wages were confronted with viewers in the studio to debate the issue. The program, therefore, went one stage further than the Polish *Forum* because it actually included discussion instead of politicians simply fielding questions. Such frankness appalled President Novotny, who complained that television was going too far and discrediting government policies. But the public response was enormous. The sight of people challenging politicians on issues like commuter trains and buses was a breath of fresh air. Each program produced a vast mailbag, which was reviewed in a half-hour follow-up the next week. What also came out was that several ministers were totally ignorant of subjects which they were supposed to control. Without a civil servant to prompt them they simply floundered. "It was a great scandal," said Pelikan. "Here were ministers revealed on television as being quite incapable of government."

While ministers had to open up more frankly on the screen, television news also became more objective. The censorship was eased, until early in 1968 Alexander Dubcek told Pelikan that television news could exercise its own judgment in deciding what to report and how to say it. The candor of the news was, of course, one factor that most incensed the Russians. But for a few months before they stepped in to control it its credibility with the Czech public soared.

Pelikan also sought to raise the standard of drama on television as part of his determination to bring good theater to the masses. He insisted that his television cameras go out and about to many of the eighty theaters in Czechoslovakia. A competition was started among the theaters for the best production suitable for television. But above all he sought to persuade Czech writers to contribute. Previously, playwrights had been very nervous about trying their hand at a TV play because of censorship. This tended to be tougher on television (as a mass audience saw it) than in the theater (with only a few hundred in the audience). After 1966, however, censorship eased considerably. Pelikan considers that between then and 1968 he conjured up twenty good plays especially for television. He also launched a very successful crime series, *Sinful City of Prague*. One episode, "Lady Macbeth from the Suburbs," won several international prizes.

He attempted also to persuade the Soviet Union to let him show some of the best drama productions put out by their own regional television stations. The trouble was he found that the Russians always wanted to let him have plays or documentaries about Lenin instead. "I told them that was quite unacceptable to our viewers," he said. "I wanted good plays from Estonia." The Russians paid no attention.

But Pelikan did succeed in increasing the activities of Intervision, the communist counterpart of Eurovision. Intervision is an offshoot of OIRT (Organisation Internationale Radiodiffusion et Television), the broadcasting union of the communist world. Actually, OIRT is a direct descendant of the prewar International Broadcasting Union, to which most broadcasting organizations throughout the world belonged. In the tense period of East-West relations in the late 1940s the communist countries tried to use this union (by then renamed Organisation Internationale Radiodiffusion, OIR) purely for propaganda purposes. So the Western countries, at British initiative, formed their own European Broadcasting Union and took over the old OIR administrative center at Geneva and the technical center in Brussels, while the rump of OIR itself moved to Prague. When television came along OIR added the T for Television. Then in 1960 OIRT, seeing the growing success of Eurovision, set up its own version, Intervision, coordinated from Prague. Although Intervision is sometimes rather pompously described as "international television in the service of Marxism-Leninism," it is essentially a clearing house for program exchange just like Eurovision. The original members were Czechoslovakia, Hungary, East Germany, and Poland; the Soviet Union, Bulgaria, and Rumania joined the club later. Finland is also a member of OIRT and Intervision, as well as being an active member of the EBU and Eurovision. The maverick Yugoslavia, of course, has thrown in its lot with the EBU.

The prime job of Intervision has been to coordinate the exchange of news and sports within the communist bloc. Sports accounts for more than 40 percent of Intervision transmissions, news for over 25 percent. A news exchange, similar to the Eurovision pattern, started in 1964. Initially the exchange was once a week, but it was gradually built up to a daily exchange by May 1970. Every morning each Intervision member must telex to Prague by 10:15 an outline of the stories on which they can offer film that day. The Intervision Program Coordination Center in Prague then distributes a complete story list, again by telex. During the afternoon there is a final story conference over the permanent Intervision sound circuit to confirm running time of each clip of film and details of its contents. The actual exchange, with all the television services linked together on a vision circuit, begins at 4:25.

The daily story list emphasizes the communist bloc's distinctive understanding of what makes news. Consider its makeup for November 3, 1970. The Soviet Union offered film of five items: a session of the Supreme Soviet to ratify a new Soviet-Finnish treaty; preparations in Moscow for a military parade; the arrival in Moscow of an Italian parliamentary delegation; an international geological exhibition in Moscow; and what was described as the reunion of a Soviet soldier and a Czechoslovakian teacher, who first became acquainted twenty-five years before, at the end of the war. The reunion was clearly an exercise to underline good Soviet-Czech relations—a theme also reflected in Czechoslovakia's own story suggestions that day. They had film of a "festive meeting and performance in a Prague theater, marking the anniversary of the October revolution and the opening of the 'month of Czechoslovak-Soviet friendship.' " Their suggestions concluded with the unveiling of a Lenin memorial in Prague. East Germany proposed "decorations and promotions of new officers and generals attended by Walter Ulbricht" and the return from Hungary of the vice-chairman of the Council of Ministers. Poland came up with the visit to Warsaw of the West German foreign minister, Walter Scheel.

The Intervision countries usually exchange about eight stories a day; the total in 1969 was 2,432 stories. A special review of the kind of story on the exchange made in June 1970 revealed that of the 224 stories, 109 were "social-political," 46 cultural, 61 science, technology and economy, and 8 sports.

The Intervision exchange is, of course, also linked to the Eurovision news exchange. The full Intervision list is telexed from Prague to Geneva, so that Western countries can pick up any items. Similarly, Intervision gets the Eurovision list. The Intervision headquarters in Prague also listens to the Eurovision story conference on a sound circuit but, at the insistence of the West Germans, is not allowed to participate in actual discussion.

Broadcasting liaison between East and West is now much easier than it was in the frosty period immediately after the forming of the European Broadcasting Union and OIR's departure for Prague. The real thaw began, appropriately enough, in a Finnish sauna bath.

A special EBU-OIRT summit meeting was arranged in 1963 in Helsinki, which was obviously a suitable meeting place, as the Finnish broadcasting organization belonged to both bodies. The presidents and vice-presidents of both the EBU and OIRT attended. When the conference began, relations between the two sides were simply very correct and businesslike. After a while, however, a group of four leading broadcasters from East and West, including Sir Hugh Greene, director general of the BBC, Olof Rydbeck of Sweden, and Sikorski of Poland left their staffs to get on with the detailed discussions and accepted an invitation to use a private sauna in Helsinki to which the Finnish cabinet repairs when it is deadlocked. As Sir Hugh Greene recalls it: "We went into the sauna at 270 degrees Fahrenheit several times. Those sessions transformed our relationship into one of warm and lasting friendship." Television relations between East and West have been better ever since.

Although Eurovision and Intervision now work together daily, tension crops up again from time to time. The toughest test was the invasion of Czechoslovakia in 1968. Intervision took a great deal of film during the next few months that had been shot by cameramen from Western agencies and was offered on the Eurovision exchange. Ostensibly the film was for the news, but it is widely believed that it was primarily to help security forces identify demonstrators. During the same crisis the Russians also offered to the West film purporting to be their side of the invasion. In fact it showed military maneuvers earlier in the year—the leafless trees revealed the fraud.

Intervision is also reluctant to pay for coverage of American moonshots. They argue that pictures of Americans landing on the moon are good propaganda and should be free. Eurovision, which handles the satellite relays to Europe on such occasions, does not agree and insists on a share of the satellite charges. Actually, most communist countries show only clips of the moon landing in their news bulletins; only Poland, for example, went for extensive live coverage of the first manned landing on the moon in 1969.

The news is naturally the most tightly controlled aspect of all television in Eastern Europe. News and comment intertwine. The Egyptians never open fire across the Suez Canal; it is always "the imperialist, aggressive Israelis." Reports from the West usually come late in the bulletins. Even the surprise announcement in July 1971 of President Nixon's proposed visit to Peking came near the end of the news.

However, in several of the communist countries it is difficult for television news to suppress stories completely. Not only do many people listen to Radio Free Europe, the Voice of America, West German radio and the Eastern European Service of the BBC, but television from the West penetrates into millions of homes. Over the last decade a spirited confrontation has been maintained between television of East and West.

15

Television
Jumps the Wall

From the topmost floor of the fourteen-story television center of Sender Freies Berlin (Radio Free Berlin) on Masurenallee in West Berlin, there is a fine panoramic view out over the entire city. At that height the gray wall topped by spikes and barbed wire that divides it so unnaturally in half is hardly visible. For a moment it seems one city again. The television producer pointing out the landmarks echoes the sentiment. "Down there you see all of Berlin. We are here to serve the whole city and I make my programs for *all* of Germany." For television, in fact, the Berlin Wall does not exist. Where people, newspapers, magazines, and books cannot pass freely, television flits daily with impunity.

Every home in East Berlin and for eighty miles all around in East Germany can watch the programs of Sender Freies Berlin just as easily as the two channels of East Germany's own network. And vice versa; West Berliners have the same chance to see television from the East.

Television has made not only the Berlin Wall, but the Iron Curtain everywhere within the range of its transmitters, totally transparent. Right up beyond the Arctic Circle, Norwegians in Kirkenes and Russians in Murmansk can watch each other's programs. In Helsinki the Finns turn to Russian television coming in from Tallinn across the Gulf of Finland to watch the ice hockey games, while the people of Tallinn are avid fans of *High Chaparral* and *Bonanza* from Finland. Farther south, Austria is ringed by the communist bloc so that television from Vienna radiates easily to Czechoslovakia, Hungary, and Yugoslavia. Indeed, the Austrians are in the curious position (like the broadcasters in West Berlin) of having more viewers for their television in surrounding nations than within their own domain. The seven million Austrian viewers are quite outnumbered by the 4 million Czechs, 3 million Hungarians and 3 million Yugo-slavs who can regularly watch two channels of the Austrian network ORF. As a Austrian television commentator, Hugo Portisch, put it: "We are rather like an aircraft carrier penetrating into foreign waters."

The communists, of course, hasten to point out that this is very much a two-way traffic. "Millions of people, especially in West Germany, West Berlin, and also in Denmark and southern Sweden, are able to re-ceive the transmissions of the Deutscher Fernsehfunk," the official guide to East German television explains. "Thus, many television viewers are able to receive truthful accounts of the peaceful economic and cultural socialist construction of our republic."

The most spirited battle to present each side's version of the truth in this television wall game is between the divided halves of Berlin. Else-where the electronic eavesdropping from one country to another is pri-marily to enjoy the normal programs put out for the local viewers, especially sports or special events not shown in the communist world. Every Easter, for example, many Catholics in Eastern Europe turn to Western television to see the Pope's annual blessing in St. Peter's Square in Rome. Communist television does not carry programs about religion.

In Berlin, however, television is actively concerned with scoring points off the other side; programs are tailored with full awareness that they may be viewed by millions in another regime. "We are an outpost, a lighthouse," said a news editor at Sender Freies Berlin (SFB), "and we believe that three quarters of the homes in the East look at us regularly." The station is one of nine comprising the West German ARD network. The majority of the programs it beams out over the wall are those of the full ARD network, so that East Germans can watch identical tele-vision most of the time not only to West Berliners, but to all West Ger-mans. SFB itself contributes 8 percent of the programs of the ARD net-work. This share of the programing is calculated basically on the 750,000 television licenses in West Berlin. Strictly speaking, these would entitle the station to only a 5 percent program contribution. However, in recognition of the city's unique political and geographical position, giving it access to another 4.5 million sets in East Germany, it is allowed 8 percent, plus a cash bonus of $6 million a year from the other ARD stations to help underwrite its operations.

SFB makes the most of what it sees as its responsibility to its East German viewers. Every year, for instance, the station produces eight or ten plays for the full network. "Our aim is always to produce plays about the problems around us in Berlin today," Dr. Erich Proebster, SFB's drama director, told me. "We aren't interested in classical or historical plays—we leave those to the other ARD stations."

During 1970 four out of SFB's eight plays were actually set in Berlin. *Kinderehen (Child Weddings)* focused on the problems created by so many West Berliners marrying much younger than is customary elsewhere in Germany. *Tatort Berlin* was a thriller based on the unique dilemma facing a criminal on the run in West Berlin. He is trapped in the city, as if on an island, for East Germany is all around. The play included a scene in which gangsters, bent on murdering their leader, tempted him close to the wall. A shot rang out from the East Berlin side and the gangster fell dead. The authorities took it for another escapee shot coming over the wall; in fact the gangsters had set it up with a gunman in East Berlin. Along with these plays the West Berliners also staged a color production of a dramatized version of Alexander Solzhenitsyn's novel *The Cancer Ward,* knowing full well that it is banned throughout Eastern Europe.

The desire to needle the East German authorities influences even the planning of SFB's school programs. "We are a window on the free world," said Paul Wallnisch, the director of school television. "Our programs are aimed partly at the children and teachers in East Germany. We realize they cannot watch officially in the schools, so we screen them in the late afternoon between 4:00 and 4:30, when they can watch at home. We have shown, for example, a series of twelve lectures on politics and economics designed to teach children here in West Berlin about their country, and for those in the East to see how capitalism really works. We also put on plenty of travel films in the geography lessons, because children in the East cannot travel easily to see for themselves what other countries are like."

When the building of the Berlin Wall in August 1961 so abruptly cut off East Berliners from half their city, SFB responded at once with a special transmission of three and a half hours of programs every morning to help them keep in touch. This early session, aimed entirely at the East, is supported by both German networks, ARD and ZDF. The actual broadcast is handled by the Berlin station, which culls the output of both networks and adds some original material of its own. The main television news magazines *Panorama, Report, Monitor,* and *ZDF Magazine* are all repeated on this morning roundup, which also includes fresh news bulletins and a daily review of the international press. Twice a week, on Wednesdays and Saturdays, SFB compiles a local magazine show on the latest news and gossip from West Berlin. To insure that every possible home in East Germany can watch this morning session, it is also relayed by transmitters of other ARD stations in Hamburg, Frankfurt, and Munich, which are nearer the border, to achieve blanket coverage.

The East Germans are naturally fully aware that millions of their people watch this "propaganda." At one time viewing of West German television was illegal, but nowadays the authorities do little to check it. They have tried marketing sets that receive only their channels, but most families find a friendly electrician who can usually adapt the set to receive the West. The law does say that it is illegal to pass on information gained from foreign television, but this is interpreted to mean it is all right to watch in the privacy of your home, though unlawful to invite a friend in to view with you.

The director general of Deutscher Fernsehfunk in East Berlin keeps a special color set in his office tuned to Sender Freies Berlin, so that he is alert to what they are showing and can decide, if necessary, how to respond. Providing, of course, that he knows what line to follow. During the Russian intervention in Czechoslovakia in 1968 he could see SFB alive with almost nonstop reports and film of Russian tanks moving into Prague but, lacking orders from Moscow, could not report the crisis at all on his own network. East German television made no mention of the invasion for twenty-four hours, so viewers got all the news from SFB over the wall.

Normally, however, the East Germans try to get their own back every Monday evening in a half-hour program, *Der Schwarze Kanal (The Black Channel)*. *The Black Channel,* say the East Germans, "deals with the transmissions of the revanchist West German television." The host, ever since the program began in 1960, has been Karl-Edoard von Schnitzel, an adroit East-West sniper. After avidly watching the news magazines on West German television, von Schnitzel culls from them material that he either denounces as propaganda or uses to demonstrate the iniquities of the capitalist system. For good measure the program is repeated twice in the daytime later in the week. When *The Black Channel* first started, the West Germans countered for a while with their own disclaimer of von Schnitzel called *Red Uptake,* but eventually decided that he was not worth answering; the less said about his programs, they felt, the better.

Plays and documentaries on East German television also seek to attack Western decadence. One favorite target has been Axel Springer, the powerful West German publisher. In a dramatized documentary, *I—Axel Casar Springer,* the East Germans explained that "the basic reactionary developmental tendencies in West Germany since 1945 are reflected in the life of Springer, in the rise of this publisher to be a dangerous manipulator of opinions and a leading personality in the psychological war." They also pulled off a rather neat coup in 1968 by getting a long interview in West Germany with Dr. Walter Becher, spokesman and self-styled president in exile of the Sudetanland Germans, whose homeland is now part of Czechoslovakia. Dr. Becher, apparently, was under the impression that he was talking to *West* German television reporters, because they said simply they were from German television. The remarks he made, thinking they were for West German consumption, naturally provided ideal propaganda for East German television intent upon showing aggressive policies in the West.

How many West Berliners regularly watch East German television is not known. Most people I asked in West Berlin simply dismissed it as "very few" and hurried on to talk of something else. But they will agree that the East German television's Little Sandman, who bids the children good night and scatters dream dust for them each evening at 7:00, is much more sympathetic to most tots than his West Berlin rival. "The trouble is he comes during an advertising period here," a West Berlin producer complained, "and in the West we don't spend money on programs during the advertising periods." So most Berlin children are sent happily to bed each evening by a communist lullaby.

But those commercials opposite the Sandman also make their impact in the East. Many viewers there watch the commercials avidly to keep abreast of the latest consumer goods and gadgets, which they ask friends and relatives to bring over during the rare occasions when visiting across the wall is permitted. And when a West German brewery started advertising its beer on television, the sales of a brewery in East Berlin, which has the same name, soared by 40 percent.

Beyond the beer sales, the real significance of this constant exposure to West German television has been to make the use of the medium in East Germany the most professional to be found anywhere in communist countries. Even the weekly television guide is lavishly produced, with many color photographs. It is laid out almost identically with the most popular TV magazines over the border. Programs are often close copies of their Western counterparts. The news—*Aktuelle Kamera*—which comes on at 7:30 each evening has the same crisp style as *Tagesschau,* which starts half an hour later on the West German ARD network. While television in several communist countries is technically poor, with snowy screens and frequent breakdowns, the East German service is acknowledged, in both East and West, as technically first class. They enjoy not only the biggest budget in Eastern Europe, but have studios at Berlin-Aldershof that are the envy of several Western European nations. And, along with the Soviet Union, they are the only communist countries to have switched to color. Their color channel opened in October 1969 and two years later was putting out more hours of color each week than even the Soviet Union. Like the Russians, they have adopted the French SECAM color system, which effectively segregates them from West Germany with PAL color. The disparity of color systems, of course, is a hurdle in the television viewing over the wall; a SECAM set will not show PAL color. The eavesdropping, therefore, will have to be done on old black and white sets.

Although SFB in West Berlin no longer bothers to respond to von Schnitzel's *Black Channel,* two other ARD stations in Hamburg and Cologne maintain a special team, Ost-West Redaktion, who make sixteen programs a year on life in East Germany. Their task is somewhat hampered by the fact that the East Germans will not allow West German television reporters and cameramen in. Film, therefore, has to be obtained in a roundabout way. Usually the Ost-West team just monitor television in the East and film items that interest them direct from the screen. Occasionally there is more subterfuge. When a Danish TV crew was permitted to make a film on life in East Germany on the implicit understanding that they would not then sell it to the West Germans, the Ost-West men just filmed the Danish program off the screen and used it anyway.

The West Germans have no qualms at such open picture stealing. "Occasionally the East German broadcaster's lawyer writes and accuses us of piracy," admitted an Ost-West editor in Hamburg, "but we just write back and say 'You do the same thing.' "

While West and East German television snipe at one another over the wall and pirate each other's pictures, the Austrians in Vienna normally have a more formal relationship with their neighboring communist television services. Vienna is the official coordinating center hooking together Eurovision with the Intervision network centered on Prague. Every morning, for instance, the list of news stories from Eastern Europe on which the Intervision countries can offer film that day is relayed down from Prague through the Eurovision coordinator at ORF in Vienna to Eurovision headquarters in Geneva. Then in late afternoon, ORF videotapes the Intervision film over the circuit from Prague and feeds it to all Eurovision members. Similarly, news and sports from the West are routed through Vienna to Prague and into the Intervision network stretching from East Berlin to Vladivostok.

This regular liaison between Vienna and Prague, which began in September 1965, enabled news editors and technicians in both cities to establish a good working relationship, which paid an unexpected dividend in August 1968. The Russian invasion of Czechoslovakia that month to snuff out the Czech spring suddenly transformed their daily link into the last precious lifeline of Czech freedom.

The pictures of Russian tanks rolling into Prague during those summer days of August 1968 must rank as one of the most moving events yet recorded in television's short history. This was the first invasion ever to be seen as it happened in living rooms around the world.

That remarkable coverage was achieved through the cool cooperation of a handful of Czech and Austrian producers and engineers. Long before the Russians moved in there was an informal understanding between the two sides that in an emergency, if normal circuits were cut out, ORF would have only to direct its antennae to certain prearranged locations in Czechoslovakia to pick up pictures from mobile transmitters. "All we had to do when the invasion started was to push the button," said an Austrian engineer. "We knew where the secret Czech transmitters would be from hour to hour."

Dodging down the side roads with their mobile transmitting flotilla, the Czechs stayed one jump ahead of the invaders, while their cameramen, covering the scene in Prague and other cities, raced with their film to constantly changing rendezvous. Their call sign was "Free Television Station of Prague." The Austrians, having locked onto the clandestine signals, kept on monitoring them, even after one or two mobile units went off the air abruptly with a quick warning from a technician: "We have to give up now, goodbye." On one occasion the Czechs actually left the camera on in a small town studio after their departure, so that the Russians moved in and took over the studio without realizing they were on television.

As the Russians gradually eliminated transmitter after transmitter, Czech and Austrian cameramen kept the film coming by driving to the border and smuggling their film through the checkpoint. In seven days in August 1968 Austrian television relayed, through the Eurovision network and by satellite to the United States and Japan, almost ten hours' coverage of the invasion. And those same pictures, of course, were seen by millions in Czechoslovakia, Hungary, and East Germany, who had only to tune to their Western station to see the whole invasion. As Horst

Jancik, the Eurovision coordinator in Vienna, said, "We screened every cough we could get from Czechoslovakia. I don't know if it helped the Czechs, but it was something we had to do."

That week all eyes were on Czechoslovakia. Normally, however, it is the Czechs and the Hungarians who gain a wider view of the world by watching Austrian television's two channels. Many Yugoslavs also look in but, since their own television service is closely allied to the Eurovision network of Western Europe anyway—and carries many American and British series—the appeal of the alternative Austrian channels is much less. For the others, however, ORF, Vienna, is a precious glimpse of the West. In Czechoslovakia, Prague itself is on the fringe of reception, but the large cities of Bratislava and Brno enjoy good pictures. In Bratislava so many aerials tuned to Vienna have proliferated on the rooftops that they are known locally as "the Vienna woods." The Austrian signal even radiates, in good conditions, as far as Budapest. "We are high on the eastern end of the Alps, on the roof of Central Europe," Alfons Dalma, the chief editor of ORF, said in Vienna, "so our pictures are carried great distances. Reception is possible even one hundred and fifty miles beyond our borders. "It's quite startling to be stopped on the streets in Prague or Budapest by strangers who say, 'You're Dalma. Thank you for your programs.' We are a major source of news for these people."

Since many of these viewers behind the Iron Curtain speak some German, they have little difficulty in following programs, and they learn the schedules by purchasing the Austrian communist daily paper, which is permitted to circulate in Eastern Europe.

What they see is a cross section of the best and worst of Western television, ranging from concerts by the Vienna Philharmonic to the local *What's My Line?* and *Lassie.* The Austrians, unlike the West Berliners, are not constantly trying to trim their programs to the tastes of their external viewers; this is Austrian television for the Austrians. Actually, since Austria is a small nation, ORF has to rely on importing 40 percent of its programs. They work closely with the second German network, ZDF, with whom they mounted sixty coproductions in 1971. Some shows, like the popular German crime detection series *File on Case XY . . . Unsolved,* go out simultaneously in West Germany and Austria. These mingle with American and British imports—*The Man from U.N.C.L.E., Daktari, The Virginian,* and *The Avengers.*

"We are the showcase for the Western world," said the television commentator Hugo Portisch. "We notice time and again that Poles, Bulgarians, or Russians, who cannot see Western television, are far more surprised by the capitalist scene when they come to Vienna than the Czechs or Hungarians, who can. The visual impact of watching the ordinary day-by-day television of another country is enormous—much more than listening, for example, to the Voice of America Radio, which everyone knows is propaganda. The real advantage here is that the Czechs and the Hungarians see the programs we make for our own people. They see all the arguments in our current affairs programs and documentaries."

Not that Austrian television's position as a show window displaying the capitalist line to communist countries nearby does not earn it some special favors in the West. When I was in Vienna, Hugo Portisch and Sepp Riff, one of the best-known cameramen in Austria, had just returned from the United States, where they had made a documentary, *Missiles for Peace,* about the American missile defense systems. The documentary was to be shown to coincide with the SALT disarmament talks in Vienna. The Austrian team had obtained special White House permission to film inside the Minuteman rocket silos in the United States— the first foreigners ever permitted to shoot there. The Americans doubtless felt that the documentary was an excellent way of showing millions in Eastern Europe their side of the arms race.

Over the border the Czech and Hungarian authorities regard these Austrian incursions with mixed feelings. For several years the Czechs were officially forbidden to watch Austrian television, but everyone did anyway. "The problem was that a good aerial was necessary," a Czech broadcaster told me. "If you went to your local TV repairman he would say, 'I cannot put it up for you because the state forbids it and I work for the state.' Then he might add, 'But I stop working for the state at five o'clock and if you like I'll do it for you afterward.' " The formal prohibition was finally withdrawn in early 1968 as part of the Czech spring.

How much Austrian television influenced that spring is hard to say. Some Austrian television commentators believe that daily viewing of their channels helped to stimulate a more refreshing climate in Prague. Certainly Jiri Pelikan, the lively director general of Czech television from 1963 to 1968, who contributed so much to the liberalizing of television there, occasionally invoked the ease with which Austrian television could be seen in Czechoslovakia as a bargaining point in winning some of his battles. One of his difficulties, Pelikan told me afterward, was getting the necessary foreign exchange from the government so that he could buy from Eurovision coverage of important soccer matches in Western Europe. The minister in charge of broadcasting was always reluctant to allocate the hard currency. Pelikan would threaten, "I shall announce to our audience that we cannot show the game as we are not given the foreign exchange. You know that every Czech will then watch it on Austrian television. You are making football a political issue." Faced with this mild blackmail the minister often relented.

Any impact, however, was short-lived. Pelikan was replaced after the Russian intervention and now lives in exile in Rome. Several distinguished television writers and commentators are in prison. The Russians made quite clear in reimposing their will on the Czechs in 1968 that "priority is to be given to control over the mass media, which must serve the cause of socialism. It is agreed that the mass media shall discontinue antisocialist pronouncements." So Czech television is back in a new dark age. The news, which was so frank for a few months in 1968, is now once again a stiff statement of the official party line. What has not been curbed is the Austrian television signal still going through to the "Vienna woods" on Czech rooftops. Those tall aerials are a reminder of how transparent the Iron Curtain has remained.

THE ARAB
WORLD AND
ISRAEL

16

The Search for
Unity

On a summer night in Beirut a little astute fiddling with the tuning of a television set conjures up the programs of no fewer than five nations, spanning between them the whole confused spectrum of Middle East politics. Quite apart from Beirut's own three channels, it is possible to get Syrian television from Damascus, Jordanian television from Amman, Egyptian television from Cairo, and, of course, Israeli television from Tel Aviv. This mosaic out of the Arabian night is made possible by a phenomenon known as "tunneling" or "ducting," which occurs at that end of the Mediterranean in the summer. The television signal, instead of radiating out into space as usual, is trapped by certain atmospheric conditions so that it "tunnels" along close to the earth over great distances. The Cairo signal, for instance, comes in quite strong to Beirut, almost five hundred miles away. The frontier-hopping thus achieved has enhanced television's role as a propaganda weapon, not only within the Arab world itself, but in the Arab-Israeli conflict. Both in Jordan and in Israel, television programing is dominated by the desire to outwit the rival station over the border. The Jordanians study Israel's schedule before making up their program patterns; the Israelis in turn try to get their own back by putting on popular programs in Arabic to conflict with the news on Jordanian television. Paradoxically, both sides have relied heavily on American advisers in establishing their television services.

No one makes any secret of the fact that television is there primarily as a propaganda weapon. "Jordanian television was set up purely as a political tool," admitted one of the Americans closely involved in the establishment of the Amman station. "The idea was to win a large audience both in Jordan and in Israel with popular programs and then slip the propaganda in between—the sugar-coated pill." The station even came equipped with a special helicopter landing pad, so that King Hussein could always arrive in an emergency and be seen instantly over the air. In Cairo Egyptian broadcasters were equally frank. "In Arab nations television is the sure way to rule people," said one of the directors of the United Arab Republic's television service. "This is how the people get to know and love their leader. Everywhere I go in the Arab world I tell the rulers, 'Learn how to be loved by your people through that marvelous machine.' Nasser himself," he went on to point out, "was not really known by our people until we had television. Before that they had only *heard* him"—he twigged his ear—"on radio, but after 1960 everyone *saw* him." The television coverage was meticulously prepared. Cameramen had precise written instructions on how to film the president if he was making a speech. "We showed him full face, concentrating on his eyes," one of the men who drafted the rules told me. "If he mopped his brow or coughed that was cut out. Everything was done to give him dignity."

The lesson has not been lost on other Arab leaders. As television has spread throughout the Arab world, from Morocco, on the shores of the Atlantic, to tiny sheikhdoms like Qatar and Abu Dhabi on the Arabian Gulf, it has been carefully installed under the wing of the Ministry of Information (the one exception is Lebanon, which has private commercial stations). In countries like Iraq, television has become a regular political weapon to demonstrate the realities of power. The Iraqi leader General Kassem was actually shot in the television station in Bagdad in 1963 and the cameras turned on his body and those of his colleagues. Since then the director general of Iraqi television has made something of a specialty of conducting "spy confessions" on the screen—a macabre *This Is Your Life* in which hapless prisoners confess their misdeeds. In the autumn of 1970, after fourteen Iranian soldiers were caught in Iraq during a border clash, they were paraded before the cameras to confess their guilt as the television commentators intoned, "Inevitable death awaits all those who seek to enter Iraq illegally."

Syria and the Sudan have used the same technique to drive home to the viewing public the success of a political coup. After the military takeover in the Sudan in the summer of 1969, extra television sets were distributed to group viewing centers so that the public could watch live coverage of a "people's tribunal" set up to impeach the rulers of the previous regime.

Television is not always so grim. From day to day there is the conventional round of Western and Arabic popular programs. In Cairo you can take your choice of *The Virginian, The Addams Family, The Avengers,* and *The Fugitive,* all with Arabic subtitles (dubbing is too expensive); in Amman *Perry Mason, The Saint, Marcus Welby, M.D.,* and *Ben Casey* are all active. But most Arab nations—and Israel, whose television must be considered in the same context—are placing increasing emphasis on television as an educational tool not just for schools, but for improving agriculture, health, and hygiene. A prospectus for Sudan television even envisages "programs transmitted for social change, such as the abolition of harmful social traditions, superstition, sorcery, and the combating of tribal and minority squabbles."

"In an underdeveloped country we must make the maximum use of television in all forms of education," said Sad Ladib, the director of programs for U.A.R. television. "We propose, during the next two or three years, to turn our second channel over completely to education for schools during the day and for adults in the evening."

The Egyptians have long been the pace setters for television in the Arab world. President Nasser realized the potential value of the medium in molding the Egyptians into a strong, united nation in the late 1950s and, in one of the first agreements signed with the United States after John Foster Dulles refused to provide funds for the Aswan Dam, approved the Radio Corporation of America's installing a television network in Egypt. So while the Russians helped with the Aswan Dam, the Americans provided television. Since the work went ahead at the time of Egypt's abortive union with Syria, RCA also installed television in Damascus as part of the same deal.

The Egyptian installation was on a grand scale. The facilities are quite unequaled anywhere in the Arab world today; indeed, few other nations anywhere have quite so much apparatus. Eleven television studios are housed in a vast, circular building crowned by a twenty-ight-story tower on the banks of the Nile. The largest studio is the size of a full-scale theater and is equipped with a revolving stage and five cameras; even the most sophisticated television stations in Britain, West Germany, and Japan don't have anything much bigger. No less than 2,500 program staff and 1,000 engineers are required to run this establishment—rather more people, as far as I can make out, than are employed in broadcasting by all the other Arab nations put together. Almost half the staff are women, who seem to be treated equally with men on the television scene: they direct programs, read the news, and even do the sports reporting. I watched a half-hour sports review in which a woman interviewer happily questioned footballers and basketball players. And a half-hour weekly program on architecture, painting, and sculpture has been written and directed for many years by the wife of one of the chief television news editors.

Ambitiously, the Egyptians pitched in almost from the beginning with three television channels, putting on programs for a total of twenty-four hours every day. The first channel, covering virtually the whole country, concentrated on popular entertainment, news, and sports. The second channel, reaching Cairo and the Nile Delta (in fact, the majority of the set-owning population), carried minority programs and imported serials, while the third channel, just for Cairo, was given over entirely to foreign programs—mainly British and American—with news in English and French. The third channel, aimed at the diplomatic community, European expatriates, and tourists, was clearly something of a luxury, but as long as President Nasser lived it was kept on. The broadcasters I talked with all said they felt it was too much of an indulgence for a relatively poor country and that it was imposed on them "from above." Shortly after President Nasser died in 1970 the third channel stopped broadcasting; no one expects it to restart.

The two remaining channels, however, are on the air for seven hours each a day, with some 60 percent of the programs locally produced. Imported entertainment programs have always come primarily from Britain and America, but Egypt's increasing involvement with the Soviet Union has naturally been reflected in more programs from communist countries. During my stay in Cairo, you could take your choice of a Bulgarian series about a Resistance hero, a Czech documentary on industrial safety (a very solid program), and Hungarian ballet. Although the Egyptians are proud of producing a high proportion of their own programs, they choose to put on a wide selection of imported shows. "Cairo has always been a cosmopolitan city," said Sad Ladib, the director of programs. "We believe in taking programs from all over the world."

There is no reliable audience research to demonstrate whether home-grown or foreign programs are the most popular, but the Egyptians can draw on the best pool of talent in the whole Arab world. Small television stations starting out in Kuwait, Saudi Arabia, and the Sudan have had virtually no tradition of acting or variety entertainment to build on. Cairo, however, has always been the artistic and film capital of the Arab world, and television has benefited accordingly. "We are the Hollywood of the Middle East," said an Egyptian producer proudly.

Along with variety shows featuring the best Arab entertainers, Egyptian television has created everything from detective serials to soap operas. The most popular when I was there was about the foibles of an aging Cairo schoolteacher and his family, who had an endless succession of visits from their relatives living in remote villages of the Nile Delta. These productions are ideal, not only for home consumption but for television stations in other Arab countries, and Egyptian entertainment can be seen nightly on screens from Rabat to Khartoum and Algiers to Aden. Egypt's ability to supply programs is especially important for nations like Syria, which, for political reasons, decline to take the normal package shows from Britain or America.

The Egyptians, understandably, are delighted at this state of affairs and use it to propagate their views widely. They are skilled at playing off one nation against another. If Kuwait, for instance, declines to take one of their programs, then they offer it free to Iraqi television for its station at Basra, which can be received clearly by everyone with a set in Kuwait. If it proves popular, the Kuwaitis come along after a while and agree to run the show, as they are not anxious for their own viewers to make a habit of watching Iraqi television. Nevertheless, several Arab nations, especially Saudi Arabia and the small sheikhdoms on the Arabian Gulf, are notably reluctant to take too many Egyptian programs because of the inevitable indoctrination slipped into them. Saudi Arabia refuses categorically to take any Egyptian productions.

But, propaganda aside, the Egyptians are trying to use television to best effect in overcoming problems of illiteracy and disease in their own country. Their television service, to its great credit, has developed school, health, and agriculture programs on its own initiative, often in the face of indifference or complete lack of cooperation from the responsible ministries. Although schools have sometimes refused to help in discussing curricula, the broadcasters have gone ahead anyway in putting out two hours of secondary school level language, physics, and mathematics programs daily. In 1968, U.A.R. television embarked on a special project to overcome illiteracy by organizing some three hundred viewing groups nationwide to watch a nine-month reading course. The experiment had mixed success because of the administrative problems involved and the lack of set maintenance, but at least the attempt was made. Now, in the seventies, senior Egyptian broadcasters are determined to build on this past experience in gradually shifting their second channel over entirely to education.

The difficulty, however, is that after more than a decade television in Egypt is still not a truly mass medium. Despite the early encouragement given it by Nasser and attempts to establish community viewing centers, television is essentially for the middle and upper class—who are probably literate anyway. There are only 600,000 sets for a nation of 34 million people; for the majority a television set is still too expensive. Moreover, only one third of the villages have electricity, so that television is often almost unknown outside the towns. "Television here isn't really serving the people," said Hamdy Kandil, one of Egypt's best-known television commentators and managing director of the Arab States Broadcasting Union. "The *fellahin*—the peasant—doesn't see it."

But that is not to decry Cairo's position as the most influential television center in the Arab world. No other Arab nation can match either its program output or its relative wealth; U.A.R. television has a budget of around $10 million a year, sustained by an annual license fee of $15 and a limited number of commercials which yield about $1 million a year. Most other Arab countries have to get by with less than $1 million a year from all sources.

The sole challenge to Cairo comes from Lebanon, where Beirut has developed as a rival production center for pan-Arabic programs. Lebanon has the only purely commercial television in the region, which has been established and run with considerable help from outside. There are two stations: Compagnie Libanaise de Television (CLT), which has extensive French backing, and Tele-Orient, which is partly owned and managed by the London-based Thomson Television International (TTI). CLT operates two channels, one broadcasting in French, English and Arabic, the other exclusively in French. And it works hard to maintain the French influence in Lebanon. Indeed, the French-language channel is almost an arm of France's own ORTF; it receives seven hours of programs free from ORTF each week, and no commercials are permitted to interrupt them. CLT's other channel shares many of its programs with Tele-Orient, under an arrangement of joint networking and combined advertising sales, which came about when the two companies decided there simply was not enough advertising in Lebanon to sustain two fully competing stations. The total commercial revenue available for all three channels is a mere $2.5 million a year, and all sales are coordinated through a single company, Advision. This cooperation, however, has not prevented Tele-Orient from developing a highly profitable sideline of its own in syndicating Arabic programs to many countries. Tele-Orient's success arises partly because Beirut is a cosmopolitan city that naturally attracts entertainers to its casinos and nightclubs, but more because, unlike the U.A.R., its programs are not trying to put over a political line. As a commercial station, Tele-Orient is concerned with popular entertainment for mass audiences; the resulting programs are welcomed by other Arab television stations that are always wary of the message infiltrated by the Egyptians. "We are apolitical," said Harold Jamieson, Tele-Orient's general manager, "and we've succeeded in selling our programs to every Arab country. This year [1971] we'll earn about $600,000 through sales."

Tele-Orient's programs are carefully conceived to avoid giving any offense in Arab countries, particularly Saudi Arabia, which adopt a high moral tone toward sex or violence. The Saudi Arabians have taken to television very slowly. When their stations in Riyadh and Jeddah were first set up by NBC International, they were most reluctant for women to appear on the screen—even wearing a veil. But, as the country had absolutely no acting or entertainment tradition to fall back on for programs, it had to import them. That has meant slowly adopting a more tolerant attitude to women. They can now be seen without the veil, but they must be very correctly dressed at all times—miniskirts, for instance, are forbidden. Adultery is frowned on, as is stealing or any kind of violence, unless the culprit is seen to be punished.

Tele-Orient has taken all this into account and, consequently, has become a major source of programs for Saudi Arabian television. The most widely distributed are variety shows featuring the top Arab singers like Sabah, but Tele-Orient tackles anything from situation comedies to a series on the lives of the great Arab philosophers. Operating from one very cramped studio, into which they somehow squeeze half a dozen sets at once, they can turn out a half-hour drama in a day at a cost of about $1,500. These productions may not be very polished or sophisticated but they far outrate imported programs with the local audience. Tele-Orient, for example, put a comedy show in Arabic against *Bonanza* (with Arabic subtitles) on CLT on Monday evenings and got more than double the audience.

Since they pay their way by advertising, both the Beirut stations concentrate heavily on popular programs and, apart from CLT's specialist French channel, have little time for education or minority programs. Although they are the only television outlets in the Middle East not under the direct control of the local Ministry of Information, they tread warily to avoid upsetting the Lebanese government. From time to time direct censorship is imposed, but normally the stations censor themselves. "We don't try to fight the horses," said one executive candidly.

Beirut's location enables its programs to be seen regularly—even without that summer ducting phenomenon—in Syria, Jordan, and Israel. The sales promotion for the stations even touts the fact that advertisers can be sure of reaching 135,000 homes in "Palestine." But the Lebanese stations have never been involved in the intense rivalry that exists between the stations in Jordan and Israel.

Jordan's television station, just outside Amman, which was completed at a cost of over $1 million in 1968, is regarded as one of the best equipped in the Arab world. The studio facilities were designed to enable the Jordanians to make plenty of local programs both for viewers in Jordan itself and in Israel. Originally, the Jordanians had invited the BBC to help them in the organization of the station and training of staff, but the British lost out to the powerful persuasions of Radio Television International (RTV), a New York-based organization that has long specialized in advising on the establishment of radio and television in developing countries.

The Jordanians and their American advisers hoped that the station would be an important propaganda weapon, but events have somehow blunted its thrust. To begin with, during the Six Day War a fine new television mast and transmitter that the Jordanians were about to install in Jerusalem fell into Israeli hands. Fortunately for the Israelis, the plans on how to erect it were packed in the captured crates of equipment and in no time at all the Israelis had it all assembled and hooked into their own television service.

After the war, the delicate situation in Jordan between King Hussein and the Palestinian guerrillas also made the station tread carefully. It played safe with *I Love Lucy, Ben Casey, The Fugitive,* and *Perry Mason* rather than tackle controversial local shows.

However, they did make a remarkably realistic twenty-six-part drama series about the guerrillas. Several of the actors were truly members of the fedayeen and everyone, quite naturally, used live ammunition. Indeed, it was often hard to discern whether skirmishes were for television or for training. One morning an American adviser driving out of Amman to the television station suddenly came upon a guerrilla roadblock; putting his foot down, he drove through it and fled at full speed. The guerrillas came tearing after him in a Land-Rover, gesticulating wildly. They caught up with him as he got to the television station and surrounded his car. It turned out to be the "actors" who were trying to stop him on the road because they needed a special microphone he was carrying. The only trouble with the series was that, by the time it was finished, King Hussein had begun his drive against the guerrillas' challenge to his authority and the program could not be shown. Other Arab countries also showed remarkable reluctance to buy it.

The high level of American series sustaining Jordanian television had one intriguing side effect on Israeli television. Many Israeli viewers began to tune in to Amman to catch the latest American shows. Israeli television, which began originally as a purely educational service and only eased reluctantly into general programs, had to respond with more popular programs.

The Israelis, in fact, have had quite a time trying to dodge programs from Arab countries. Apart from the strong Jordanian signal, the ducting in summer means that Egyptian television can be received in Tel Aviv. In an attempt to avoid these foreign incursions the Israelis decided in 1970 to switch over to UHF television (Jordan, Egypt, and Lebanon are VHF). At the same time, however, they try hard to seduce large Arab audiences with their own programing. Since 1969, they have put on two hours of popular shows in Arabic early each evening aimed not only at Arabs still living in Israel, but at refugees who fled from the west bank of the River Jordan in 1967, and at Jordanians themselves. From time to time they even resort to showing old Egyptian films to woo the Arab audience.

Israeli television itself, however, has had a somewhat checkered career. The whole notion of television was firmly rejected until the mid-1960s; Ben-Gurion was implacably opposed to it as long as he was prime minister since he felt that Israel had to give priority to more important tasks. Finally, an Instructional Television Center under the Ministry of Education began daytime programing in 1966. The attraction of entertainment, however, that could be picked up from Jordan, Lebanon, Egypt, and even Cyprus, eventually forced Israel to respond with some popular programs. The Israel Broadcasting Authority started general programing in the summer of 1969 and extended this to a daily service later that year. There was great argument for a while on whether television could broadcast on the eve of the Sabbath. The government tried to prevent it, but an enterprising private citizen took the issue to the Supreme Court, which ruled in favor of television on the Sabbath eve. The national network is now given over to the Instructional Television Center from 8:00 in the morning until 6:00 in the evening and to the Israel Broadcasting Authority from then until 11:00 at night. But progress has been erratic. One director of television departed in the summer of 1970 and his successor lasted barely eight months. At the same time, a proposal to introduce commercials to help out the service's minuscule budget was vetoed at the very last minute by the Israeli Prime Minister, Mrs. Golda Meir, on the grounds that advertising on TV would "foster conspicuous consumption." "Our television," conceded an Israeli journalist, "is constantly in a rather precarious state."

The development of television in Israel has, nevertheless, caused great debate in all the Arab countries. The Arab League considered the possibility of jamming the Israeli signal, but ruled it out as technically impractical. They decided, instead, that all Arab countries should help Jordan with contributions of free programs. Most Arab countries, however, chose to ignore developments in Israel in their own programing. The one exception is Kuwait, which regularly puts out a report on the Israeli scene: *Know Your Enemy.*

Kuwait television is among the most advanced in the Middle East, for the simple reason that the country is so small it can be blanketed with one transmitter, while the profits accruing from oil comfortably sustain the high costs. Moreover, the majority of the population can afford a set; Kuwait has almost 100,000 television sets—one for every five people, compared to one for every fifty people in Egypt, or one for every three hundred in the Sudan. Originally, Kuwait got television through the imagination of the local RCA salesman and without the official approval of the ruling sheikhs. The RCA man was anxious to sell TV sets; there was no TV, so he just went ahead and started his own station using imported programs. Later the government took over. Soon two modern studios were built and by 1970 Kuwait was putting on seven hours of TV a day with more than half the programs locally produced. Kuwait was also the first Arab country to install an earth station, enabling it to pick up live pictures, from the Indian Ocean satellite, of moonwalks and sports events. Most other Arab nations still have to wait to receive film a day or two later. "Kuwait television," said an Egyptian television executive admiringly, "is very sophisticated."

It will become more so. Plans were going ahead in 1971 on a $35 million project to give Kuwait three color television channels—one with popular programs, one cultural, and the third educational. Every school in Kuwait is being equipped with a special room for audiovisual teaching, complete with television set and cassette player.

Kuwait television has also branched out in the Arabian Gulf in managing the station at Dubai, the little sheikhdom in the Trucial States, which is one of the world's great gold- and watch-smuggling centers. To match Kuwait and Dubai, the other sheikhdoms along the gulf have also installed television. Previously, the only station along the gulf had been run by an American oil company at Dhahran for its employees, and several sheikhs had installed enormous antennae to pluck *Bonanza,* like a mirage, out of the desert air. Abu Dhabi, Bahrein, and Qatar all had television by 1971, while Oman, finally emerging from centuries of feudal rule after a coup in 1970, was busy negotiating for a station. With virtually no local talent to draw on initially (Qatar has a population of only 80,000), these stations inevitably run almost solely imported programs from America, Cairo, and Beirut. There is a marked preference for Beirut's Arabic output along the gulf, because the station managers fear the disguised propaganda in the most innocent-seeming Egyptian shows.

The Egyptians, of course, are not alone in seeking to use television to promote their cause. The Americans, the French, the British, and the Japanese are always anxious to provide both technical and program advisers to fledgling television stations in any developing country of Asia or Africa. Having a hand in television is a very good way of maintaining a sphere of influence. Embassies of many nations are always delighted to dole out free "tourist" and other films to television stations that cannot afford to buy all their programs on the open market. The French are particularly adroit at this; they seek to maintain a sphere of influence in television in all their former colonies. We have noted already ORTF's assistance to the French-language channel in Beirut; equal ties are established along the North African coast with Morocco, Algeria, and Tunisia. These countries all take a high proportion of their imported programs from France. Educational television in Tunisia, for instance, has been coordinated and paid for by the French. And a special division within ORTF devotes itself to studying their requirements. They judiciously select programs to match the spirit of the regime. "If we have a promonarchy program we try to sell it to Morocco," said ORTF's liaison man with North Africa. "If it's anti-monarchy we try Algeria."

These North African countries also have close links with the European Broadcasting Union and are consequently much more integrated into the European television scene than most of the Arab world. Morocco is hooked into the Eurovision network across the Straits of Gibraltar, Algeria is linked via Majorca and Barcelona, while Tunisia is connected through Sicily. This enables them not only to take all Eurovision programs live but to participate, if they wish, in the Eurovision news exchange. Tunisia, for instance, joins the European story conference every morning and takes almost all the news items offered. These three Arab countries also tried a limited live program exchange among themselves for a month at the end of 1970.

The real breakthrough, however, will be to link these North African countries, at the western end of the Mediterranean, with Libya, Egypt, and beyond. For potentially, if individual political differences can be overcome, there is a natural network to be developed embracing all 120 million Arabic-speaking people from the Atlantic to the Arabian Gulf. Indeed, along with the Spanish-speaking countries of South America, the Arab world represents an ideal basis for interchange of programs between nations with a common language and culture.

This is one of the targets of the Arab States Broadcasting Union (ASBU), which was established in Cairo in 1969. Within two years, all the major Arab nations, except Morocco and Tunisia, had joined this newest of the broadcasting unions. Although European broadcasters are inclined to view the union as a purely political association to further the Arab cause, it undoubtedly makes considerable broadcasting sense. Previously, the Arab countries of North Africa had close associations with the EBU, while Egypt and most other Arab nations of Asia belonged—and still do—to the Asian Broadcasting Union. Yet in practical terms the Egyptians, for example, have little common interest with broadcasters in Japan, New Zealand, or the Philippines, who also subscribe to the ABU. An Arab States Broadcasting Union, therefore, is a logical development. The main distinction between the new ASBU and the EBU—or the ABU —is that the ASBU is clearly an intergovernmental organization, while the others pride themselves on being associations of broadcasters. The ASBU makes no secret of its political links. "We are created within the framework of the Arab League," said Hamdy Kandil, the managing director of the ASBU in Cairo. "Of course we are under the influence of governments —but you show me broadcasters who are not in some way. We are a natural union sharing a common religion and language." The union states that one of its main tasks is "making known the nature, aims, and aspirations of the Arab nation and carrying out the objectives of the League of Arab States charter." But together with this political goal, the union proposes not only to encourage the interchange of programs between Arab countries but to coordinate all their requirements in the same way that the EBU handles its members' needs at major news or sporting events. The ASBU plans to open an office in Beirut for the joint purchasing and marketing of programs and hopes to establish an Arab Television News Agency. Their most ambitious project, looking ahead five or six years to the late 1970s, is for a communications satellite for the Arab nations that could be used primarily for educational television. A preliminary report, prepared by UNESCO and the International Telecommunications Union in 1971, stated that complete television coverage of several Arab nations, notably the Sudan, Saudi Arabia, and Algeria, would be prohibitively expensive by conventional microwave networks; an Arab satellite could do the job.

But the real necessity before any firm satellite plans are made is for all the Arab countries to agree on a strong commitment to educational television. At the moment, as the UNESCO-ITU report pointed out, existing television facilities are being underused for educational television. Only when they are used to capacity, and all the Arab countries agree to accept common educational programs, can a satellite really be worthwhile. The Egyptians, naturally, are great campaigners for the satellite and the ASBU for, as major producers of television programs, they stand to gain most. But for that very reason, the essential agreement may be hard to achieve. As Tele-Orient in Beirut has shown so clearly, what most Arab nations really want to pick up from anyone else is nice, innocuous entertainment; they prefer to do the propaganda themselves.

ASIA

17

Waste Land into Fertile

A few miles out into the country beyond New Delhi our driver spun the jeep off the road down a narrow dirt track. For a while we bumped along past fields ghostly in the full moon and then, by a low pile of haystacks, turned into a walled farmyard. Half a dozen black Indian buffalo were dozing in one corner. We parked by them and stepped out across the dusty compound toward a group of perhaps twenty men sitting or squatting on the ground before a twenty-three-inch TV set in a small open porch in front of the farmhouse. The men were wrapped in blankets to ward off the chill of the December evening. One of them took occasional satisfying pulls at the long stem of a hookah, another was busy writing notes in an exercise book. The men belonged to the teleclub of the village of Chattarpur and they were all engrossed in the "prime time" show— *Krishi Darshan,* a half-hour agriculture lesson. The program, which goes on from 7:30 to 8:00 three nights a week, demonstrates the scientific techniques of farming and encourages farmers to make the best use of fertilizers and insecticides. Almost every farmer in Chattarpur turns up to watch. Tonight the program began with a short film about a woman who was running her own poultry farm near Delhi, went on to explain the latest bank credit facilities available for farmers and finally turned to the spraying of sugar cane with insecticides. Everyone watched with deep satisfaction.

"We relate these agricultural programs exactly to the farming calendar," said the television producer from All India Radio, who had guided me to the village. "If it's sugar cane planting time, then our program shows exactly how it should be planted and protected from disease."

The village headman, in whose farmyard this community TV watching took place, told me how much the programs really helped the farmers in the village. "It has changed all our farming," he said. "I used to plant one crop a year, now I find I can take three crops a year off my land. We no longer plant our wheat three or four inches deep; television has shown us to plant it only one inch into the soil. We had heard these things on the radio, but that was only sounds; on television we see exactly the best way to plough or to spray insecticides."

For these farmers in Chattarpur and in eighty other villages near New Delhi that also have teleclubs, television, for once, is not a wasteland, but a medium that can help transform waste into fertile land. Although television in India is still in its infancy, its potential for educating a nation, not only to read and write, but in agricultural skills, social welfare and family planning, is already being explored.

By day All India Radio's television service puts on two hours of school programs, which are seen by 20,000 children in 400 schools around New Delhi; in the evening most of its three hours of programs from 6:30 until 9:30 are devoted to education or information, with the occasional lightweight English film. These initial experiments, limited to the New Delhi area, have been painfully slow; there has been little expansion in almost ten years, but India's Prime Minister, Indira Gandhi, is finally beginning to encourage television as one possible way of helping to solve the country's massive problems of illiteracy and poverty. Before becoming Prime Minister she was Minister of Information, where her portfolio included All India Radio. The firsthand experience gained there convinced her that television must be developed. Progress is still tentative. Until 1971, All India Radio's television service reached only a twenty-mile radius around the capital of New Delhi. There were a mere 20,000 privately owned television sets plus a few hundred others at village tele-clubs and in schools—in a nation of 600 million people. More recently stations have opened at Bombay and Srinagar, while others are planned for Madras, Calcutta and Lucknow. Yet it will be a couple of decades before television in India becomes the mass medium it is in Europe, America and Japan. The simple cost of the television set is still at least two months' salary for many upper-middle-class people; for the millions of India's poor it is more than their income for a year.

The possible shortcut to television as a method of mass education in India is a satellite, beaming pictures directly down to 5,000 community receivers scattered in villages throughout the subcontinent. The project is a joint venture between the Indian Atomic Energy Authority and NASA, in the United States, under which NASA will launch two Application Technology Satellites (ATS) during the early seventies, each equipped with a VHF-FM transmitter capable of relaying one television and two radio channels. The Indians will provide all the programs, transmitting them up to the satellites from a ground station the Atomic Energy Authority is building at Ahmedabad; the satellites will bounce the pictures back to the community receivers scattered in villages throughout India.

This experiment, which was initiated by Dr. Vikram Sarabai, the director of India's Atomic Energy Authority, will be a crucial test of how effective satellites can be, not only in India, but throughout the developing countries, both in educating villagers when no integrated school system exists and also for building a national identity.

"We hope that by providing both entertainment and education of a high standard on television we can produce a genuine improvement in rural life," Dr. Sarabai explained, "and that way we may reduce the attraction of migration to our overcrowded cities. The potentials are truly staggering for improving India's agriculture, wiping out illiteracy and uniting isolated villages."

This satellite project could switch on television in Asia. With the very notable exception of Japan, it does not yet exist there as a mass medium; there are probably more people who have never seen it than those who have. Indeed, in all Asia, discounting Japan, there is only one television set for every five hundred people, compared with one for every 2.5 people in the United States. Even when television does become a mass medium, it is likely to fulfill an educational rather than an entertainment role throughout most of Asia. In India, Malaysia, Singapore and Iran this is already the priority.

Singapore has what is widely regarded as one of the best educational television systems in the world, with a high degree of coordination between the television teachers and the schools. Programs are specifically tailored to meet weak points in the conventional syllabus. And in Iran the government actually bought out, in 1969, the existing commercial television network, which had been run for several years by the family holding the local Pepsi-Cola bottling concession; it is now extending the coverage to provide primarily an educational service throughout Iran.

Asian television is not, of course, entirely harnessed to the alphabet or the plough. In Bangkok you can watch *Bonanza, Mission Impossible* or *Peyton Place* with live dubbing into Thai as the story unfolds (or turn down the sound on TV and hear the English soundtrack on FM radio); in Hong Kong *The Man from U.N.C.L.E., The Flying Nun,* and *Marcus Welby, M.D.* are all speaking fluent Cantonese on the Chinese channels. *The Lucy Show* seems to be on all the time whether you are in Singapore, Karachi or Manila; *Ironside* travels just as widely, around what the trade in the Far East calls "the Sampan Circuit."

The prices paid around the Sampan Circuit for these programs often hardly justify their distribution. Malaysia, Singapore, South Korea and Taiwan, for instance, pay only $40 to $60 for a half-hour episode. Yet every country that I visited in Asia was at pains to explain at once how much less they relied on package programs nowadays; instead they are all pressing ahead with local programing, despite shoestring budgets. In Pakistan the normal expenditure on a local half-hour program is about $150 to cover all costs of writers, actors and incidental expenses. To save a little money they never have television there on Mondays. And throughout most of Asia television is still limited to four or five evening hours.

Coverage rarely extends outside the main centers of population; microwave links creating nationwide audiences do not exist (always excepting Japan). The real problem, of course, is money. Governments cannot afford to finance television services themselves; there are too few sets to make any worthwhile revenue from license fees. The only alternative, therefore, is commercial television. Sir Charles Moses, Secretary General of the Asian Broadcasting Union, believes: "Television in most Asian countries can only be financed by advertising, but that does not mean a free-for-all. I think the best combination is a public broadcasting organization earning money from a limited number of commercials. You must control the ads—don't let them control you."

Whatever the precise formula, no government in Asia these days is likely to let television develop independently; all of them are anxious to keep it strictly under their own control. In India it is part of the Ministry of Information. In Pakistan, where television began in 1964, the government has a 51 percent stake in the commercial Pakistan Television Corporation. The secretary of the Ministry of Information is chairman of the board of directors, while the managing director, the finance director and the director of program administration are all government appointees. Until 1970, when Pakistan was under the direct rule of a president nominated by the army, television simply avoided any political coverage at all. This policy was relaxed only during the elections in 1970 to allow each of the fifteen political parties equal time.

In Thailand, the public relations department of the Ministry of Information runs one commercial station and supervises the program of another, while the army has two channels of its own.

The Thai army's television station, HSTV, is unique. The chief of the programing department, Tawon Chueyprasit, is a full-fledged colonel in the signal corps, who spends his mornings on more conventional army assignments and the afternoons supervising television. Resplendent in his olive green army uniform with three gold stars on the shoulder, the colonel explained that the army originally went into television because they felt their signal corps should be fully conversant with this new medium of communications; they also thought it might be useful for training soldiers. Moreover, on maneuvers or in battle, television could give commanders a view of action right up at the front. They quickly discovered, however, that the expense of running TV was far more than the army could afford. "So," said the colonel cheerfully, "we became a commercial station." HSTV now operates one black and white and one color channel in Bangkok showing *The Andy Williams Show, Bonanza* and *The Saint* along with several rather charming local soap operas. Their most popular show is *Pipop Mujjurag,* about the King of the Hill to which all Thai souls go when they die. The news department is run, very appropriately, by army intelligence. Just to keep up its army image HSTV still tucks in one military program a month, normally explaining how to combat the communist guerrillas who are infiltrating Thailand. As the colonel said, "Everything is aimed against communist insurgence." The whole operation, apparently, is remarkably profitable so that the signal corps is one of the most popular branches of the army to join. The true profits are a well-kept military secret but, according to one officer-turned-program-executive, they have been as high as $600,000 a year. "But perhaps," he said, "you had better not write too much about the profit."

In Hong Kong the control of television by the British authorities is more subtle. The worry is not so much program content as limiting the viewers. The policy is that the programs should *not* be seen by people in Communist China just a few miles away. The delicate diplomacy of keeping this toehold on the Chinese mainland apparently dictates that the Chinese should have no grounds for complaining that their population is being bombarded with Western propaganda. "There isn't any written rule about this," said a Hong Kong broadcaster. "The government just arranges things so that our television is sealed off from China." For ten years all television in Hong Kong was closed-circuit cable.

The British company, Rediffusion, started a closed-circuit English-language commercial channel in 1957, which has developed into the world's largest cable system. Rediffusion added a Chinese channel in 1963 and by 1971 more than 110,000 Hong Kong homes were hooked directly into their cables. This closed-circuit network insured no viewers over the border in China but, in 1967, the Hong Kong authorities relaxed enough to allow the establishment of a conventional commercial television station, TVB, with English and Chinese channels; the English channel is christened Pearl, the Chinese is Jade. Although all the directors of TVB are local businessmen, NBC and Time-Life from the United States and Anglia and Thames from Britain hold shares in the station. Its transmitters, however, are very carefully positioned to give good coverage to Hong Kong itself and also limited reception in the Portuguese colony of Macao just across the Pearl River, but preclude reception within mainland China. Programs are subject to censorship in case they might give offense to China; but the censors are normally reasonably benevolent. A forthright Yorkshire Television documentary on the twenty-year struggle for China was passed without query. Local political issues are ignored by television, a decision based on the theory that Hong Kong as a British Crown Colony has no party politics. Coverage of church services is expressly banned in case they appear to be "advertising" Western religion, thus giving offense to the 3.5 million Chinese in the colony.

Just across the border in China itself, television is still recovering from the cultural revolution, which shut it down completely for many months. Not that it was a very going concern even before the Red Guards came along in 1967. Although the Central People's Television Broadcasting Station opened in Peking in 1958, growth was slow. The very size of China makes network television an expensive business, so it has developed city by city on a regional basis. The only linkup before the cultural revolution was between Peking and the nearby port of Tientsin. Elsewhere in Nanking, Wuhan, Shanghai, and Canton the programing relied on local production or "bicycled" film from one city to another. Chairman Mao could not—and still cannot—expound his thoughts to the assembled nation at once.

Chinese television studios are very primitive and reminded one visiting British broadcaster of an English church hall. Their equipment was a mélange of Russian, East German, and British cameras and lenses. And no real attempt was made to "present" programs. The technique of "mixing" pictures from several cameras in a studio was not used. Instead someone would step before one camera, announce, say, an acrobatic or juggling act, step back out of view and the artists would then move into the picture to perform.

Shortly before the cultural revolution, however, Chinese television was becoming a little more enterprising. In 1965 the Chinese signed up with Visnews, the international news film agency in London, both to take their service and to provide them with news pictures out of China. Their leading broadcasters were showing keen interest in learning more about the uses of television. The Red Guards stopped that abruptly. Television closed down throughout China, several leading broadcasters disappeared, and some have not been heard of since.

The comeback was slow. Since the cultural revolution had made all art and culture suspect, no one was sure what could be presented. The simplest and safest tactic was to show nothing. Even in 1970, by which time television was back on the air for three or four evenings a week, much of the time was taken up just showing captions of the thoughts of Chairman Mao on the screen. A British broadcaster, who visited Peking in October 1970, counted up that eighteen minutes out of a total twenty-six minutes of the main evening news bulletin one night were rolling captions of Mao's thoughts with background music of "The East Is Red."

The uncertainty as to what was permissible meant that the handful of programs known to be officially approved were repeated again and again. The schedule, therefore, differed little. The staple fare most evenings after the news at 7:00 was yet another screening of one of the "Peking operas" approved by Mao's wife. The operas, *Taking Tiger Mountain by Strategy, White-Haired Girl* and *The Red Lantern,* together with a ballet, *The Red Detachment of Women,* all glorify the communist guerrilla campaigns against the old Chinese regime and the Japanese. *The Red Lantern* tells how communist railway workers sabotaged Japanese troop trains. The operas were all shown in live performances direct from theaters. Since many theatrical groups put them on, the repetition at least had the benefit of a different cast each night.

As television regained confidence, however, the choice of programs widened. The great May Day parade in 1971, for example, was shown for five hours, with relatively elaborate coverage from five outside broadcast cameras. The pictures were then relayed direct to other cities by landline—where it existed—or by videotape to cities throughout the country. The international Ping-Pong tournament in Peking, which marked the beginning of the relaxation in China's relations with the outside world, was also shown live. A much heralded documentary, *Red Flag Canal,* reported on the building of an irrigation canal through treacherous mountain country in Honan province. Even on the evening news, Mao's thoughts gave way to world news, as Peking agreed to start taking agency news film again.

But television is clearly far from being a mass medium in China. In all some fifty cities are now reported to have television stations. Even Lhasa in Tibet is due to open a station shortly. But millions in China are still outside television's range. The easiest way to cover the whole country would undoubtedly be a domestic communications satellite, relaying pictures to community antennae.

Television's role, however, is likely to be very different from the way we know it. Sets are not owned privately; they are all in factory canteens, hotels, and other communal centers. Thus everyone can be assembled together to watch an educational program or some speech by Mao calling for greater industrial or agricultural production: an ideal captive audience. And, as television grows up in China, it is likely to be harnessed even more than in the Soviet Union to both educational and political indoctrination.

By contrast the most casual government direction of television in Asia is in the Philippines, where commercial channels have proliferated and most are losing a fortune. Manila has seven television channels all competing for a mere ten million dollars' potential advertising revenue. Profits, however, are less important than the prestige they bring to the wealthy Philippine families who own them; a television station here, as in South America, is a status symbol. Thus the most successful station, ABS-CBN, with two channels, is part of the Lopez family empire which embraces newspapers, radio stations, insurance, and even the Manila electric light company. The Elizalde family, whose fortune is based on rum, steel, and newspapers, owns Channel 11; the Soriano family added Channel 13 to their ownership of San Miguel beer, the Coca-Cola concession, and various engineering enterprises. "The result," said Almeida Lopez, the general manager of ABS-CBN, "is a disaster."

The stations are so busy fighting each other for ratings that no one has time to consider a more rational growth of television throughout the Philippines. Television is concentrated almost entirely in Manila; 320,000 of the 400,000 sets in the Philippines are in the city and its suburbs. There are a handful of regional and relay stations, but no comprehensive national plan to extend the networks in an orderly way throughout the islands. "We are so busy competing here in Manila," said Almeida Lopez, "that there's no time or money to think of expansion."

Moreover, their costs are constantly rising because viewers in the Philippines, as in every other country these days, are clamoring for locally produced shows. All top fifteen programs in the Philippine ratings are local, mostly live variety programs or talk shows. ABS-CBN, which has all the top ten programs, runs 80 percent live shows on its Channel 2. What they lack in polish is often made up for in enthusiasm and sheer local topicality.

In the early evening ABS-CBN runs a two-hour program called *Patrol,* which is really just a public bulletin board for the city of Manila. All kinds of local tidbits turn up. Insurance agents are advised that their exams have been postponed. Boy Scouts are told when and where to report for a jamboree. Payment is offered for 500 cc. of a rare type of blood urgently required to help a 14-year-old boy suffering from bone cancer; anyone who can offer a transfusion is asked to phone the studio immediately. Even photographs and descriptions of several children missing from home in the slums of Manila are given. *Patrol* calls itself "the public service program that makes a city move," and it outranks the imported *Bonanza* in the ratings.

Rather surprisingly, amid all the commercial frenzy, the Philippines also has the beginnings of one of the better educational television systems in the Far East. The development comes through the Center for Educational Television, a nonprofit educational foundation, which has backing from the Ford Foundation and the World Bank. The Center is run by a lanky Jesuit priest, Father Leo Larkin, who explained, "We have an emergency in education. Thousands of children have to be turned away from schools every year because of an acute shortage of teachers. We cannot train enough new teachers overnight, so what do we do with the sheer numbers who must be educated *now?* I am convinced that television at its best can make all the difference in a nation like the Philippines between quality education and none at all."

The priority is in elementary and secondary schools. Larkin hopes that his Center can develop eight completely new courses for these schools each year and, by repeating programs over several years, build up a total library of fifty different courses covering a major part of the school syllabus. Initially, the Center broadcast programs to schools in Manila by its own small transmitter, but Larkin has persuaded Andres Soriano, owner of commercial Channel 13, to allow his network to be used for the school programs during the day. This spreads the coverage to most of Luzon province around Manila and to four other cities where Channel 13 has affiliates. Over one hundred schools watch the programs regularly. Yet even this still leaves 80 percent of the Philippines' school population outside the range of television. The real stumbling block to further expansion is not just the absence of TV stations, but simple lack of electricity. Until electrification is extended to rural areas, television cannot follow. "I get so frustrated when I see how little coverage we actually have," said Father Larkin sadly.

For all its limitations, the Philippine experiment is setting an important precedent for television in Asia. Father Larkin finds that half his mail is requests from other Asian countries to come and advise them on how to start their own educational television. While he is always ready to help, he believes that, in the long run, it is much better for each country to devise its own educational television system tailored to the particular deficiencies of its schools. "Frankly, every single developing country ought to have its own Center for Educational Television," he said, "where the local educators could come and learn the theory of educational television and get some practical experience; then they can help their country develop its own network. I find we never get down to the nitty-gritty unless people think it out for themselves."

The interchange of ideas between Asian broadcasters is now being increasingly coordinated by the Asian Broadcasting Union, which was created in 1964 after several years of sustained campaigning by the Japanese. The ABU has a sprawling parish extending halfway around the world; it accepts a very broad definition of "Asia," so that its membership includes nations as far apart as Egypt and Samoa, South Korea and Australia. The broadcasting experience of these nations ranges from the sophistication of Japan to India and Indonesia, which are just starting to come to terms with television, and to Afghanistan and Ceylon where it has not yet arrived. Initially, one of the problems of starting an Asian Broadcasting Union was this enormous diversity among its broadcasters; the Japanese were so far ahead that they were bound to dominate. Ultimately the Australian Broadcasting Commission was persuaded to join the proposed union, thus bringing into the fold a nation where television was also relatively advanced. "The participation of Australia and later of New Zealand filled in the gap between Japan and the smaller countries," said Ichiro Matsui, the ABU's Honorary Deputy Secretary General in Tokyo. The ABU thus established its headquarters in Tokyo, but the secretary general's office is in Sydney where Sir Charles Moses, the former General Manager of the Australian Broadcasting Commission, is the secretary general.

The real challenge facing the ABU is to aid the developing nations within its domain in improving their broadcasting skills, without falling afoul of the politicians who are increasingly dabbling in communications. Their first major achievement has been to organize, with UNESCO, a regional training school for Asian broadcasters which will open in Kuala Lumpur, Malaysia, in 1972. They have also persuaded their members to take advantage of Japan's expert understanding of satellite communication by setting up a coordinating center at NHK, Japan's public service broadcasting corporation, in Tokyo for all satellite relays for Asia. Eventually, the ABU would like to have its own satellite to help bridge the vast distances not only between its members but within their own countries. "We need one here for Australia if we are ever to serve the outback," said Sir Charles Moses in Sydney, "but that's nothing to the problems facing India, Malaysia, or Indonesia. You realize Indonesia is made up of 3,000 islands scattered over 3,000 miles of ocean? You're never going to cover a country like that without a satellite. Satellites and the future of broadcasting in Asia go hand in hand."

18

Japan:
The Golden Samurai

Precisely at six o'clock every weekday morning, as the sun rises behind Mount Fuji, more than nine million Japanese bound out of bed and switch on their television sets to catch the opening programs of the day. Two hundred thousand of them settle down to watch a choice of English conversation lessons offered by the educational channel of NHK, Japan's public service broadcasting corporation, plus a commercial station; 250,000 more are immediately engrossed in a computer lecture on another commercial network, while nearly nine million energetically follow a brisk calisthenics course on NHK's general channel. Thus enlightened or refreshed, they become part of a 31 million audience—almost one third of the entire Japanese nation—who watch NHK's first major news bulletin of the day at 7 A.M.

As this early morning appetite for television suggests, the Japanese have become the world's most compulsive viewers. The majority of them spend almost half of all their leisure time before the box. Although television was introduced into Japan relatively late—the first programs were in 1953—they have exploited it with their customary diligence, giving it several twists that no one else has yet thought of.

Today, in wealth and number of sets (23 million, including 5 million color), Japanese television is second only to the United States. They began regular color programs as far back as 1960—long before anyone in Europe—and their harnessing of computer technology to television is the envy of broadcasters everywhere. In concocting a formula combining public service and commercial television, they have sought to extract every possible advantage from the medium. NHK, the public service corporation, runs the world's most comprehensive educational channel for eighteen hours a day, seven days a week, as well as an all-color, general network for eighteen hours daily; even the commercial stations pitch in with self-improving programs.

The diet is not as serious-minded all the time. On my first evening in Tokyo, I watched a program called *Play Girls,* on a commercial channel run by the Japan Science Foundation, displaying a bevy of three gorgeous girl private eyes who knifed, shot, and stripped their way through an hour-long crime series; in the course of outwitting the crooks one of them posed nude for artists in a club, while another took a revealing shower. The Japan Science Foundation's television license actually specifies that 60 percent of their programs should be "of scientific educational" content; *Play Girls,* therefore, is a little light relief among all those computer lectures.

The term "educational," however, has an extraordinarily wide interpretation on Japanese television. Another of Tokyo's commercial stations is National Educational Television (NET), a name suggesting that it is indeed an educational station. Sure enough, its license duly requires it to carry 50 percent educational programs, 30 percent cultural, and a mere 20 percent of entertainment; NET's interpretation of "educational" is, as one of their program executives put it rather charmingly, "very subtle." He pulled out a program chart in which all the educational programs were crayoned in in yellow; they included, besides normal morning school programs, coverage of a golf tournament and even an hour's professional wrestling. Was that really education? "Of course, it helps people to understand wrestling."

Most evenings during the peak hours of 7:00 to 10:00 P.M., which the Japanese call "golden time," NET keeps up its "educational" quota with samurai dramas. These samurai series, set in feudal Japan and showing roving young warlords routing out the baddies, are the westerns of Japanese TV. They have the same essential recipe as any western, except that guns are replaced by splendid curved swords and no one seems to own a horse. The swords are much more dramatic than guns on TV because there can be swashbuckling duels, full of grunts and groans, before the sword is plunged into the victim's writhing body. Moreover, the design of the Japanese house, with sliding walls instead of doors, makes for spectacular confrontation; just as the innocent is about to be disemboweled, the wall flies back and in leaps the samurai to the rescue. Whether such antics are educational is highly debatable. NET responds to the suggestion that by the same token *Bonanza* or *The Virginian* must also be labeled educational by agreeing politely that indeed they are. "After all," said an executive, "the story of a sheriff in the West is teaching Americans about their heritage." He added, "Perhaps you might say it is a typical Japanese solution."

Actually, the solution has much to do with the economics of running a commercial television station; advertisers do not queue up to buy time on a Chinese lesson, but they will pay $1,400 for a thirty-second spot on an "educational" samurai show.

NET's definition of "education" has earned it the nickname of National Erotic Television among Japan's more caustic TV critics.

Japan's prosperity has enabled its television to produce 85 percent of its own programs. Every single program in the top twenty is Japanese. American programs were widely shown during the early years, but nowadays the Japanese are highly selective in their overseas buying. They can afford to be. NHK earns more money from license fees—$280 million a year—than any other public service television organization in the world, out of which it finances the two television channels and three radio networks. The commercial networks compete for a television advertising cake of $600 million a year—the largest anywhere outside the United States. Tokyo has five commercial stations, of which four "key" stations have programing networks throughout Japan, operating up to twenty hours every day, with all "golden time" programs in color. The majority of Japanese, therefore, have a choice of six channels; in Tokyo it is seven. Actual ownership of commercial stations is strictly controlled; no individual or company is allowed to be a major shareholder in more than one station. But this restriction has not prevented the development of networks for programing purposes, controlled by the four major commercial stations in Tokyo: Tokyo Broadcasting System (TBS), Nippon Television Network (NTV), Fuji, and National Educational Television (NET). The Japan Science Foundation's Channel 12 in Tokyo has no affiliates.

The frequency of the commercials is not officially controlled, but the stations claim to adhere to a voluntary limit of 10 percent of total broadcast hours given over to advertising, with up to ten minutes per hour during "golden time." However, with Japanese flair, they have developed simultaneous programs and advertising; the message is superimposed over the continuing program with no commercial break. So just as the samurai drama reaches its climax, a caption flashes up FLY JAPAN AIRLINES, BUY SAKURA COLOR FILM, or DRINK HONEY WINE, before the struggling swordsmen on the screens. Sponsors normally have three of these plugs in each half hour. At news time the sponsor's name is superimposed over the breast pocket of the news reader as he gives the headlines. The blending of ads with programs may well seem the nadir of commercial television, yet in some ways it is much less distracting than an actual commercial break at the crucial moment in a film or play, especially as the ad is never more than a three- or four-word caption. It is no more worrying than a subtitle in a foreign movie.

A surprising number of the full commercials are in English or use English phrases; potato chips are "super duper," one sports car is the "now" car, another is a "souped up" coupe. A Lux soap commercial begins, "Yes, Lux from England," over the pictures of a guardsman marching up and down. The strident drumming home of the message in so many American commercials is absent; instead a commercial for a washing machine shows a Japanese housewife getting on with her delicate flower arrangement while the machine does the work. And the Japanese do not appear to be plagued by those perpetual headaches, stomach upsets, and ghastly colds for which remedies are so constantly promoted on American television. Instead, they listen to Mozart through the fine tones of the latest hi-fi equipment advertised by SONY or Hitachi.

When Japanese commercial television began in 1955 three of the major newspaper groups, Mainichi, Asahi, and Yomiuri, invested in TBS but, as commercial TV expanded, the newspaper groups reshuffled their holdings, leaving Mainichi linked with TBS, Yomiuri with NTV, and Asahi with NET (the American ABC network also has a 5 percent stake in NET). The fourth major newspaper group, Sankei, has always been tied with Fuji. The prosperity of television, however, is increasingly making the stations the most prominent partners in these ideals. Sankei newspapers, for example, are now a subsidiary of Fuji-TV.

These four commercial stations in Tokyo are responsible either for making or for purchasing from local production companies most of the programs for their networks; their affiliated stations in other cities mainly produce their own local news and regional magazines. The exception is the city of Osaka, which, like Tokyo, has four "key" stations. Each is affiliated with a Tokyo station, but they originate many more programs for their local viewers and contribute two or three hours each week to the commercial networks. Since the Osaka stations are one stage removed from main network programing, they are much freer to experiment and try out new ideas on their local audience; if a show succeeds then they can push it for the network. "The Tokyo stations are always cautious and conservative," a TV critic told me, "but two Osaka stations, ABC and MBS, are giving their producers a much freer hand. All the new talent is coming from there. MBS has one *Laugh-In*-type show built around all the young talent in the city and encouraging audience participation that is the most original entertainment in years."

The commercial networks, naturally, are geared to entertainment. Although they may schedule English conversation at 6:00 A.M., there is no pretense of culture at 6:00 P.M. In the evenings they pump out a steady diet of variety shows with pop singers belting out their latest hits, samurai dramas, home dramas (local for soap operas), and a Japanese phenomenon known as "hard training" dramas. "The Japanese people like series about characters training hard to achieve some special goal, either in their job or in sports," a TBS program director explained. "They love the theme of dedication to the almost impossible." TBS itself sets the pace with a hard training series *V for Victory* about a girls' high school volley ball team toiling to win a local championship. Once victory was indeed obtained the series fizzled out—"training" slackens off, and so does the audience. TBS replaced it promptly with *Attention Please,* a fictionalized account of the trials, tribulations, and loves of seven Japan Airlines hostesses learning how to cater to the 340 individual whims of passengers on a Boeing 747 Jumbo Jet.

The home dramas, of course, are very like soap operas everywhere. The most popular one in 1971 was *Wife at Eighteen,* a tale set in a Tokyo high school in which a student of eighteen and her history teacher are trying to keep their marriage secret. Another epic, produced by MBS in Osaka for NET's network, chronicles a dentist's love affair with a lady pediatrician.

The most popular home dramas, however, cannot quench the Japanese love of action, whether it is provided by a sixteenth-century samurai saga or a twentieth-century crime series. Hour after hour private eyes, both ancient and modern, snap necks with karate chops, send thugs hurtling into oblivion with the flick of a well-judo-trained wrist, or, in fine kick-boxing style, administer a flying scissors kick on some villain's jaw. These traditional Japanese sporting skills are heaven-sent to the TV producer. And while the samurai cut swathes through the armies of evil with their swords, the modern private eyes all throw a deadly knife. Guns are out of fashion, but gore is in.

No one seems unduly worried by all the violence. The commercial stations took considerable comfort from a survey by a sociologist at Kyoto University of 448 juvenile delinquents in Osaka who had been charged with murder or manslaughter. This inquiry, apparently, indicated that only 2.4 percent of the boys and 3.5 percent of the girls had been influenced in their crime by television; most of them claimed to have drawn their inspiration from films and magazines.

The commercial broadcasters are more worried about the free rein of sex on the screen. The ethics committee of the National Association of Commercial Broadcasters stopped a variation of strip poker on NTV in which the clothes of losing contestants in a quiz·show are gradually snipped away with a pair of scissors. They also ruled out women's professional wrestling on the Japan Science Foundation's Channel 12, which they felt was stretching the interpretation of science education just a little too far.

Controls, however, are few; the industry is left to police itself. The Ministry of Posts and Telecommunications has overall responsibility for licensing the stations, but is concerned primarily with administration rather than program content. The minister accepts without apparent qualms, for example, National Educational Television's far-reaching definition of "educational" programs. There is no equivalent of the U.S. Federal Communications Commission, Britain's Independent Television Authority, or the Australian Broadcasting Control Board to call the commercial broadcasters to account.

The maintenance of program standards, however, in face of the rising costs of television, is beginning to tax even the most prosperous commercial stations. All four key stations in Tokyo make profits, but the competition is intense. According to Nobue Shiga, a leading Japanese television critic, there is really only enough advertising in Tokyo to sustain two and a half commercial stations if they are to keep up good standards and develop their technical facilities; the fact that there are five, including the Science Foundation's channel, means the profits—and the plots—are thin.

For many years the TBS network, with twenty-five affiliated stations, has been the most profitable; frequently TBS had ten or twelve of the shows in the top twenty ratings. TBS's undoubted lead is now being challenged strongly by Fuji, which has cornered most of the new UHF stations; the Fuji network now comprises twenty-seven stations, including nineteen UHF, and is the biggest in Japan.

The success of networks is often seasonal. NTV, which is strongly oriented toward sports, does well during the summer months for the simple reason that it owns one of Japan's favorite baseball teams, the Yomiuri Giants. They are guaranteed exclusive coverage of all the Giants games and, as the team plays five nights a week from 8:00 P.M till

9:30 from April to September, NTV is assured of fine ratings for those six months. Actually, the Giants owe their existence to Matsutaro Shoriki, the founder and for many years president of NTV, who was also known as the father of baseball in Japan. While securing for NTV the first commercial TV license he was also organizing baseball teams.

NTV's preoccupation with sports persists throughout the year; they promote most of the major kick-boxing events and are now trying to encourage the Japanese to play soccer. Their most popular winter programs are two cartoon series about a boy baseball player and professional wrestling. They are the only Japanese network not to have succumbed to the samurai craze. Instead, they have developed a documentary department, under Junichi Ushiyama, which has won an international reputation reporting everything from the gorgeous girl pearl fishers of the Ainu, to the Stone Age peoples of New Guinea and a journey by wood-fired train across South America. They are now linked with Yorkshire Television, the Canadian Broadcasting Corporation, and Swedish and Russian television in a long-running coproduction series, *Under One Sky*. One initial project was for each contributing country to make a ten-minute film on a child genius; the film from each nation was then blended into a worldwide view of exceptional children. NTV hopes that this cooperation can be expanded into building up an international film encyclopedia for the dawning cassette age.

Despite their preoccupation with entertainment, the commercial stations all devote a considerable proportion of their budgets and program time to news. TBS, which has always had a strong reputation for news reporting, devotes 14 percent of its budget to news and has a news staff of three hundred and five foreign bureaus. NTV has three hours of news bulletins and news magazines every day. The rivalry to be first with a news story is fierce; all have radio cars, helicopters, and mobile units ready to leave instantly on any major story. The six senior news editors at TBS all carry electronic bleepers to alert them in a crisis if they are within a twenty-mile radius of their office. Stations delight in broadcasting that they are first with the news. Once, when a Boeing 727 crashed in Tokyo Bay, TBS just beat all its rivals to the nearest pier with a mobile unit, commandeered the only boat, and was first to locate the wreckage; the other networks were fuming back on the quay. The rivalry ceases only for satellite transmissions, which are normally shared through a pool because of the high costs.

The real people to beat on news, however, are NHK. They take their role as Japan's public service broadcasting organization exceptionally seriously. NHK was modeled originally on the BBC in the days when the image of Lord Reith was extremely strong. Lord Reith, whose ideals of high thinking and plain living earned the BBC the affectionate nickname "Auntie," has persisted longer as an influence at NHK than at the BBC. Their mission, NHK likes to remind visitors, is "to contribute to the elevation of the cultural level of the nation."

For almost ten years the president of NHK (i.e., director general) has been a remarkable man named Yoshinori Maeda, who was perhaps the single most influential man in television in Japan, or indeed in Asia, during the 1960s. Maeda began his career as a foreign correspondent with the Asahi newspaper group, then worked his way up through NHK's news service to the presidency of the corporation. He is still, at heart, a journalist, a great believer in the potential role of television in disseminating news and information to the Japanese people, not only about their own nation, but about the world at large. "Maeda," says one of his colleagues, "has always insisted that NHK is not just a Japanese broadcasting organization, but a world broadcasting organization, dedicated to international cooperation with other broadcasters."

His great preoccupation is with NHK's news coverage in trying to preserve its independence from any kind of government or other pressures. "We must be quite free from pressure from any quarter," he insists. His own position at NHK depends on the approval of a board of twelve governors, who selected him initially and can renew his term every three years. The governors, like those of the BBC on which NHK's constitution is largely based, are chosen from a cross section of leading Japanese citizens; during 1970 the board was composed of five industrialists, two diplomats, a lawyer, a scientist, a college president, and representatives of the fisheries and farming industries. The prime minister appoints the all-male board, but he must have the approval of both houses of the Diet. Left-wingers in Japan often charge NHK with following the government line and, like many other public service broadcasting corporations, it has an inevitable reputation of giving the "official" view. However, the government must be exceptionally careful of trying to control the broadcasters' views. As in Germany, there are many bitter memories of government manipulation of radio before and during World War II, which have established especially strong resentments at any attempts to meddle in radio or television today.

Maeda's concern with news occasionally makes it seem as if NHK's general service is putting out nothing else; almost six hours a day—one third of total broadcast time—is given over to news and news analysis.

The general news bulletins are amplified by three special reports from overseas correspondents, together with a five-minute bulletin for children. The news division obtains its foreign reporting chiefly from the largest corps of foreign correspondents maintained by any broadcasting organization in the world. The network was originally established by Maeda himself as director of NHK news in the 1950s, and comprises twenty-four foreign bureaus (the BBC has fourteen and CBS has nine). The news division can preempt all other program time for major stories. During my own stay in Tokyo four hours every afternoon on three consecutive days were given over to live coverage of a crucial debate in the lower house of the Diet on pollution. This extended coverage is accepted at NHK as a natural part of its responsibility to the Japanese public.

Besides this heavy allotment of news, NHK describes a further nine hours of its programs each day as "cultural" or "educational," leaving a mere five hours or less for entertainment. Even in its entertainment programs NHK tries to carry through that feeling of cultural uplift. "Our aim," explained an NHK executive, "is fair and healthy entertainment. We have our duty to raise the level of understanding of the Japanese public." Their most successful evening program, for example, is a regular Sunday night samurai drama, *Ten to Chi to (Heaven and Earth),* which is about the only occasion in the week when they can beat their commercial rivals in the ratings during golden time. While swordplay abounds, the producer explains, "We try to make our samurai play on a higher level than the commercial stations. We include much more about the ancient customs of our people."

This Reithian concern for achievement and moral virtue pervades everything that NHK produces. One of their very best documentary series of fifteen programs in color looked at the accomplishments of the early Meiji pioneers who introduced Western civilization into Japan and began the modernization of the nation. NHK campaigns constantly, both in news and in documentary programs, on everything from pollution to stopping traffic accidents. One major undertaking, which they hope will run right through the present decade, is a monthly ninety-minute color documentary, *Our World in the Seventies,* based on coverage by NHK teams around the globe of important trends—the problems of youth in France or America, the increasing infiltration in almost every phase of life of computers.

NHK's educational channel, of course, is even more serious-minded and it is watched by a small, but remarkably constant audience. From the moment it comes on the air at 6:00 A.M. until midnight it rarely has less than 100,000 viewers or more than 400,000. Over three quarters of its programs are strictly educational; the remainder are billed as cultural, which may mean a symphony concert, a ballet, or Kenneth Clark's successful BBC series *Civilisation*. Six hours each day are devoted to school programs, which are viewed extensively at all levels of the Japanese educational system; the science programs for primary schools, for example, are watched by 82 percent of all primary students. Outside school hours, half an hour every day is given over to special programs for handicapped or mentally retarded children. There are lessons in English, French, German, Spanish, and Chinese; university courses in sociology, jurisprudence, mathematics, history, and economics, together with lectures for women on running the home, on shop management and, for teenagers, playing the guitar.

Both of NHK's television channels, together with three radio networks, are financed out of license fees of $10.80 a year for a black and white set and $15.60 for color. Unlike all other public service broadcasting organizations whose fees are collected by a third party, NHK itself signs a contract with every household that has a TV set, and its own staff go door to door collecting the fees. License evasion, so NHK claims, is almost nonexistent. "Everyone," they say, "is very honest." This method of license collecting gives NHK a unique relationship with its viewers; on the doorstep you are bound to get the full vent of any public dissatisfaction.

Whether NHK pays enough attention to complaints is debatable. Television critics often suggest that the corporation is so busy giving the masses its version of enlightenment that it has no time to heed their views. Rather curiously for an organization that has a large public opinion research department, NHK does no daily audience research; they rely on ratings provided by an outside commercial company and on two or three major surveys of their own each year. Maeda and his program executives clearly watch the ratings as closely as anyone else in television. Nevertheless, they go to some lengths to explain that they are not slaves to the ratings game. "Clearly we like a good audience," says Tadashi Yoshida, deputy director of the general network, "but we don't follow commercial formulas." NHK is, in fact, on that endless high-wire act that faces all public service broadcasters in nations which also allow commercial television—trying to maintain a balance between reasonable standards and a large enough slice of the viewing audience to justify the compulsory license fee.

Actually, NHK is consistently at the top of the ratings by day and, almost as consistently, at the bottom in the evenings. Between 6:00 A.M. and 6:00 P.M. NHK normally holds the top seven positions in the ratings, and a total of fifteen out of the top twenty; in "golden time" it is lucky to get two places low down in the top twenty (for the samurai drama on Sundays and a Folk Song Festival on Thursdays). Rarely does NHK's evening audience equal that peak of 31 million it achieves with its news at 7:00 every morning. No other major television organization that I know gains its maximum audience at dawn.

Moreover, only a handful of programs on the commercial networks, even in "golden time," ever win as large an audience as NHK does with the breakfast news; a 20 million audience for an evening program is excellent.

While NHK's earnestness makes for admirable and highly professional television, one does wish for a few more touches of frivolity. The phrase "our responsibility to the public" came up almost too frequently. A little irreverence might be fun from time to time and amplify NHK's unquestioned daytime leadership into nighttime superiority also.

"The trouble with NHK," says TV critic Nobue Shiga, "is that they are so sober that new creative talent simply cannot express itself in their programs." Shiga's recent book, *Naked NHK* (which made him persona non grata at NHK), suggested that all the creative genius in the corporation was being channeled into technical wizardry rather than programs.

Certainly NHK's automated Broadcast Control Center in Tokyo is regarded as the ultimate technical showplace by broadcasters everywhere. "When you get to Tokyo," everyone urges, "you *must* see that center."

Well, they are right. If you sit for the afternoon in the Technical Operations Center there, which handles the transmission of 2,000 programs a week on NHK's two TV and three radio networks, you begin to wonder after a while why the four young men on duty did not just stay out for a long lunch. Two IBM 360 computers are doing all the work.

Occasionally, just to reassure themselves that the computers are on the job, these technicians glance at a formidable galaxy of television monitors and computer display screens. On five display screens an IBM 360 has spelled out just what it is doing with each network. On the GTV monitor the computer has printed out in red letters that it is supervising a keep-fit program for housewives, which will end at 4:15; the educational TV display alongside reports that a science lecture is being transmitted. The computer has also printed out in green letters on each screen details of the next scheduled program. The GTV will have a children's puppet show from NHK's Osaka studios. The computer knows that the videotape of this show is already loaded on the videotape recorder in Osaka. Naturally, it has already thoughtfully double-checked a coding on the puppet show tape against a similar coding in its program schedule memory bank to confirm that no foolish human in Osaka has inadvertently put on the wrong tape. (If they have, the computer sounds the alarm, so that the correct tape can be installed well before broadcast time.) Then, precisely at 4:15' the computer switches out the keep-fit lesson and switches on the puppet show; in the same moment it also remembers to change from a science to a Chinese lesson on the educational channel. Radio programs are transposed with equal adroitness. An automatic apology can even be interjected in the event of a temporary fault.

Since the majority of NHK's programs are prerecorded on video-tape, the essential role of all this automation is simply switching tapes on and off at the right split second. The computers are equally adept, however, at coping with a live news program. NHK's News Center is hooked into the computer complex and the entire sequence of each newscast is mapped out on plastic cards which are slotted into a gadget known as the Resources Random Selector. All the producer has to do is push a single button which commands the selector to "read" the next card and, following that instruction, automatically switch in a studio camera on the news reader, a news film projector, a videotape recorder, or even a live satellite transmission from halfway around the world. The system is so flexible that if a late story comes in while the news is on, the whole running order can be altered just by rearranging the sequence of plastic cards. Sudden news breaks outside regular news time can also be accommodated by ordering the computers to bypass the regular program schedule and cut immediately to the news studio; the computers need just two minutes to reorganize their thoughts and comply.

The transmission of programs is merely the final chore in a complex computer operation, which NHK has christened Total On-line Program and Information Control (TOPICS). Earlier, TOPICS has presided over every moment of a program's progress, from the first vague plan to the finished taping. Two hundred offices at NHK are hooked into TOPICS through their own computer terminal and display screens. This enables a program's birth to be charted so closely that critics occasionally suggest that computers have replaced people completely at the corporation. TOPICS, in fact, coordinates all requests for actors, musicians, designers, lighting experts, announcers and outside broadcast units, and juggles the bookings for all NHK's thirty-six videotape recorders and twenty-one studios. A producer working out his schedule can call up the computer and find in an instant when a particular studio is available and tap out a reservation on his keyboard. At any moment the computer will obligingly print up on any one of the two hundred display screens a complete briefing on the status of the project, outlining whether the script is complete, who are the actors and technicians assigned, when and where all rehearsals and the final taping will take place, together with a provisional airing date. Alternatively, the computer can conjure up the entire network schedule weeks ahead for instantaneous review or alteration.

"TOPICS can handle eighty different types of production facilities," says Yoshinori Maeda proudly. "Previously our staff were writing out 5,000 requests a day for studios or announcers or mobile units; it often took hours for these to be delivered and for them to get an answer—now it's instantaneous."

NHK's latest notion is to ask its computers to memorize their entire film library. At the moment, if a producer wants to get a shot of Mount Fuji from the north at dawn he may have to look through fifty rolls of film to locate the precise view he has in mind. Once the computers have added the library to their repertoire, they will advise the producer in a few seconds on precisely which roll of film he can find the view of Fuji on. Hours of frustrating viewing will be eliminated.

While squeezing every last advantage from its computers, NHK displays equal efficiency in planning such mundane things as floor coverings. The endless miles of studio corridors are laid with three different colors of floor tiles; green tiles indicate a special visitors' route through the building, so that the 7,000 daily sightseers can find their own way through the building without a guide—they are just told, "Stay on green floor"; orange tiles guide artists and performers direct to the dressing and makeup rooms; gray-tiled corridors are for staff only—they are supposed to know their way through the maze.

Those 7,000 sightseers trudging down the green tourist corridors of NHK every day reflect the Japanese fascination, almost obsession, with television. They have the most voracious appetite for TV of any nation in the world; 80 percent of the population spend at least two hours every day watching TV, 30 percent spend four hours or more. The average Japanese man views for two hours and forty-five minutes on weekdays and three and a half hours on Sundays; his wife is even keener—she looks in for three hours and fifteen minutes during the week and three hours and forty minutes on Sundays. This represents a major slice of their leisure time; indeed, according to Naomichi Nakanishi of NHK's Public Opinion Research Institute, the Japanese spend almost twice as much of their leisure time watching television as do the Americans. The housewife in Japan spends 56 percent of all her leisure before the box—compared with 24 percent for the American housewife.

The moment she has seen her husband off to work and the children are on their way to school, she tunes in to a cozy little fifteen-minute home drama, *Rainbow,* on NHK's general channel. *Rainbow* chronicles the life of a Mrs. Tanaka, who is married to an archeologist. They have several children, one of whom, appropriately, works for NHK. After 8:30 she has the choice of several *Today*-type shows, all aimed at women; there is *Hello Madam* on NHK, the *Kazu Nara Morning Show* on NET, the *Hiroshi Ogawa Morning Show* on Fuji, or the *Jiro Kimbara Show* on NTV. The remainder of the day is whiled away with cooking lessons, keep-fit classes, several traditional Japanese tea ceremonies, and a good choice of short home dramas normally about the conflict between parents and children in some modern Japanese family.

Traditionally the Japanese wife has always been obedient and even subservient to her husband: her role has been one of complying with his every whim, having a boiling-hot bath ready for him when he comes home, scrubbing his weary back, then serving him a delicious dinner. Moreover, as Nakanishi points out, "The majority of Japanese housewives have never had any opportunities to train themselves on how to spend their leisure hours." Television, consequently, has become "indispensable," a new window to a wider world in which men are not always such superior beings. Can that arduous back-scrubbing ever be quite so dutiful again? The Japanese housewife is not yet in open rebellion, but the new perspectives she observes through television are clearly slowly changing the rigid family structures. NHK, probing the influence of TV on its viewers, found that in 1970 one fifth of them reported, "TV programs have promoted the democratization of human relationships within the family."

The same inquiry also revealed that television viewing time is still increasing, especially in the 30 percent of Japanese homes that now have two or more television sets, as family conflicts over which program to watch are reduced.

The prospect for the future is that the Japanese will have an even greater choice of programs, although most of them are likely to be embellishments of the educational pattern already established. The government has one channel reserved on the UHF wave band for an Open University of the Air, relying heavily on television for its teaching. The issue is whether the government runs this itself or pays NHK to do it for them. NHK, always anxious to preserve its independent status, is extremely reluctant to undertake the production of government programs. Moreover, they have their own ideas for expanding their educational projects.

But everyone in Japan, of course, is really brimming with plans for the era of cassettes. All the commercial networks have set up special subsidiary companies linked with electronics firms to exploit the cassette potential. The electronics industry's exceptional expertise at miniaturization and its competitive costs may well mean that the Japanese will be the first to produce a cassette player that is cheap enough for the ordinary home. The initial players that went on the market in Tokyo in 1971 cost about $300 each, with the program cassette costing $100 for a half hour's tape. "Although these first cassette players are beyond the budget of the ordinary Japanese family," said an executive of the National Association of Commercial Broadcasters, "I am quite sure we can develop cheap video packages for home use by the late 1970s." If the Japanese appetite for television is anything to judge by, the country could become the first mass market for the cassette.

Japan's leadership in television in Asia is so great that it is impossible to envisage any other countries there even beginning to challenge her. Already the Japanese sphere of influence is spreading swiftly. Three Japanese directors are on the board of the Pakistan Television Corporation, where all the equipment is Japanese. More than 500 engineers and broadcasters from other Asian nations have already been trained by NHK's Central Training Institute in Tokyo and scores more fly in every year.

En route from New Delhi to Bangkok I traveled next to a young Indian girl on her way to Tokyo to join her husband, who was learning how to make television sets; once he had the skill he was to return to India to start manufacturing sets there. "No one in India really knows how to make television sets," she said to me. "The Japanese are so far ahead of us."

AUSTRALIA

19

Linking Up
Down Under

For two hundred years after Captain James Cook made his first landfall at Botany Bay in 1770, Australia always seemed at the ends of the earth; an enormous, almost empty continent of red, brown, and orange deserts and sheep farms with, perched around its rim, a handful of cities reached only after weeks aboard ship or some tedious thirty hours in a jet. That isolation ended, in one sense anyway, in November 1966 when the first Pacific Intelsat satellite relayed television pictures of a small group of English migrants, specially gathered at a portable earth station at Carnarvon in Western Australia, to their relatives assembled at a BBC television studio in London. "It was not a fantastic piece of television programing," Walter Hamilton, Assistant General Manager of the Australian Broadcasting Commission (ABC), conceded later, "but the world was shrinking for us at last."

The satellite bridge to Australia really proved itself, however, in July 1969 when Neil Armstrong first stepped from Apollo 11 onto the surface of the moon. A special NASA tracking station at Honeysuckle Creek near Canberra and Australia's own giant radio telescope at Parkes were the first to home in on the scene on the moon and relay it via the Pacific satellite to Houston, Texas, and the watching world. "Just for one big occasion Australia had the picture first, at least 300 milliseconds before anyone else," ABC's Hamilton added proudly. "Just for once we were not at the end of the line, our accustomed place 'down under.'" [1] Regularly now, thanks to Intelsat, Australians can watch their tennis stars winning at Wimbledon and Forest Hills or their cricketers trouncing England.

[1] W. S. Hamilton, "Australia's Dwindling Isolation," *EBU Review,* November 1969.

Australia may have been at the end of the line before satellites, but she was by no means bottom of the viewing league. Although the Outback can be cut off five hundred miles from the nearest TV station, in the big cities of Sydney, Melbourne, Brisbane, and Adelaide there is a choice of the ABC's public service and three commercial channels. Over half of Australia's twelve million population is gathered together in these cities, where they can enjoy a choice of more television channels than anyone in Europe (always excepting those addicts with high roof aerials in Brussels, who pick up programs from four surrounding countries). They can also watch for longer hours because the commercial stations are on the air at least seventeen hours a day. Indeed, only in the United States and Japan is the quantity of television offered greater; total TV programing in Sydney is an extraordinary 445 hours each week—in Britain and West Germany, by comparison, it is just under 200 hours. While this may sound like an achievement, television down under is, in fact, an object lesson in what happens with too much programing and too little money. The results can be as barren as Australia's deserts.

The splendid submissions of prospective programs made by some commercial operators in applying for their licenses have fallen forgotten by the wayside. One applicant in Melbourne grandly announced that his station's output "would reflect an Australian environment, encourage an awareness of the achievements of Australia, and advance the arts and culture of the nation." Yet in 1970, the amount of program time devoted to "the arts" on Australian commercial television was so small that it could not be rated in official program content analysis; a footnote merely remarked, "less than 0.05 percent." The general manager of one commercial station told me frankly, "Our promises in applying for the license bear no resemblance to what we are doing now."

The Australian Broadcasting Control Board, from the best of motives, simply adds to the trouble. In granting the licenses and regulating the commercial stations the board insists that half their programs must be locally produced. They also specify that six hours of Australian drama must be transmitted by each commercial station weekly. While this policy has the admirable aim of limiting the flood of imported package programs and stimulating home production, in effect it places too great a strain on local resources. Australia has little theatrical or filmmaking tradition on which television can draw. Television has had to pull together its own group of talents from scratch to satisfy a colossal demand; in Sydney or Melbourne more hours of local programing each week are decreed than is created either by the BBC or commercial television in Britain, or indeed, by any European television organization. Not surprisingly, standards suffer. One Australian television tycoon, explaining why he objected strongly to any increase in the proportion of Australian programs, stated flatly that he was not going to be responsible for foisting "muck" on the Australian people.

With two hundred broadcasting hours still left to fill each week, after the local quota has been aired, Australian television has long been a lure for international program salesmen. The BBC sold almost eight hundred productions there in 1969, earning a third of the total income of BBC Television Enterprises. The British viewer visiting Australia consequently feels entirely at home: he can watch *Softly, Softly, Dr. Finlay's Casebook, The Troubleshooters,* and *The Power Game.* Sir Lew Grade at Associated Television also has a long-running contract with Channel 7 in Sydney, supplying everything from *The Saint* to *Tom Jones.* There is a special fondness for British programs among the commercial stations that has nothing to do with sentiment: commercial stations are allowed to count a half of each program as "local production" in fulfilling their domestic quota.

Yet the Americans sell just as well. Australia is one of the few countries with a well-developed television system where American programs still gallop into the top ten. "Australia is by far our best market," said Bill Fineschreiber of the Motion Picture Export Association of America, rubbing his hands happily. For some years, to prevent costly bidding and to keep prices down, the commercial stations and the ABC formed a pool for their American buying. Each station listed the programs it wanted and a vote was then held to determine who should be the lucky one to show *Lucy* or *Ironside.* At one point, the Americans countered by refusing to sell to the pool for almost a year. It only came to an end when Channel 7 in Sydney broke loose and went on a grand American buying spree.

Amazingly, the avalanche of programs is transmitted without a true commercial network. The ownership of commercial stations is tightly regulated; control of more than two television stations by any person or company is forbidden. Only loose program-producing groups have been formed; a Melbourne station embarking on a new series will seek assurances from outlets in Sydney, Brisbane, and Adelaide that they will take the show, but essentially the stations in the cities operate independently. Anyone from Sydney traveling to Melbourne or Adelaide may find that his favorite program goes on on a different night of the week. Only the ABC has a true network carrying programs simultaneously nationwide.

Outside the major cities of Sydney, Melbourne, Brisbane, and Adelaide, each with three commercial stations, and Perth with two, there are thirty "country" stations, generally owned by small newspapers or local businessmen. These country stations have no direct link with the metropolitan stations. They originate few programs, apart from local news, but simply shop around the big city stations to fill the few hours that they are on the air each evening. This unsystematic purchasing hampers the metropolitan stations, since it never guarantees countrywide sales for any program. With three main groups of commercial producers, the program market is overcrowded, and countless shows are never aired outside the major cities.

Although commercial networks are prohibited, formidable concentrations of power have arisen in Australian television through major newspaper groups. With no more than the two stations that the government permits to any one owner, newspaper owners still find it possible to wield great influence in television's development throughout the country. Newspaper magnates' dominance of television in Australia is perhaps more potent than anywhere else in the world.

Leading the field is Sir Frank Packer, renowned as both newspaper owner and yachtsman, whose Australian Consolidated Press publishes the Sydney *Daily Telegraph* and several magazines. He owns TCN Channel 9 in Sydney (the very first commercial station in Australia) and GTV Channel 9 in Melbourne. The John Fairfax group, owners of the *Sydney Morning Herald,* control ATN Channel 7 in that city and are major shareholders in BTQ in Brisbane. Down in Melbourne, Sir John Williams' *Herald* newspaper owns HSV Channel 7. Rupert Murdoch, who is now extending his empire into Britain with his purchases of the *Sun, The News of the World,* and a slice of London Weekend Television, has a large stake in ADS Channel 7 in Adelaide through his company, Advertiser Newspapers. *The News* in Adelaide is also owner of NWS Channel 9.

The lone nonnewspaper tycoon in Australian commercial television is the airline millionaire, Sir Reginald Ansett, who owns stations in Melbourne and Brisbane. Ansett arrived in television rather late, when the third commercial stations were licensed in the main cities. He has had a hard time breaking into the market. As his losses and those of the two other stations not owned by newspapers, in Adelaide and Sydney, mount, their executives often criticize the newspaper alliances of their rivals or lament that they have no such link themselves. "The newspapers that own television stations promote them quite shamelessly," complained one bitter executive. And Talbot Duckmanton, the quiet, pipe-smoking general manager of the Australian Broadcasting Commission, explained, "You will find hardly any newspaper outlets that are not linked to television. It's very hard for us at ABC to get writeups of our programs."

A check of these complaints reveals that they are often justified. The *Sydney Morning Herald,* for instance, publishes a weekly four-page pull-out TV guide, including a full page of articles previewing programs. Not only are the programs for its own Channel 7 listed first, although the natural sequence is to print Channel 2 (ABC) first and then Channel 7, 9, and 10, but *all* articles in guides I have seen preview only programs on their own channel.

Newspaper partiality for its own channel is understandable, but the exclusion of editorial comment on the others is a different matter. Blatant pressure on TV critics is also unmasked from time to time. One television critic was fired by a well-known newspaper baron for criticizing programs on his paper's station. When the critic protested he was trying to be impartial, the magnate snapped, "What about being impartial our way?"

The stations with newspaper tie-ups hotly deny any one-sidedness. "The newspaper interest is not all that important," protested Clyde Packer, Sir Frank's son, who runs TCN in Sydney. "Look, we're top station in Brisbane and Melbourne where we don't even own newspapers."

With and without newspapers, the metropolitan and country commercial stations comfortably beat the public service ABC ratings. The concept of the Australian Broadcasting Commission is close to that of the BBC in Britain and of NHK in Japan. The ruling body consists of nine government-appointed commissioners selected from prominent Australians in business, education, and the professions; the commissioners must include one woman. They, in turn, appoint the general manager (director general) of the ABC, who presides over day-to-day running and policies. But one crucial difference in organization distinguishes the ABC from the BBC and NHK—the ABC's revenue does not come from license fees. Although there is a license costing $14 (U.S. $15.60) a year for owning a TV set in Australia, the money from the 2,300,000 licenses goes into the government's general revenue kitty. Each year, the general manager of the ABC has to go, cap in hand, to the government and ask for money, which is then paid out of government funds. This means the ABC does not have a guaranteed income based on the number of television sets in the country. Normally the ABC's grant is close to license fee revenue (about U.S. $56 million a year in the early 1970s), but its isolation from that fee can be crucial. Equally inhibiting is the fact that the appointment of all ABC's staff paid over $7,500 (U.S. $8,250) has to be approved by the government's Public Service Board. If the ABC wants to offer a high salary to a good director from a commercial station, they have to seek approval from the Board to pay him above the standard rate for directors. "Unfortunately, our reputation for independence is not as strong as the BBC's," an ABC executive admitted, "but we are now trying to build it up."

The ABC successfully rebuffed the Postmaster General, Alan Hulme, in 1970 when he threatened a curb of their current affairs budget because he objected to the tone of the programs. The Commission pointed out that the Broadcasting and Television Act clearly gave them control over program policy and, eventually, the minister backed down. "The government here is very afraid of television," said the same ABC executive, "and we need a strong chairman of the Commission to stop them interfering."

The ABC's brief is also much vaguer than for most other public service broadcasting organizations; they are required simply to provide "adequate and comprehensive programs." Understandably, just what that means is open to many interpretations. For several years the ABC left entertainment mostly to the commercial channels and concentrated instead on a rather solid diet of programs with a nice moral tone. "We assumed there was an ABC viewer who came home at 7:00 and sat down to watch 'worthy' television," one ABC man told me. "We offered a little bit of everything that was good for him." This policy gained the ABC a microscopic proportion of the audience.

Since Talbot Duckmanton became general manager in 1965, the ABC has suddenly become more conscious of how to please large audiences with popular entertainment. "We must compete for audiences," said Duckmanton. "If we don't, our audience will diminish beyond the level at which we can claim we are a national broadcasting authority. Some people would like to see us maintained merely for the satisfaction of minority audiences, while they themselves were free to attend to the majority audiences. But we could then no longer be regarded as a national body. If public service broadcasting is to be effective, it must be comprehensive."

The ABC's most conspicuous audience winner has been a gossipy little fifteen-minute soap opera, *Bellbird,* about life and loves in a small Australian town. *Bellbird* is shown each weekday evening just before the main news at 7:00 P.M. and occasionally slips into the top twenty programs. But even then it attracts barely 25 percent of the audience in the cities. A more enterprising ABC series, *Dynasty,* a saga of a newspaper-television tycoon and his family, took a swipe at newspaper control of commercial television. The script was carefully tailored to avoid libel suits by identifying too closely with any single Australian newspaper-owning family, but there were no prizes for guessing the autocrat on whom the series was modeled.

The real achievement of the Australian Broadcasting Commission, however, has been to reach a high level of current affairs and documentary programs, a field almost completely ignored by the commercial stations (they gave a mere 1.1 percent of their time to current affairs in peak evening periods during 1969–70). Every evening, from 7:00 until 8:00, the ABC boldly presents a full hour of news and current affairs, which wins them consistently their best audiences of the day (apart from *Bellbird*). The audience for this evening hour is actually double that for almost any other time; on the graph of their ratings it stands out like Mount Everest.

The dilemma facing producers, both at the ABC and the commercial stations, is that their audiences have long been accustomed to the professional standards of imported programs, which they find very difficult to match. "It's a tragedy that we didn't have much stricter quotas to begin with," an ABC drama producer said. "By the time we started making more of our own shows the audience was already accustomed to overseas standards. Now they can reject our efforts." But the problem is not necessarily one of quotas; the Australians simply have too many television stations on the air for too long each day. The money and the talent available cannot make the programs worthwhile.

Of the homegrown dramas the most successful have been two police series, *Division Four* and *Homicide,* but several others have been dropped at considerable cost after poor audiences for the opening episodes. Nowadays all the commercial stations and ABC are hunting overseas for partners for coproductions to be made in Australia. Channel 7 in Sydney has been making pilot programs for CBS, and Channel 9 worked with Paramount on a series, *Flea Force,* about a team of Australian commandos in the Pacific in World War II. ABC has joined up with the BBC for a thirteen-part down-under western on Ben Hall, an Australian bushranger of the Jesse James brand.

Any attempt at liveliness on the part of local producers has often been curbed, however, by one of the strictest rule books of television standards anywhere. Australia's stand as the last bastion against the permissive society is clearly reflected in her television. There is no television on Sunday mornings and all stations must put on at least thirty minutes of religious services each week. Sex education on television is explicitly ruled out. "References to sex relations should be treated with discretion," says the rule book, "reference to illicit sex relations should be avoided where possible and should on no account be presented as commendable." The rules also specify, "Respect for the state of marriage and the importance of the home and family should be maintained."

Attitudes have eased slightly, however, in the last few years. "I remember a script a few years ago in which an unmarried couple met in a bar," recalled an ABC drama producer. "This had to be changed so that they met over a ham sandwich in a sandwich bar." The relaxation is due not so much to Australian boldness as to imported BBC shows. "The BBC has been an icebreaker in pushing forward the frontiers of permissiveness all round the world," said the ABC producer. "It's helped us enormously— we just argue that if the BBC does it, then we can too."

Nevertheless, all imported films destined for television are still subject to the approval of the Commonwealth Film Censorship Board. The Board grades them either G, indicating they may be shown on television at any time; A, meaning they are not recommended for children and must not be shown before 7:30 in the evenings; or AO, adults only, which may be shown only after 8:30 P.M. The censorship rules also spell out that before 7:30 P.M. "parents should be able to feel secure in allowing children to watch television without supervision." This responsibility is taken seriously by the television companies and after 7:30 it is quite usual to see the caption over the opening titles, "This programme is not suitable for children."

While Australia's television producers are working to nourish local writing and acting talent, the technical challenge of the seventies is to extend television into the Outback. Although 96 percent of Australia's population already live within television range, the remaining 4 percent are thinly scattered over thousands of square miles. The cost of bringing television to them, as demanded by the ABC's public service concept, will be enormous. Thirty-eight new low-power ABC television stations are being built in the Outback in 1972–73, but these will bring only a further 110,000 people before the box. Communities like Darwin and Alice Springs, which are well over a thousand miles from the nearest city, cannot be hooked neatly into a microwave network. Indeed, the answer for them, as for so many other small settlements in Australia, is a satellite to feed community receivers. Just as the Pacific Intelsat satellite finally ended Australia's visual isolation from Europe and America, so eventually an Australian or Asian satellite tuned to bounce signals into every corner of the desert could end the loneliness of the Outback.

AFRICA

20

A Symbol
of Independence

Africa is proving as hard for television to penetrate as it was for Livingstone and Stanley. Steamy tropical climates wreak havoc with sensitive electrical equipment, colossal distances defy the establishment of networks, electricity often does not extend more than a few miles outside main towns, while television sets are quite beyond the means of the average family. In Sierra Leone there were still less than one thousand sets eight years after the beginning of television—and no one was sure how many of those were working. Only two television sets out of one hundred installed for an educational television project in Ghana survived the first two years without succumbing to heat and humidity. Upper Volta, on the southern fringes of the Sahara Desert, started television with a flourish, but gave up daily programing after a few months through lack of money. They now have television only two nights a week. "Television is still in its infancy in Africa," said Levinson Nguru, the director of the Kenya Institute for Mass Communications. "Ownership of a set here is still a matter of prestige—a set costs £150 [$360]. None of my friends can afford that."

As late as 1971 there were just 250,000 television sets in the whole of Africa south of the Sahara; or one television set for every thousand people. Nations as diverse as Tanzania, Malawi, Angola, Mozambique, and South Africa had no television at all. South Africa, the last developed country anywhere without television, is finally proposing to take the plunge in 1975 when it will introduce an all-color channel in English and Afrikaans for the European population and later a separate color channel for the Africans. Despite this late start South Africa will have the only color TV in Africa and conceivably more sets in use almost from the beginning than the rest of Africa combined; the commission which recommended the establishment of television estimated 700,000 sets would be sold in the republic in five years.

This is entirely feasible since in Rhodesia, which has had television since 1960, there are fifty thousand sets, ten times more per head of the population than in Africa as a whole. Rhodesian television, however, is very much the odd man out; it is aimed at the white population. Moreover, since that country's unilateral declaration of independence from Britain in 1965 resulted in United Nations sanctions, it has not been able to buy programs openly from Britain or America, although this has not prevented it from getting prints of the latest shows by various roundabout methods.

Television's slow start in Africa has surprised many people who felt a decade ago that it would be a mass medium there within a matter of years. Not only the British, American, and French equipment manufacturers who competed for contracts have been disappointed; even educators, who believe that television can be an invaluable tool in both adult and school education, have felt thwarted. They often wonder if, for the time being, they should put more emphasis on radio. The cheap transistor radio is firmly implanted in most homes even in the remotest villages and seems much less sensitive to the hazards of climate. Politicians are aware of this. "Most African nations are being created out of what was previously just a collection of tribes," a Kenyan broadcaster pointed out. "If you want to mobilize these people you must use radio."

This has not discouraged most African leaders from enthusiastically approving the opening of every television station. Indeed, television has widely become a symbol of newly won independence, along with a flag and an airline. Everywhere it is under the close supervision of the ministry of information and, for all its present limitations, is regarded as a formative influence in welding together disparate tribes into one nation. Much of the local programing tends to be given over to nation-building propaganda, with news cameras dutifully following presidents and ministers as they open hospitals, schools, and roads. When I was in Kenya enormous efforts were being made on television to persuade everyone in the country to plant one tree: the Minister for the Environment gave a ten-minute special broadcast exhorting everyone to plant a tree the next day.

Limited treasuries have forced almost every African country to accept advertising on television as one source of income, supplemented by license fees or direct grants. Advice on the kind of station that a country can afford has poured in from all sides. Together with the major American, European, and Japanese equipment manufacturers, organizations such as Thomson Television International (TTI) and Television International Enterprises (TIE) in Britain, L'Office du Co-operation Radiophonique (OCRA) in Paris (now merged with ORTF), and Radio Television International (RTV) and NBC International from New York have been bustling all over the continent. They offer package television stations to suit all pockets, management expertise, program and advertising representation, and training programs for local staff. In former British colonies both radio and television have often been modeled on the BBC, while ORTF's influence is strong in former French colonies and in the territory of Afars and Issas (formerly French Somaliland) and the island of Réunion out in the Indian Ocean. The French have been particularly tenacious in maintaining a hold on television in several countries. The Ivory Coast at one time considered signing up with Thomson Television International in London for a package station, until the French reminded the government of the Ivory Coast that their economy relied heavily on exporting coffee to France. The French won the TV contract. They also outmaneuvered the Americans from RTV in the Congo (Brazzaville) by simply offering to train television personnel for free, which RTV, as a commercial organization, could not afford to do. The competition for contracts has now become even keener with the arrival of the Japanese in force. Their first major coup was to win the reequipping of Uganda's television network.

Package television stations come in all shapes and sizes and can be tailored to the requirements of the country. The cheapest cost $150,000 for equipment and installation and can be run for about $200,000 a year (about the same as it costs to make one episode of *Bonanza* for American television). "We created 'tailor-made' television stations," explained Desmond O'Donovan, the managing director of Thomson Television International, who helped set up TV in Kenya, Sierra Leone, and Ethiopia. Actually, stations are sometimes "off the rack" rather than "tailor-made," for governments have a notorious tendency to dither for years about whether or not to have TV and then demand overnight that it be ready for some celebration next month.

The record for swift installation is held, by general consent, by TTI, which had a television station operating in Addis Ababa just nineteen days after Emperor Haile Selassie suddenly ordered that it must be open for coverage of the anniversary celebration of his coronation—then less than three weeks away. All the equipment had to be air-freighted in from London, and set up in makeshift studios on half a floor of the Addis Ababa municipal office building. Matters were not helped because the head of customs in Ethiopia was personally against the introduction of television and, despite the fact that it was the Emperor's express command that it be installed, insisted that all the normal formalities be carried out in clearing the equipment at the airport. However, right on time, the station went on the air with the Emperor in the studio to watch the transmission. Moreover, the Ethiopians themselves, who had never even seen a television set, let alone sophisticated cameras, control console, or transmitter until a couple of weeks before, handled everything. The British advisers, who had installed the equipment and given them instant training, stood to one side with fingers crossed. All went off perfectly, and the Emperor was delighted.

From that auspicious beginning in 1964 the Ethiopians have continued to run their station, putting on about three hours of programs a night, nearly half of them locally produced. Several of the senior staff have been to Britain for short training courses at the Thomson Foundation's television school near Glasgow, and TTI still supplies a chief engineer, but otherwise there is no outside advice. Admittedly, it is hardly a grand setup. All the props are stored in the passage outside the director general's office; there is a small news studio about the size of a modest bedroom and the main studio is little larger than a family living room. Yet the Ethiopian Television Service's half dozen producers have shown an instinctive flair for the medium and conjure up all kinds of programs; they have even produced a Chekhov play translated into Amharic.

I spent an afternoon watching one young producer tape a half-hour variety show. The studio, which is ventilated simply by opening the windows, was like a sweat box. Somehow, a nine-man band and a squad of singers and dancers were working away in there before two cameras. Every now and then the producer would leap up from the control panel, dash into the studio and move around, himself, one or two arches that formed the scenery. With a little bit of manipulation of the arches and the cameras he could make the studio floor look like half an acre. The whole show was taped on the station's one videotape recorder—a rather ancient piece of apparatus acquired second hand (the station originally managed without a VTR at all and did all local programs live). Considering the heat and the cramped conditions, everyone was remarkably good-natured. The producer sustained himself with long pulls at an enormous bottle of fizzy mineral water between his forays into the studio to change the scenery. "You should have been here when we did those variety programs live," he said. "That really wore us out."

Although their television is partly financed by commercials, the Ethiopians take a serious view of their role as educators and builders of national unity. "People don't move around very much in this country," said Kassaye Damena, the director of programs, "so it is our job to make people in villages aware of what the rest of their country looks like, to create a national consciousness. Just now we are making a series of documentaries about the historic towns of Ethiopia and their role in our development."

Inevitably, the Ethiopians have to rely on buying many of their entertainment programs from abroad; quite apart from their limited studio facilities they simply cannot afford too much local output. Their income is just $200,000 a year. Since it costs them $800 to make a half-hour show of their own, but they can buy *Bonanza* for $50, they end up purchasing about half their programs. They also get a few free; the French Embassy in Addis Ababa provides them with *Panorama* in French once a fortnight. But most evenings, you can hope to catch *Star Trek, UFO,* or *Land of the Giants.* All are presented in English without subtitling or dubbing, which is too expensive. "Most of those American stories are so simple that you can understand them even without speaking English," said Kassaye Damena. "My father loves *Bonanza* although he doesn't know the language." One of the few programs the Ethiopians steered clear of was *The Avengers.* "We didn't take to *that lady,*" said Damena, referring to Steed's judo-adept partner. "Ethiopian women don't throw people around like that."

The real challenge for Ethiopian television is to extend its network; at the moment pictures can be received only within a few miles of Addis Ababa, and there are a mere 15,000 television sets. The aim is to extend the service as rapidly as possible to the northern city of Asmara and thence to the other main population centers.

While Ethiopia has the distinction of possessing the fastest-installed television station in Africa, Nigeria had the earliest. This was a commercial station, WNTV, set up with the help of the British company Overseas Rediffusion in 1959 at Ibadan in Western Nigeria. WNTV is run by the provincial government and is conceived purely as a commercial operation, relying heavily on imported American programs. A relay station boosts its signal into the capital of Lagos, where it has a sharp rivalry with the federal Nigerian Broadcasting Corporation's television service. The corporation, which is a public service organization loosely modeled on the British Broadcasting Corporation, got into television much later. When television first started in Africa, the corporation was still run by BBC men, who had been sent to Lagos to establish a nationwide radio network in Nigeria. The director general, an Englishman, argued that the corporation was still too preoccupied establishing radio to become involved in television and the federal government should wait. The government, however, enjoying the first heady moments of independence from Britain, was eager to have television, especially as the provincial government of Western Nigeria already had WNTV. So they simply shopped elsewhere. They signed a five-year contract with NBC International of New York to install and manage a television station. This new federal television service opened in 1962 and was operated by NBC International until 1967. By that time the Nigerian Broadcasting Corporation was run by the Nigerians themselves, and they felt ready to cope with television as well as radio. The American contract was not renewed, and the Nigerian Broadcasting Corporation took television under its umbrella.

Under the corporation's wing the television service has become one of the most ambitious in Africa. Despite the fact that it has only two studios and its signal is received by a mere 50,000 sets in the Lagos area, it produces 45 percent of its own programs. The director of television, Michael Olumide, believes strongly that his programs must reflect the local culture and way of life. "If I were to put out imported programs all the time that just showed the American or the British heritage, I wouldn't be beginning to broadcast," he told me. "In Nigeria we are very fortunate in having more writing, acting, and musical talent to draw on than most other African countries." The real problem is money. The NBC exists on a government grant and commercials, but the total budget for television is no more than one million dollars a year. "The government just does not realize the importance of television," said Olumide. "We have the most potent medium in the country, but we are starved of money so that many of our artists are really working for us from charity. Nigeria has creative talent, but we cannot really pay enough to nourish it. We have a weekly drama series called *Village Headmaster*—about a schoolmaster in a little village—but we can pay the leading actor only $25 for a half-hour play." The NBC's most popular program, an hour's live variety show, *The Bar Beach Show* on Saturday nights, gets by on a budget of under $250. "The real danger of all this is that you settle for mediocrity," said Olumide, "that you accept substandard work just so you can keep going. But I would rather cut our time on the air than do that."

The real difficulty, of course, is that television in Nigeria, as elsewhere in Africa, is still available only to the upper classes living in the capital city. Until the network extends throughout the country and sets are counted in hundreds of thousands, no government is going to give television priority for funds. Meanwhile they stagger along as best they can. "I was showing some visiting American television people our studios recently," said Michael Olumide, "and explained that we made half-hour dramas using two cameras and, as we have no videotape editing equipment, we simply shoot the whole thing nonstop from beginning to end. They just did not believe me."

The West African nation that began television with the highest hopes was Ghana. While Kwame Nkrumah was President he determined to build a nationwide network to produce most of its own material, including many educational programs. "Originally Ghana's plans were the most pragmatic conceived anywhere in Africa," said Frank Goodship, a Canadian broadcaster, who helped establish Ghanaian television. "They planned a nationwide network, good production facilities, and trained plenty of people before they went on the air. They aimed at five hours of local material every day including educational television every morning." Initially the Ghanaians did not buy much packaged entertainment or westerns from overseas. Africans who are new to television will sit glued to the set for hours watching instructional films about farming or fisheries —until you show the first western. That opens the floodgates and they then want nothing else. "If you really want to use television to teach people about the world, then you must not import cowboy shows," said Frank Goodship. The Ghanaians under Nkrumah, ambitiously determined not to develop the appetite for cowboy pictures. They began producing more than 80 percent of their own programs. The only trouble was that the money simply was not there to sustain them. With less than 15,000 sets in the country, the annual license fee of $12 could not provide enough revenue. After a while, Ghanaian television began to accept advertising and, as a corollary, the advertisers demanded popular shows. So the floodgates to the western opened after all, and today Ghana's television service produces only 40 percent of its output.

Yet even advertising cannot really raise enough money to sustain television in Ghana or other African countries. With a mere 15,000 to 20,000 sets in most countries no advertiser is prepared to spend more than a few dollars per minute for spots. The scarcity of sets means that even the combined income from licenses and advertising just does not add up to a worthwhile television budget. Only commercial radio is a profitable operation anywhere in Africa.

Zambia and Kenya, for instance, each with about 20,000 sets, face exactly the same problem of miniuscule budgets. "My total program budget is about $140,000 a year," said Morris Mwendar, controller of television at Voice of Kenya (VOK) in Nairobi. "We manage to do about 40 percent of our own programs, but our facilities weren't really designed for extensive local production—and there is very limited local talent." The

Kenyans and Zambians concentrate on news (introduced naturally with a beating of message drums) and nightly news magazines. The Kenya magazine *Mambo Leo* from 6:30 to 7:15 each evening follows very closely the old BBC *Tonight* or NBC's *Today Show* format of interviews and filmed reports. The one difference is that it is conducted in two languages: English and Swahili. The two anchormen switch happily back and forth from one language to the other according to the linguistic ability of their guests. The local politicians love it, and are forever calling up seeking to get on to expound their views—African politicians, apparently, have become just as addicted to appearing before the cameras as politicians everywhere else.

For more general entertainment the Kenyans fall back heavily on imported programs. The exception is a delightful weekly local comedy show, *Mzee Pimbi,* about an amiable old rogue called Pimbi and his wife, Mana Tefi, who live in a small village outside Nairobi. Pimbi is a game little fellow who feels he must get involved in everything that's going on. During the East African Safari motor rally he naturally turns up to participate in a beat-up jalopy, and if there is a local boxing championship, he's in the ring mixing it with all comers. The show is sponsored by a local dairy, so he is also seen drinking gallons of milk. *Mzee Pimbi* is popular with everyone in Nairobi except European expatriates (who tend to be the people who can afford television anyway) because all their servants are falling about with laughter in front of the set instead of serving dinner. The best place to watch the show is in one of the local police stations around Nairobi: they are all equipped with television and become a social viewing center for the neighborhood. Often a hundred people may be gathered before one police set.

Whatever they may be viewing, you can be sure of one thing—there is no violence on television. Kenya has quite the strictest rules I have encountered anywhere regarding violence on TV—no killing, no shooting, no fighting, no poisoning, no stealing may be shown. That, of course, rules out many imported shows. The Kenyans have to restrict themselves to a fairly light diet of *Tom Jones, Rolf Harris,* the *Andy Stewart Show, The Planemakers,* and *Not in Front of the Children* from Britain, plus carefully selected episodes of *Peyton Place* and *The World of Disney.*

The reason for the violence ban, according to Morris Mwendar, is that "people here believe what they see. Out in the villages many of them have seen films on mobile cinemas—these are usually educational—showing them how to grow coffee or tea. So they see a film as speaking the truth. If they see somebody shot on television they believe he is dead, and you can't tell them that he isn't: they've seen the gun fired and the blood coming out."

The restriction on violence is, of course, an extension of the strict political censorship that is part of the way of life of television in every African country. No one makes any secret of the fact that censorship exists. The usual justification for it is exactly the same as that given for not allowing violence, namely that the people are totally unsophisticated: they believe everything they see on the box, so it is much the best that they see a nice government line and nothing else. Not that everyone is taken in. I met a well-known BBC news reader in one African country where he was spending a month, teaching the local television announcers how to present the news. That afternoon one of them had inquired politely at the end of his lecture, "When you are giving the television news on BBC and you know that what you have to read is lies, how do you present it?"

Television stations are true seats of power, and some that I visited were as difficult to get into as a gold vault, for they are the natural first place to capture in the event of a coup d'état. Occasionally, the precautions have quite embarrassing results. In Zambia, when President Kaunda was away at the Commonwealth Prime Ministers' Conference in Singapore early in 1971, the military decided to run through their anticoup drill to make sure all was secure in the President's absence. A squad of troops came rolling up to the television station in late afternoon and surrounded it: no one was permitted to enter or leave. Inside the broadcasters were busy putting the finishing touches to the *Tonight* show. But the troops outside would not allow any of their guests in. When the time finally came for the program, the anchorman went on the air alone and said, "I'm sorry we don't have a program for you this evening. Our station is surrounded by troops who will not let the guests through to the studio. If any senior army officer is watching perhaps he would come down here and change the orders." An embarrassed officer arrived post haste and the program went ahead, rather late.

One of the real dilemmas facing television in Africa has been shortage of trained staff. Most African nations, quite naturally, want their stations run by their own people, but sometimes the technical standards are so bad as to make the whole effort meaningless. I saw a long interview with General Gowan of Nigeria over VOK in Nairobi, when the General was on a state visit there, in which the sound quality was so bad that the General's remarks were totally unintelligible.

Happily, the Kenyans are now making a serious effort to raise their whole training standard. They have established in Nairobi at the Kenya Institute for Mass Communications the only television training school in Africa. To begin with, it is a modest affair training ten students at a time in one small studio with three cameras. They are not only thoroughly briefed on all the equipment, but also make their own television programs. One or two that I saw were already as good as anything being put on on Voice of Kenya. The potential importance of the Institute is not just the training, but that the Kenyans are receiving it in their own environment. If the Kenya Institute develops, it could become the major source for television talent that not only Kenya but all Africa requires.

The great debate is how much educational television can really advance in Africa over the next few years. Ethiopia, Ghana, Nigeria, Zambia, and Uganda already have educational programs shown on the general television service during the day, but their effect has been often blunted through lack of cooperation from schools, the limited coverage of transmitters, or simply through inadequate knowledge of how to operate the sets and maintain them. A teacher training college in Ghana received its first set in 1965, but it never worked; the following year a new set was put in—that did not work either. In all it was three and a half years between the time the college first had a set and it received decent pictures.

In Ethiopia, which has a very good educational television service, putting on nearly two hours of programs five days a week since 1965, sheer lack of transport makes regular maintenance of sets impossible. When I visited Addis Ababa, the Mass Media Center of the Ministry of Education, which runs the service with help from the British Council, was sitting on 130 television sets which it could not deliver to schools in outlying villages because no transport was available. Despite the excellent intentions of everyone working there, the educational television service, which transmits its program in the daytime over the Ethiopian Television Service transmitters, lives a hand-to-mouth existence, never knowing when the next money will come in. Once they got down to sixteen cents in the kitty. Even so the programs on geography, mathematics, social studies and English are seen by some 60,000 Ethiopian children every week. And their response shows how significant television could be in raising education and living standards everywhere in Africa if it can be more extensively used. "You go to these schools in the villages," one of the British Council's advisers told me, "and there are children in rags with no shoes sitting on the floor—there are no chairs or desks—bellowing back answers to questions on television. Often there is no teacher there to supervise them, but they are quite entranced."

"The pity is that many countries still do not fully realize the advantages of educational television," said Tom Singleton, the director of the Centre for Educational Television Overseas (CETO) in London (now merged with the Centre for Educational Development Overseas). But he believes that this picture may change radically in the 1970s. "Ministers of Education in developing countries are now being brought face to face with the financial realities of education. They want five years of primary education for everyone—but the cost makes it a dream many years away. This is where television should come in, not only in educating classes but in helping to upgrade the whole standard of teaching."

The real test case for Africa is in the former French West African colony of the Ivory Coast. Faced with a soaring bill for education and a desperate shortage of qualified teachers, so that less than 50 percent of the children had any chance even of primary school education, the Ivory Coast, with the advice and help of UNESCO, has staked $500 million over the next twelve years on a nationwide educational television project. They hope that by 1975 more than half a million children will be watching the daily television lessons, and that by the mid-1980s television's shouldering of much of the burden of education will enable all children to be enrolled in primary schools. The educational programs will all be made in the Ivory Coast at a fine new production center in Bouake, a city in the interior 150 miles north of the capital of Abidjan. The World Bank, in its first major investment in educational television, has contributed $11 million to the building of the center and the French government has chipped in with a further $1 million.

The TV lessons will cover the whole range of primary school education and should, for the first time, provide a high quality of instruction throughout the country. The problem in the past has been that the capital, Abidjan, and one or two large towns had good schools with quite high enrollment, but elsewhere schools have been almost nonexistent—less than 10 percent of the children receive any education in the rural areas of the north. Besides nearly three hours of TV lessons daily, there will be an hour's live briefing for teachers over the network at 7:00 each morning. This will outline the day's programing, advise the teachers on how to prepare the class and deal with any queries arising out of earlier lessons. The programs will be transmitted over the existing commercial television network, which already covers more than two thirds of the country. Since many of the rural areas have no electricity, hundreds of battery-operated television sets are being supplied to schools and schemes worked out for maintenance because of the ravages of the humid tropical climate.

The Ivory Coast experiment will be watched closely, not only in Africa but throughout the Third World. If it is successful, many other countries will certainly turn much more rapidly to harnessing television to education. While educational schemes expand, the other real requirement is for closer liaison between African broadcasters on all aspects of television. The nucleus for cooperation already exists in the Union of National Radio and Television Organizations of Africa (URTOA), but its membership is limited primarily to West African countries and it has not yet been a potent coordinating force. "We haven't really started to explore the possibilities of cooperation yet," said Morris Mwendar in Nairobi. "I am sure that television in Africa will not play its full role unless and until we use it to show what is going on elsewhere on this continent. Most of us have no idea what other television services are doing; we ought to be working with them on coproductions, trying to create television that is truly African in character." That ideal, however, may be difficult to achieve before television has really found its feet within the individual countries. At the moment, most governments see it as one means of welding together a complex conglomeration of tribes into a nation; while that fragile task proceeds they are likely to keep television very much within their own control.

But at the heart of the matter really is Africa's need for a cheap durable television set and more electrification. Until these requirements are fulfilled, television can do little to penetrate the continent. Television sets are being assembled locally in Nigeria, Ghana, and Kenya. They are cheaper than imported models, but they are still beyond the means of, say, a Masai tribesman—even assuming he wanted to buy one. And an enterprising firm in Nairobi has also developed a small, gasoline-driven generator especially to power a television set. But again, the combined cost of generator and set is too high for the individual family and can only really be used for community viewing in villages without electricity. "The real trouble, you know," an African broadcaster admitted, "is that we all rushed into television for prestige reasons long before we were ready for it. Often we were oversold on the idea by manufacturers of equipment. They all said, 'It'll turn you on.' So one country got it and then it became a matter of keeping up with them to maintain face."

CONCLUSION

21

Toward 1984

Television channels these days resemble an amoeba—constantly dividing and multiplying. Looking back ten years from now, the choice of two, three, or even half a dozen channels that most of us in Western Europe, America, Japan, or Australia now enjoy, may seem tremendously restrictive. The advance in technology since World War II, which has already made television so dominant in our lives, will propel its expansion even faster in the future. The latest series of Intelsat IV communications satellites lofted above the equator during 1971 can handle no less than twelve color television channels simultaneously (plus 9,000 two-way telephone conversations). In San Jose, California, a cable system capable of disseminating forty-two different channels is already hooked into many homes.

What is in store for television, in fact, is so exciting that it makes fiction pall. Electronics engineers talk quite seriously of the prospect of multichannel television sets on which the viewer can dial up, not only a wide selection of conventional programs or films, but his bank for a screening of his statement or the supermarket for a display of the day's top bargains. Against this potential, today's broadcasting becomes, as the chairman of the American National Cable Television Association put it, "rather like a narrow cart track to a forty-lane superhighway."

Effectively television is moving forward on three fronts: satellites, cable, and cassettes. The satellites will shortly become so high-powered and sophisticated that they will be able to relay pictures direct to home receivers by the 1980s. A United Nations study of the likely timetable has revealed that within five years direct broadcasting from satellites into specially augmented home television sets will be feasible; the ordinary family set, the report indicated, could be augmented for between $40 and $270. Relays from nuclear-powered satellites direct to unaugmented home receivers are predicted for the mid-1980s.

Such a breakthrough could be of immense advantage in the developing countries, where television has still hardly established a foothold. A single regional satellite could reach every village in Africa or India or the pattern of islands that make up Indonesia. The expensive infrastructure of microwave networks to span the vast distances need never be contemplated. Regional satellites could lift television out of the cities of the Third World into the backwoods. A village of five hundred people in some remote valley that would inevitably be bypassed by microwave links can be enfolded overnight.

The delicate question, of course, is going to be who makes the programs? The Arab States Broadcasting Union, for example, are very eager to have a regional satellite for educational television throughout the Arab world—but who actually prepares the television lessons? The Egyptians? Will the Libyans or the Sudanese accept their version of history? South America faces the same dilemma: does right-wing Argentina make the programs that will also be beamed to schools in left-wing Chile? The political hurdles of the age of satellites are likely to be much more difficult to overcome than the technical ones.

For this reason I am sure that although satellites will prove invaluable eventually for education in developing nations, their prime use will remain for sports and news events of universal importance. The current form certainly suggests this. Of the 996 hours of television relayed on the Intelsat system in 1970, the majority were of sports. During the World Cup football in Mexico City, for instance, three different matches were being relayed simultaneously to Europe by satellite. The additional channels now available on Intelsat IV mean that for the next World Cup half a dozen or more matches could be covered at once, insuring that every country can see its own team play.

One afternoon in Washington, D.C., in the offices of COMSAT, which manages the Intelsat system on behalf of the seventy-seven participating nations, I looked over the individual pattern of transmissions, country by country, for 1970. Japan, for example, transmitted 56 hours of television to the Pacific and Indian Ocean satellites and received 32 hours of pictures relayed by them; Britain sent 62 and received 114. But the little island of Puerto Rico took 135 hours of satellite transmission and Venezuela 99 hours. The explanation of this enormous—and expensive—satellite usage by such small countries was simple: they take the baseball games every weekend from the United States.

While broadcasters speak quite rightly of our being in the age of global television, most of us are really interested in our own backyard—unless the home team is playing away. Although technology may make it possible for us to tune in in the 1980s to a Chinese satellite relaying Peking's version of *Bonanza,* the mass audience may look at it out of curiosity but after that will probably switch back promptly to their own home channels.

Moreover, those channels may well become more absorbing if cable television and cassettes live up to their advance billing. So far, apart from the special case of Hong Kong, cable television has made the most impact in Canada, where a quarter of the homes are plugged in to twelve Canadian and American channels. The United States is catching up fast, particularly now that the FCC has finally decided to permit rapid expansion of cable systems. The lead was given by President Johnson's Task Force on Communications Policy, which recommended late in 1968: "We conclude that one of the most promising avenues to diversity [of programing] is the distribution of television to the home by cable." The FCC's new chairman, Dean Burch, told the National Cable Television Association's annual convention in 1970: "The time is ripe for a breakthrough in your industry." Already the number of homes linked to cable systems has doubled between 1968 and 1971; by the end of this decade at least a third of all American homes are expected to be connected.

Europe has moved toward cable much more slowly, primarily because the public service television networks there have always covered the whole of their countries with a conventional signal, eliminating the need to bring in distant signals by cable to remote towns or villages. However, most new apartment blocks in the Netherlands and Belgium now have cable, bringing them television from West Germany and France. And one Munich suburb has its own closed-circuit television service. In Britain, apart from an abortive pay-TV experiment in London, its use has been limited mainly to closed-circuit educational systems in London and Glasgow. But the prospect of the "wired nation"—of cable television in every home—is foreshadowed in the new town of Washington in County Durham, which is laid out with ducts for cable TV's lifeline—the coaxial cable. The real advantage of cable over conventional television is that while airwaves become jammed with relatively few channels, a coaxial cable can easily pipe twenty, forty or even eighty channels into every home. Many systems now being installed in American towns have the option of twenty channels and, as noted earlier, San Jose in California has forty-two.

But how much genuine diversity will cable really offer? Although American systems with over 3,500 subscribers now have to originate their own programs, in addition to relaying normal television stations, the choice is hardly scintillating. They rely heavily on local news and sports events. "Cable TV is best at local programing," Wallace Briscoe of the National Cable Television Association told me. "We can identify with a community just like a local newspaper covering politics or high school events." A technological revolution to relay the local school plays seems pointless.

At the moment the cable scene in America and Canada is fragmented; there is no nationwide network. But once systems do begin to link up first into regional associations, then possibly into a national system, the opportunities for good programing are greater. So are the potential profits. The Ali-Frazier fight in 1971, although not carried by cable systems, started everyone counting up how much the purse might have been if it had been piped into 10 million American homes at a special price of $10. Although most cable systems charge a fixed monthly fee, it is possible to scramble signals so that certain channels are received only after extra payments.

What every viewer really cares about is what he finally sees. His best hope is the cassette. This newcomer, quickly nicknamed "Son of TV," is the visual cousin of a tape recorder. The equipment consists of a video player, which can be plugged into the aerial socket of any normal television set, and cartridges or cassettes of programs. The cassette is simply inserted in the player—rather like putting a tape on a tape recorder—and the program is seen on a spare channel on the TV set.

What is widely called "the cassette revolution" was originally pioneered by Dr. Peter Goldmark of CBS, the man who also invented the long-playing record back in 1948. Dr. Goldmark's system, known as EVR (for Electronic Video Recording) uses miniaturized photographic film. CBS, together with ICI in Britain and the Swiss chemical firm CIBA, has invested nearly $50 million in launching EVR in the United States, Japan, and Europe during 1971 and 1972. But EVR's lead is being challenged by a cluster of rivals. Phillips and Sony have devised a player using magnetic tape rather than film. Decca and Telefunken prefer plastic discs (not unlike refined long-playing records), while RCA's Selectavision uses a laser beam to imprint images on vinyl tape. The only trouble is that none of the rival systems is compatible: an EVR cartridge will not function on a Sony or a Decca player.

Each manufacturer, however, is eagerly lining up all kinds of programs for his own version. CBS bought 1,500 old movies from Twentieth Century-Fox and is busy putting them on EVR film. They have also tapped the BBC's archives in Britain for a series of travel films and have signed up the great Italian publishing corporation, Mondadori, to make educational films for them. Everyone else is rushing around trying to corner a slice of the cassette market—and to decide which of all the different systems is really going to prevail in the long run. Time-Life has Robert Redford signed up to make a series of skiing lessons for cassettes and Leonard Bernstein contracted to lecture on music. David Frost has joined the board of a New York company, Optronics, which has scooped up the rights to over 6,000 films, documentaries, and cartoons. Out in Japan all the major commercial television networks have formed cassette subsidiaries, while the mighty NHK is trying to decide how to get the maximum advantage from converting the great treasure house of video tapes, produced for its eighteen-hour-a-day educational channel, into cassettes. In Britain Sir Lew Grade, together with the ABC network in the United States, has concluded a five-year contract with the National Theatre to film all their productions for cassettes. Thames Television in London has made a series of thirteen half-hour programs on the British Museum. They will be shown first on television, but Thames regards them as perfect cassette material.

Initially, the first players that trickled onto the market in 1971 were too expensive for the family buyer: they all cost upward of $400 for the player itself, with at least another $40 to $50 for each half-hour cassette. They appealed much more, therefore, to schools and universities. A school, for instance, will soon be able to buy a complete set of cassettes of Shakespeare's plays and use them again and again. The great advantage for educational use is that the film or tape can be stopped at any point for a single frame to be studied. It can also be reversed so that a short sequence can be repeated immediately—most useful for studying a complex dramatic scene in *Hamlet* or even the arm action for serving in a tennis lesson.

Obviously the costs will come down eventually until the ordinary family can afford the cassette. And cassette libraries will enable viewers to hire their favorite old Cary Grant or Gary Cooper film (or a golf lesson) for a weekend at less than the cost of going to the movies.

But cassettes are unlikely to be for regular home use in the 1970s; most broadcasters foresee their full impact being felt during the 1980s. They point to the relatively slow growth of color television as an indication that although the technology may exist, the private purse cannot necessarily afford it. Even in 1971, rather fewer than 40 million of the 250 million television sets in the world were in color (and of those about 30 million were in the United States, and 5 million in Japan). According to most television executives, the 1970s will be the decade for color to take off. The BBC in Britain is looking for most of its increased income to the higher license fee from color; Italy and Spain are still waiting to take the final plunge in selecting PAL instead of SECAM. The 1970s, therefore, will come to terms with color, the 1980s with cassettes and cable.

As for the Third World, television there still has to become a mass medium. It can do so only when the cost of a set comes within the means of the ordinary man. At the moment his budget stretches at best to a transistor radio. In Copenhagen, Laurits Bindslov, the director of Danish television, pointed out that a survey in Denmark had revealed that a skilled worker there had to work the same number of hours in 1929 to earn enough money to buy a radio as in 1953 to earn enough for a black and white TV set and in 1968 for a color set. Africa and India, by the same token, are really at the 1929 level today. Although their development will undoubtedly be telescoped, it does suggest that television will only really get into its stride there in the 1980s.

The prospect, therefore, for the first man to step out of his space craft onto the surface of Mars some time during the 1980s is that perhaps 3 billion people—or rather more than three quarters of the world's population—will be watching him. That makes the audience of 723 million who watched Neil Armstrong step onto the moon in 1969 seem like a turnout for a matinee. So far we have really had only a preview of what television can do. As a leading European broadcaster, reviewing the difficulties of keeping up with the latest technological breakthroughs, remarked: "We already have such fantastic tools at our disposal that I find it impossible to understand what broadcasting will be like by 2000 A.D. I often feel like a village boy suddenly placed at the wheel of a Rolls-Royce already in motion."

Bibliography

This bibliography is a general guide to other books on the world television scene today or to useful books giving more detailed background on the development of television in individual countries.

Erik Barnouw, *A History of Broadcasting in the United States,* 3 vols. (*A Tower in Babel, The Golden Web, The Image Empire*), Oxford University Press, 1966–70.

J. G. Blumler and Denis McQuail, *Television in Politics: Its Uses and Influence,* Faber & Faber, London, 1968; University of Chicago Press, 1969.

Asa Briggs, *The History of Broadcasting in the United Kingdom,* Oxford University Press, 1965 (3 vols. published to date).

Wilson P. Dizard, *Television: A World View,* Syracuse University Press, Syracuse, New York, 1966.

Walter B. Emery, *National and International Systems of Broadcasting: The History, Operation and Control,* Michigan State University Press, East Lansing, Michigan, 1969.

Fred Friendly, *Due to Circumstances Beyond Our Control,* Random House, New York, 1967.

Hugh Greene, *The Third Floor Front: A View of Broadcasting in the Sixties,* The Bodley Head, London, 1969.

History of Broadcasting in Japan, NHK, Tokyo, 1967.

Stuart Hood, *A Survey of Television,* Heinemann, London, 1967.

Alexander Kendrick, *Prime Time: The Life of Edward R. Murrow,* Little, Brown & Co., Boston, 1969.

Joe McGinniss, *The Selling of the President 1968,* Trident Press, New York, 1969.

Robert MacNeil, *The People Machine,* Harper & Row, New York, 1968.

James W. Markham, *Voices of the Red Giants: Communications in Russia and China,* Iowa State University Press, Ames, Iowa, 1967.

Burton Paulu, *Radio and Television Broadcasting on the European Continent,* University of Minnesota Press, Minneapolis, 1967.

Public Television, A Program for Action: The Report of the Carnegie Commission on Educational Television, Bantam Books, New York, 1967.

Anthony Sampson, *Anatomy of Britain Today,* Hodder and Stoughton, London; Harper & Row, New York, 1965.

————, *The New Europeans,* Hodder and Stoughton, London, 1968.

UNESCO, *Communications in the Space Age: The Use of Satellites by the Mass Media,* 1968.

E. G. Wedell, *Broadcasting and Public Policy,* Michael Joseph, London, 1968.

John Whale, *The Half Shut Eye: Television and Politics in Britain and America,* Macmillan, London; St. Martin's, New York, 1969.

Magazines and Reviews:

Educational Television International, Journal of the Centre for Educational Television Overseas, London.

EBU Review, European Broadcasting Union, Geneva.

Radio, Television, Review of the International Radio and Television Organization, Prague.

The following broadcasting organizations also publish valuable yearbooks: ARD, West Germany; BBC and ITA, Britain; JRT, Yugoslavia; NHK, Japan; ORF, Austria.

Index

267